THE POLICE, PUBLIC ORDER AND THE STATE

The Police, Public Order and the State

Policing in Great Britain, Northern Ireland, the Irish Republic, the USA, Israel, South Africa and China

John D. Brewer
Professor of Sociology
The Queen's University of Belfast

Adrian Guelke
Lecturer in Politics
The Queen's University of Belfast

Ian Hume
Inspector of Education in Wales

Edward Moxon-Browne
Jean Monnet Professor of European Integration
University of Limerick

Rick Wilford
Senior Lecturer in Politics
The Queen's University of Belfast

Second Edition

Published in Great Britain by
MACMILLAN PRESS LTD
Houndmills, Basingstoke, Hampshire RG21 6XS
and London
Companies and representatives
throughout the world

First edition 1988
Second edition 1996

A catalogue record for this book is available
from the British Library.

ISBN 0–333–65487–0 hardcover
ISBN 0–333–65488–9 paperback

First published in the United States of America 1996 by
ST. MARTIN'S PRESS, INC.,
Scholarly and Reference Division,
175 Fifth Avenue,
New York, N.Y. 10010

ISBN 0–312–15946–3

Library of Congress Cataloging-in-Publication Data
The police, public order, and the state : policing in Great Britain,
Northern Ireland, the Irish Republic, the USA, Israel, South Africa,
and China / John D. Brewer . . .[et al.]. — 2nd ed.
p.   cm.
Includes bibliographical references and index.
ISBN 0–312–15946–3 (cloth)
1. Police.   2. Police administration.   3. Public relations–
–Police.   I. Brewer, John D.
HV7921.P572   1996
363.2—dc20

95–51278
CIP

© John D. Brewer, Adrian Guelke, Ian Hume, Edward Moxon-Browne
and Rick Wilford 1988, 1996

10   9   8   7   6   5   4   3   2   1
05   04   03   02   01   00   99   98   97   96

Printed and bound in Great Britain by
Antony Rowe Ltd, Chippenham, Wiltshire

Contents

List of Tables

Preface

'I found myself kitted up with gas mask, baton gun, flameproof suit, crash helmet – I was elevated into a very aggressive role. The next day I was back in my Dixon of Dock Green role knocking on someone's door asking to see his driving licence. I think really it's a very unfair position to expect us to be in.'

'We can't pat kids on the head one day and shoot at them with plastic bullets the next.'

(British police officers speaking on BBC Television, October 1986)

These two views crystallise the problems posed by public order policing – both for the officers themselves and for the public who are policed by it. These are not problems unique to Britain, for all states face the imperative of maintaining public order. They have all evolved strategies for order-maintenance, which affords the opportunity to draw lessons from the experience of others. But while there is an immense range of national studies of the police, there is a dearth of material which sets police functions and organisation in a comparative perspective. This book seeks to remedy this deficiency.

There is a second impulse behind the study. We intend to respond to the growing public interest in policing issues by writing a book which is free of jargon and accessible to a wider readership. We have compensated for the lack of detailed footnote citations by providing a select bibliography. Each chapter has been written by a single author although the book is truly a collective product. The structure of the separate chapters follows an agreed form and contributions have been subjected to an exhaustive process of discussion and revision. The frequent and intensive meetings we have held have generated a corporate identity which is reflected in the authorship – and, it is to be hoped, in the contents – of the book.

Throughout, we have received assistance from a number of individuals and institutions. We would specially like to acknowledge the help and co-operation of the Commandant and Librarian of the Police Staff College, Bramshill; Diana Kirkpatrick and Shao Li, librarians at Queen's University of Belfast; assistants at the library of the London School of Economics; Peter Edwards; Glenda Dry, First Secretary (Information) at the South African Embassy in London; Jacquie Griffin; T.D. Bland, Police Authority of Northern Ireland;

David Capitanchik, University of Aberdeen; Ruth Geva of the Ministry of Police in Israel; Israeli Embassy in London; Ronald Weitzer, University of Puget Sound; Derek Beattie and Frank Wright of Queen's University of Belfast.

Finally, we would like to thank our wives and children, without whose tolerance, support and encouragement this book would not have been written. It is to them that we wish to dedicate this book.

JOHN D. BREWER
ADRIAN GUELKE
IAN HUME
EDWARD MOXON-BROWNE
RICK WILFORD

Acknowledgements

The authors and publishers wish to thank the following for permission to reproduce tables and extracts from published material included in the text:

The Controller of Her Majesty's, Stationery Office, for Tables 2.1, 2.2, 2.3, 2.4, 3.3, 3.4.
Northern Irish Digest of Statistics, for Tables 3.1, 3.2.
The Police Authority of Northern Ireland, for Table 3.3.
The Stationery Office, Dublin, for Tables 4.1, 4.2.
Clarendon Press, Oxford, for Table 7.6, from J.D. Brewer, *After Soweto: An Unfinished Journey* (1986).

Every effort has been made to trace all the copyright holders, but if any have been inadvertently overlooked the publishers will be pleased to make the necessary arrangement at the first opportunity.

Introduction to the Second Edition

INTRODUCTION

When this book was originally published in 1988 it was very much a product of its time. In Britain there was an immediacy about policing and public order issues, we were in the midst of changes to the relationship between the police and public, there was a growing politicisation of policing and what appeared to be an increasing use of the police force for partisan political ends. Popular culture was pervaded with negative images of the police, rooted in direct experience of a deteriorating service delivery to the public and flashpoints of disorder and violence. Memories of the miners' strike and inner city disturbances were still fresh. We conceived and wrote the book, therefore, in the context of a cultural and ideological milieu which, looking back from the vantage point of the mid-1990s, made it one of a trend of studies which addressed the changing face of policing.

But we were also seeking to deepen the state of our knowledge of a neglected dimension. What was new in our approach was to link policing overtly to the nature and project of the state and to set the changes occurring in police-state relations in Britain in a wider international and comparative framework.

With hindsight it is possible to identify the trends in Britain that went to define this cultural and ideological setting. Changes in the nature of policing in Britain in the 1970s and 1980s led critical observers of the police to detect various tendencies towards centralisation,[1] the emergence of paramilitary style policing,[2] and a deterioration in police relations with the public. The reasons for such mounting criticism were several, including the ineffectiveness of the police in stemming the rise in crime,[3] notorious public order incidents which damaged the police image, racial bias in dealing with ethnic minorities in the inner cities,[4] and the exposure of blatant miscarriages of justice. Critics argued that Britain thus displayed features of colonial policing, including the habit of 'policing by strangers', as Brogden showed in Liverpool,[5] and the excessive use of force in policing industrial disputes.[6]

These changes in policing have to be related to a cultural context in which greater social heterogeneity and division were emerging in Britain during the 1970s and 1980s; British society had changed dramatically in the decades following the second world war. There were clashes between ethnic minorities and members of the dominant society. Unemployment rose dramatically. An underclass of ultra-poor and exploitable human capital emerged in depressed and de-industrialised areas. Industrial disputes, flying pickets, violent clashes, poll tax protesters and inner city riots all came to symbolise a changing Britain. Consequently, the police, benefiting from enhanced resources and powers bestowed by a supportive government, increasingly intervened in social and political conflict.

The ideological milieu was also one of change, with shifts occurring in the nature of the British state under the Thatcher governments of the 1980s, to which changes in policing were also allied. Thus, the paramilitarism, centralisation and partisanship of the police were linked in various studies to trends towards authoritarianism and centralisation in the British state and its legitimacy crisis; a legitimacy crisis which expressed itself in a whole panoply of public order challenges to the government and in inner city riots, in all of which critics saw the police intervening aggressively on behalf of the state.[7] The fanning of moral panic by the government's assertion of moral decline, not least with the prime minister urging a return to Victorian values, consolidated the position of the police as a key beneficiary of both symbolic and material largesse by the state.

It was not surprising, then, that at this time police researchers increasingly portrayed policing as a political activity, especially Robert Reiner, the doyen of British police research, whose book in 1985 seemed to start the trend.[8] Research on the British police had entered what Reiner called its 'conflict stage', within which it became paradigmatic to claim that policing was political. This contrasted with what he termed the 'consensus stage' of British police research, up to the 1970s, in which policing was perceived as an apolitical activity, valorised in the 'British bobby', the avuncular figure who stood as a metaphor for Britain's consensual political and social value system. But by the 1980s, with the country becoming less socially homogeneous and more divisive, the police were presented with an array of social and political conflicts in which they had to intervene on behalf of the state, with deleterious consequences for police-public relations in Britain and the image of the

British bobby. In this cultural and ideological context, the liberal or British model of policing came under almost universal attack in the police studies literature.

Police, Public Order and the State was part of this debate, and thus truly reflected its time. But we attempted to extend the level of understanding by establishing whether similar patterns in public order policing were occurring in six other societies besides Great Britain, allowing a comparison with all societies in the British Isles and beyond, taking in countries with more extreme social divisions, such as Israel and South Africa, and with less, such as the United States and the highly secretive and enigmatic People's Republic of China. We challenged the liberal model of policing by demonstrating both that policing in all seven societies needed to be understood in terms of the symbiotic relationship between police and state, and that the claim that policing is apolitical was hollow. The survey of each case country followed the same format as we sought to demonstrate that the state, to a lesser or greater degree, influenced the structure, organisation and finance of the police, affected formal structures of authority within the police, conditioned or reinforced a militarisation and politicisation of policing, and provoked many public order situations in which the police had to intervene.

Because the book so clearly reflected the climate of the late 1980s, we have decided not to rewrite each individual chapter, but rather to let the chapters stand as barometers of that time. There have been changes within some of the case countries; most obviously democratisation and the abolition of apartheid have occurred in South Africa, the peace process is underway in Israeli-Palestinian relations, and ceasefires, if not yet peace, have created a window of opportunity in Northern Ireland. Liberalisation was briefly attempted in China and brutally snuffed out in the massacre of students in 1989. Moreover, new issues in public order have emerged, notably the effects of European integration on public order policing and police cooperation.[9]

Yet in another sense time has not moved on that much. We wrote in the Introduction to the First Edition that public order was at once both a topical and enduring issue, and it has proved to be so in the intervening years. In his review of contemporary issues in public disorder in the 1990s, David Waddington referred to the 'turbulent years' of British public order.[10] So widespread has this turbulence been in Britain and elsewhere, that the central thrust of the chapters remains the same despite the superficial changes, although more recent examples could obviously be used instead to illustrate the arguments. For example, the recruitment of Palestinians to the police by the Palestine Liberation Organisation to establish order in the Gaza Strip has not created social and political stability but inflamed relationships between Arafat and those opposed to his attempts to reach agreement with Israel. But rather than update chapters which would be in all other respects remain the same save for illustrative material, we have decided to provide a new Introduction to this edition. We again seek to take the debate further by attempting to theorise the relationship between policing and politics which structures the association between policing and the state. First, however, it is worth further expanding upon the theorisation offered in the Conclusion to *Police, Public Order and the State* in order to demonstrate how state strategies for public order policing operate in practice in one of the case countries covered in the volume. We end by examining some public order and policing issues in contemporary Britain.

STATE STRATEGIES FOR PUBLIC ORDER POLICING IN SOUTH AFRICA

We conclude this volume by developing a typology to identify the strategies by which states engage in public order policing, arguing that it falls into a combination of three broad categories: criminalisation, accommodation and suppression. These strategies are defined much more fully in the Conclusion but, briefly, accommodation attempts to meet the demands of the groups from which disorder emanates, criminalisation renders political acts as criminal and suppression confronts challenges to the state's authority through repression. The Conclusion does not apply this typology to a concrete case, so it is useful to exemplify the typology by illustrating how the various strategies operated in South Africa prior to democratisation and Mandela's government of the national unity.[11]

In the reform period of the Botha presidency, the South African state responded in some measure to the demands of Black South Africans, although the form of accommodation it deployed rejected equality and integration in favour of policies of cultural pluralism designed to meet separately the needs and interests of the respective racial and ethnic groups. The state was encouraging reform in social and economic life whilst trying to maintain White political supremacy. Accommodation thus became a vital strategy. The South African Police (SAP) were passive actors in this form of accommodation, such as when they facilitated the election of Black local government and parliamentary candidates by protecting them from their critics, or enforced some of the 'deracialisation' measures, such as policing multiracial events and facilities. However, the SAP were also deliberately used by the South African state as a means of achieving accommodation, ensuring that their role in politics was more proactive. Thus they were used by the state both to police reform measures and as a vehicle for measured reform. For example, reforms of police recruitment, staffing and deployment were introduced, including the monitoring of the SAP's operation of the security legislation and controls over the use of force, all of which was presented by the state as an index of its commitment to a wider process of political reform. The SAP was held as a model for 'deracialisation', as the apartheid which operated in its own structures and organisation was slowly eroded in the 1980s. The development of local Black police forces was the culmination of this process of accommodation. The 'own areas' policing strategy, by which Blacks policed themselves in their own segregated areas, while attempting to ensure greater compliance with the law, attempted primarily to accommodate Black South Africans by meeting some of their demands for normal policing.

The paradox of reform under the Botha presidency was, however, that the state extended rights and protections to its Black citizens within tight limits while still severely repressing activity which fell outside these parameters. The scope of activities which the state defined for its Black citizens as lawful and legitimate was small because of the strategy of criminalisation. That is, the process whereby formerly legal and peaceful acts and various forms of political action are criminalised in order for them to become the object of police action. Thus, the law was extended beyond direct manifestations of opposition to cover acts previously regarded as innocent of criminal intent. For instance, the 1982 Intimidation Act made it an offence to encourage someone to participate in collective action or industrial disputes. Similarly, the Demonstrations In Or Near Court Buildings Prohibition Act banned any form of activity in support of prisoners near court buildings, whilst the blunt instrument of the State of Emergency, declared in 1985, promulgated a number of new offences, many of which were previously innocuous, such as 'causing fear, panic and alarm or weakening public confidence'. While in prison, detainees were forbidden to sing or whistle or make unnecessary noise. However, the most flagrant example of criminalisation was the definitions of 'terrorism' and 'sabotage' in the 1982 Internal Security Act, which were so broad that under this guise the police could act against workers in industrial disputes, nuns singing carols and schoolchildren boycotting classes.

In this instance, criminalisation involves the police treating public disorder as ordinary breaches of the law devoid of political content and extending the scope of the criminal law to cover actions previously regarded as innocent of criminal intent. Another form of criminalisation is affixing the label 'political' to action that is lawful under ordinary criminal law in order for it to be portrayed as falling outside the realm of legitimate behaviour because of its ascribed political motivation. Portraying a lawful act as politically motivated expands the powers of discretion available to the police, enabling them to operate with a narrower definition of legitimate behaviour than is available in the criminal law. In South Africa, a number of acts were criminalised in the sense that while they were still legal, their ascribed political intent allowed them either to be made the object of police action or to fall within the ambit of emergency powers which suspended ordinary criminal law. This affected such behaviour as funeral processions, church services, carol singing, the wearing of certain T-shirts and the formation of people's education classes in the townships. The SAP were masters at discovering so-called political intent through infiltration of lawful organisations and the nefarious activities of the Special Branch.

The criminalisation strategy can also involve the representation of political acts as simple breaches of the law, ostensibly disregarding their political content. This represents a strategy to delegitimise behaviour by preventing the perpetrators from claiming that political motivation makes otherwise unlawful activities legitimate. A subtle application of this approach was the treatment of intra-Black violence in the 1980s as a form of mindless anarchy rather than a political struggle between competing factions. The more obvious illustration was the denial of political intent behind guerrilla activity, reinforced by making the police primarily responsible for defeating the guerrilla war. Initially it was the SAP which policed the border, and tours of duty in the operational areas were once the norm for all policemen under fifty years of age. It was not until 1985 that the SAP was withdrawn from the border areas to concentrate on the unrest in urban townships. The training of the police reflected their responsibility for dealing with guerrilla activity; basic training covered weapons knowledge, instruction and familiarisation in the use of mortars and machine guns, as well as aspects of anti-vehicle and anti-personnel mine warfare. Special powers were available to the police in border areas, empowering them to search without warrant any person, premises, vehicle, aircraft or 'receptacle of any nature', and to seize anything found. This power was extended to the whole country in 1983. By such means, the police treated guerrillas as ordinary criminals devoid of any political motivation.

Suppression was the more obvious strategy by which the SAP dealt with public order policing in Botha's South Africa and before. This suppression was effected by means of repressive powers granted to the police by legislation and harsh and brutal tactics in dealing with people perceived to be threatening public order. The deaths in detention or in street riots as a result of police misconduct are the infamies on which the SAP's reputation was built. But these infamies had to be situated in the context of the legislative powers given the police which limited disclosure of police misconduct, the massive firearms and weaponry available to them, the permissive conditions under which lethal force could be used legally and the absence of mechanisms of public accountability. All such powers were fully consistent with the occupational culture of the SAP, which stereotyped Black South Africans as potential threats to the state and public order. [12]

One of the benefits of our typology is to demonstrate that the police use a combination of strategies in public order policing even in extreme cases like South Africa, where the common sense impression before the abolition of apartheid was that the state relied upon suppression as the single response to threats of public order from its Black citizens. In its tentative reform process during the 1980s, the Botha government clearly saw the need to move away from depending upon the strategy of suppression, and linked it to accommodation and criminalisation. Pure coercion was insufficient: this required that the SAP change some of their long-established patterns of policing and act differently in quelling public disorder, if only to try and achieve the same result as naked suppression had in the past – the continuance of White political supremacy. We know, however, that none of this worked in the end: both the strategy and the regime were wholly impoverished. The South African state failed to prevent democratisation and Black majority rule, but this welcome fact presents no problem for our typology. Rather, it demonstrates the inexorability of change which the South African state could not forestall, no matter how it shuffled its order-maintenance strategies. What this case illustrates is that the state will attempt to use a sophisticated combination of order-maintenance strategies to try to deal with the threats that confront it.

THEORISING THE RELATIONSHIP BETWEEN POLICING AND POLITICS

Ours is a typology of strategies by which the state engages in public order policing, and while it is pioneering in identifying a chain of relations connecting the state, police and society, it does not theorise the relationship between policing and politics which underpins the police-state nexus. Under our typology of state strategies for public order policing, the police can be mere ciphers, dutifully implementing whatever strategy or combination the state has arrived at, be active and partisan supporters of the state against its opponents, or autonomous agents, working independently of the state either to undermine it as a whole or advance a particular state elite in competition for power. In other words, a variety of political positions can be adopted by the police within this typology. The typology leaves unaddressed, therefore, the vexed issue of the relationship between policing and politics.

In beginning to theorise this relationship, a basic distinction needs to be drawn between the state and specific state institutions. The police are, like the military, custodians of the state's monopoly of legitimate force and thus are by definition guardians of the state's interests. But while the police are servants of the state in the sense of expressing its monopoly of legitimate force, the police are not duty-bound to defend specific state institutions like governments and political parties. The state is also not an uncontentious entity. There may well be competing state elites, and while the police are not compelled to become involved in the competition for power, they may be unable to stand aloof from it. Therefore, the involvement of the police in politics can be multifarious within our typology of order-maintenance strategies, and we need to extend the typology by theorising the broader issue of the nature and extent of the relationship between policing and politics.

Since police studies has entered what Reiner terms its 'conflict stage',[13] many commentators have asserted that there is a relationship between policing and politics,[14] although such claims have tended to be imprecise. We contend that one or more of six claims can be implied when advancing the assertion and that they constitute six dimensions which define the police-politics relationship. Each dimension is a continuum from weaker to stronger, which, to aid clarity, are presented here in stark contrast.[15]

1. The first concerns political beliefs. In its weak version the claim is that policemen and women are political animals who, like other citizens, hold political beliefs and opinions. In its strong version, this becomes the argument that police conduct is structured by these beliefs.
2. A second claim concerns the politicisation of policing as an issue. In its weak form the claim is that policing has become a subject of dispute in party politics and in competition for power between different state elites. In its strong form, the claim is that the police identify with one party or faction rather than another, and thus directly engage in party political disputes.
3. The third claim relates to police resources. In its weak form, the claim is that the police are part of the government's expenditure, so that the resources devoted to it reflect the political and other priorities of the state. In its strong version, this becomes the claim that the police manipulate the government's priorities, through crime scares, security threats and so on, in order to obtain a disproportionate share of resources.
4. The fourth claim concerns the police relationship to government policies. In its weak version the argument is that the police implement government policies impartially through enforcement of the laws which enact them. The strong form of this claim is that the police are partisan in the way they support these policies and the bias they exhibit against legitimate and lawful opposition to them.
5. Another claim concerns the permeation of the government's values and ideology within the police. In its weak form, the argument is that the police are affected by the values and ideology of the government. In its strong version, the claim is that the police actively support these values and ideology and reinforce them by denying legitimate opposition to them or in the expression of alternative values and ideologies.
6. The final claim posits, in its weak form, that the conduct of the police affects people's perceptions of the state and specific state institutions, and thus influences politics indirectly. The strong version of this claims that the police manipulate these perceptions by

trying both to deliberately manufacture positive images by careful presentation of its conduct, and avoid negative images arising from the deleterious consequences of police misconduct.

It is possible to conceptualise the relationship between policing and politics along these six dimensions. Each dimension is a continuum from weak to strong, and since these dimensions define the police-politics relationship, the relationship itself is a continuum, coming in weaker or stronger forms depending upon how it is constituted by each dimension. This can be presented diagramatically in Figure 1.

Figure 1. A model of the relationship between policing and politics

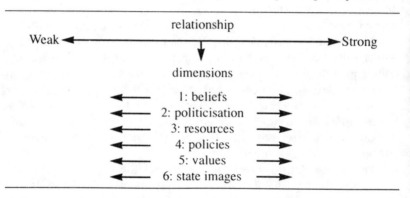

Different conclusions about the relationship between the police and politics emerge from the weak and strong versions of the relationship. Even the weak version denies the arguments of the British liberal model of policing, which presents the police as apolitical, neutral and independent of the state. However, the weak version casts the relationship between the police and politics as one-way. Policing is political in that the police manifestly come within the domain of the government's influence and are always affected by politics, but the police are passive in this relationship and largely reactive to government or state influence. In this form, the relationship describes a truism, since there is no institution which cannot in some way claim to be influenced by the political process and state power. In this sense schooling, broadcasting or medical care are also political, since they are influenced by the political process.

Like all truisms, this view of the relationship between policing and politics tells us relatively little: it advances our understanding only by making apparent something that was neglected by proponents of the liberal model of policing, who suggested that the police were apolitical. However, in the stronger version, the relationship between politics and the police is two-way. The police are proactive in politics, and partisanly advance the policies and ideology of the state, specific governments or competing state elites.

Theoretical models, however, become useful only when they can be applied in practice. The specific relationship that pertains between policing and politics in any society can be usefully described by means of these dimensions and mapped for each continuum. Since each dimension is a continuum from weak to strong, in practice particular police forces will vary in their location on the axis over different time periods and under different circumstances. For example, the extent to which Protestant members of the Royal Ulster Constabulary, who comprise nine out of every ten members of the force, allow their Unionist or Loyalist political beliefs to influence their conduct may vary depending upon whom they are policing, where they are stationed, the type of police work they undertake and the circumstances under which it's carried out. This reinforces the need to see each dimension as a continuum, with the location of the police along its axis being a substantive issue for investigation and judgement.

It is also the case that the police-politics relationship will be stronger or weaker in one dimension compared to another. For example, members of a police force may be partisan in holding beliefs which influence their conduct, and in advancing the policies and values of the state (or competing state elites), but care so little about how their conduct affects people's perceptions of the state that they are unconcerned to disguise or conceal police misconduct. It is not difficult to imagine this happening in a totalitarian state which is unaffected by how its image is perceived among the populace. Critics of the SAP alleged this was the case under the worst excesses of apartheid, at least with respect to Black South Africans, although certainly from the reform period of the mid-1970s even the SAP needed to be mindful of how its misconduct affected the state's image. Therefore, the relationship can be weaker or stronger on one or more dimension than another. However, depending upon how it is constituted along each dimension, the overall police-politics relationship, itself a continuum, will in particular cases veer identifiably more toward one pole than the other. A hypothetical case is diagramatically presented in Figure 2, where for illustrative purposes the police tend toward the weak form of the relationship in the degrees to which they are located on each dimension save that of resources, where they are orientated toward the stronger form because they manipulate a disproportionate benefit from the state's public expenditure.

Figure 2. The relationship between policing and politics in practice:
a hypothetical case

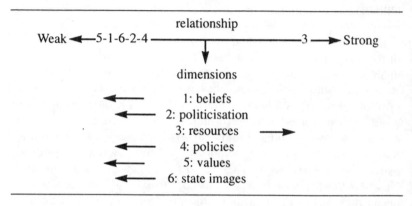

The relationship between policing and politics will also vary across different societies. The seven case countries considered in this volume, for example, fall at different places along the continuum from the weak to the strong version of the relationship between policing and politics. In no society is it possible to say that policing is apolitical, because with this theorisation even policing under the weak form of this relationship is shaped by the political process. Policing everywhere will thus be political at least in a weak sense. Police-state relations in some countries, however, will ensure that policing is political in the stronger sense.

It should be clear from this discussion, however, that societies will not fall neatly at one end or other of the continuum of the police-politics relationship, because they will not display along the six dimensions of the relationship either a consistently weak or strong form. Extreme cases at the weak or strong poles are unlikely in practice because each dimension which comprises the police-politics relationship is itself a continuum with different degrees along its axis and not all the dimensions are mutually exclusive. The personal beliefs of policemen and women in a particular society may tend toward the weaker form of the relationship for example, in that while they hold political beliefs and opinions these do not influence their conduct, whereas police manipulation of government or public opinion concerning fear of crime or threats to public order, among other things, can be used to strengthen their bargaining position over the allocation of public expenditure. Great Britain is a case in point. Northern Ireland offers an example of a police force which used civil unrest to its financial and strategic benefit, although some critics of the police in Northern Ireland deny that its members are ever politically impartial in their conduct.

Likewise, a particular police force might veer toward the strong form of the relationship on many of the dimensions but, for example, may be unable to manipulate an advantageous position for itself within the state's allocation of resources. South Africa prior to democratisation provides an illustration, as presented in Figure 3. The SAP under apartheid was perhaps one of the clearest examples of the stronger form of the police-politics relationship on virtually all dimensions (although their location on each axis differed because the degree of political partisanship and involvement varied). Nonetheless the SAP was always under-funded and under-staffed, sometimes excessively under-resourced, primarily because police functions were diffused throughout South African society and social control embedded in every apartheid institution.[16]

Figure 3. The relationship between policing and politics in apartheid South Africa

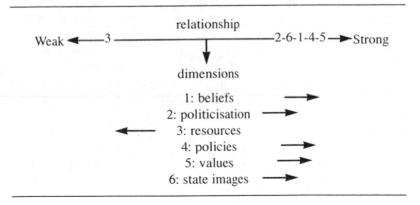

However, some of the dimensions are mutually exclusive, so that most societies empirically will have police forces which are identifiably toward one end of the continuum on most dimensions. Dimensions one, two, four and five particularly coalesce toward one end or other of the continuum. It tends to be the case, for example, that police forces which veer toward the strong form of the police-politics relationship in terms of the politicisation of policing as an issue (in that they 'side' with one party and engage in party dispute), are also toward that end of the continuum in terms of their active support for the policies of the government or rival elites, in the manner in which their personal political beliefs affect their conduct, and in the extent to which state values and ideology permeate their own values and beliefs.

For all these reasons, the theoretical model used here to conceptualise the police-politics relationship is also an empirical model, and in practice police forces can be classified according to the strength or weakness of the police-politics relationship that prevails. For example, in terms of the case countries considered in this volume, South Africa, Northern Ireland, Israel and the People's Republic of China have police forces which incline toward the stronger form of the relationship between policing and politics, while Great Britain, the Irish Republic and the United States evince the weaker version of the relationship.

However, since variation occurs within societies as the relationship between policing and politics varies over time, it is clear that some of the case countries considered in this volume have the prospect of considerable shift from one pole to the other under wider structural changes presently occurring in society. Thus, South Africa, one of the clearest examples of the strong form of the relationship before democratisation, now has the opportunity, in the current debate about police reform, of reforming the SAP to ensure it tends towards the weaker form of the police-politics relationship. The recent change in name to the South African Police Service seems to presage this. A similar shift could occur in Northern Ireland with the prospect of a permanent ceasefire and peace, allowing the Royal Ulster Constabulary to relinquish its paramilitary role and to establish meaningful relations with all sections of the community. This would facilitate a move toward a weaker form of the police-politics relationship in Northern Ireland. Critics of the police in Great Britain, however, still detect continuing movement in the opposite direction toward a stronger version of the police-politics relationship.

PUBLIC ORDER AND POLICING ISSUES IN CONTEMPORARY BRITAIN

The numbers exercised by the extension of police powers and the aggressive tactics employed by police officers have grown in scope and character since the 1980s. In the following decade Britain, as elsewhere, witnessed the burgeoning growth of new social movements which have created some unlikely strategic interest coalitions. Youthful animal rights protestors have, for instance, found common cause with suburban housewives in protesting against the export of live animals. Similarly, new age travellers and environmentalists have become unlikely bedfellows of property owners throughout middle England in seeking to protect the countryside from the development of new roads. Earlier in the 1990s, anarchists mingled with the middle classes in demonstrating against the poll tax, occasioning virtually unprecedented disorder in the heart of London. What middle-minded Britons have discovered at such events is the ubiquity of the powers available to the police and their readiness to deploy them against self-regarding law-abiding citizens.

Increasing proportions of the population have realised that what, misguidedly, they believed to be their right to engage in protest has been ever more tightly circumscribed. In such a context the thread of public consent in relation to policing has continued to fray. For instance, a MORI poll in 1993 showed that the proportion expressing satisfaction with the way their local area was policed had fallen from 75 per cent in 1981 to 51 per cent, while the dissatisfaction had risen from 23 per cent to 35 per cent in the same period.[17]

The particular affinity between the police and successive Conservative governments that we documented in 1988, far from restoring police credibility, has continued to undermine it. Moreover, the party that regards itself as one of law and order has, in a relatively short period of time, succeeded in estranging the police through its relentless pursuit of efficiencies across the public sector. This objective was given impetus by the Sheehy Report[18] which, *inter alia*, recommended the introduction of fixed term contracts and performance-related pay for all police officers, which, if implemented, would have broken the tradition of a national pay formula. These proposals alienated the vast majority of police officers of all ranks and provoked threats of resignation from a number of Chief Constables.

Coupled with proposals to alter the terms and conditions of employment, including pension rights, the Committee's recommendations led to an unprecedented meeting at the Wembly Conference Centre in July 1993 and the threat of strike action: an act which would have been illegal. In the event, the government had to retreat from the more radical recommendations and opted for an appraisal system for pay, introduced fixed-term contracts only for the most senior ranks and rationalised the rank structure. Irrespective of the merits or demerits of the Sheehy Report, what was compelling was its reception amongst the police. Through their representative bodies, a concerted and highly public campaign of opposition was mounted, exemplifying the confidence of the police to resist government proposals which they perceived to be inimical to their interests. In short, it signalled the continuing politicisation of policing.

However, the police have been unable to prevent the publication by the Audit Commission of performance tables for each of the country's forces.[19] These appeared for the first time in 1995, enabling 'consumers' of police services to draw comparisons among each of the 43 forces in England and Wales. The appearance of the figures, which show large variations in police performance, has occurred against a background of historically unseen rises in crime. In 1980, after the first full year of the Thatcher government, the total number of recorded offences was 2.52m, in December 1994 the comparable figure was 5.25m. Whilst the true crime rate is notoriously difficult to estimate, the 1992 British Crime Survey, which is funded by the Home Office, calculated that only about one in three offences is recorded in official crime statistics. Home Office statistics also show a fall in clear-up rates from 41 per cent in 1979 to 26 per cent in 1992.[20]

There is a paradox here: with more personnel and massively increased resources, the success of the police in the detection and solving of crime has fallen.[21] The paradox is all the more acute given the government's portrayal of the police as crime-fighters engaged in an unrelenting war against crime. While the Home Secretary talks in terms of renewing a 'partnership' between the police and the public,[22] such gladiatorial imagery sits uneasily with the service orientation preferred by many senior officers and large sections of the public. The emphasis on crime-control does contrast with the recent emphasis placed on crime prevention by the Labour Party, signalling the still yawning gap that exists between the major political parties on how best to tackle crime.

This is evinced not least in the Labour Party's stress on the social and economic causes of crime compared to the government's focus upon apparent moral decline and individual responsibility.[23]

Recent extensions of police powers, notably in the shape of the Criminal Justice and Public Order Act of 1994, which among other things has delegitimised the life styles of new age travellers, hunt saboteurs and rave-goers, epitomises the criminalisation strategy favoured by the government. This was welcomed by the police, as have been the ending of the right to silence, the creation of a national DNA databank, new powers to take non-intimate samples from suspects and to evict squatters. Such powers present the task of law enforcement to be concerned primarily with the deterrence rather than prevention of crime.

If anything, the discretion of Chief Officers has been compromised by the powers newly granted to the Home Secretary to specify national policing objectives. First enunciated for the year 1994–95, their introduction consolidates the drift towards the centralisation of policing we documented in 1988. Moreover, the role of local authorities has continued to be undermined via the Police and Magistrates Courts Act 1994, further subverting the tripartite model of police governance embodied in the 1964 Police Act.[24] The reduction in the number of elected members of police authorities which the legislation has caused does nothing to buttress the localism or the democratic accountability of the British policing system. Instead, there has been the official encouragement of neighbourhood watch schemes, wherein citizens are advised to 'walk with a purpose', a drive to recruit special constables and the unregulated growth of private security firms. Such developments have not commended themselves to the police who fear that they may merely encourage the growth of vigilantism and actually cause offences to occur by the vigilantes themselves.[25]

An audit of the period in Britain since 1988, therefore, does seem to amount to an increased deficit in police-public relations. Arming the police with more powers, personnel and financial resources, and criminalising more forms of protest activity, whilst simultaneously reducing the scope of police discretion and increasing the range of custodial sentences, has failed to reverse crime rates and succeeded in ensuring that policing matters remain at the top of the political agenda. The division between the major political parties on how best to tackle crime and its underlying causes, remains as wide as ever. Furthermore, the police themselves have demonstrated their preparedness to enter the political arena and set out their stall on what they believe is required to address the enforcement of law and order. Opposed to the narrowing of their operational autonomy, the police have shown a continuing willingness to enter the field of political controversy.

Policing in Britain is clearly at a crossroads. Rising trends in crime, new scenes of public disorder, increased use of armed-response, and a decline in public support for the police mark a persistent public concern over policing. The relationship between policing and politics has thus become more pronounced in Britain in the period since 1988, and the British police are moving toward the stronger form of the relationship. In this context, the need to debate the relationship between the police, public and the state is even more urgent than it was when we wrote the original volume.

Notes

1. See, for example, Fine and Miller (1985).
2. See, for example, Jefferson (1990), and his debates with Peter Waddington (1987, 1993).
3. See, for example, Kinsey, Lea and Young (1986).
4. See, for example, Cashmore and McLaughlin (1991).
5. See Brogden (1991).
6. See Geary (1985).
7. For a selection of this literature see Bridges (1983), Fielding (1991), Fine and Miller (1985), Hain (1980), Hall and colleagues (1978), Hillyard and Percy-Smith (1988), Scraton (1985), Uglow (1988).
8. See Reiner (1985, 1989).
9. On which see, for example, Benyon (1994a).
10. See David Waddington (1992).
11. These arguments are expanded upon further in Brewer (1988: 258-279).
12. A good discussion of the SAP's occupational culture is provided by Nico Steytler (1990).
13. See Reiner (1989).
14. For a selection see Fielding (1991), Fine and Miller (1985), Grimshaw and Jefferson (1987: 282-97), Turk (1982).
15. These arguments are a refinement and considerable extension of those found in Brewer (1994a, 1994b).
16. On the persistent under-funding and under-staffing of the SAP see

Brewer (1994a). For an application of an earlier version of this model to the SAP see Brewer (1994b).

17. Cited in Beynon (1994b). For data from the 1992 British Crime Survey which also documents the deterioration in the public image of the police, see Skogan (1994).
18. See HMSO (1993a).
19. See Audit Commission (1995).
20. See Mayhew *et al* (1993).
21. Benyon (1994b) shows that between 1981 and 1991, there was an increase of 10,000 police officers, and between 1982 and 1992, an increase in public expenditure on the police from £2.7bn to £7.1bn.
22. Quoted in HMSO (1993b).
23. See Loveday (1994).
24. See Marshall and Loveday (1994).
25. See Loveday (1994).

1 Introduction

The maintenance of internal order is at once both a topical and an enduring issue. The increasing frequency of disorder, the manner in which it is expressed and the responses of governments to more or less violent forms of protest and dissent have combined to propel policing to the forefront of the public mind. One symptom of the saliency of this issue has been a growing volume of research on both the police as an institution and policing as a set of functional activities, which has been especially notable in Britain. However, much of this work has tended towards an explicitly national and therefore insular approach, thereby neglecting a comparative dimension. This book represents an attempt to repair that neglect by setting public order policing in a comparative framework.

The enduring nature of order-maintenance is derived from the fact that it fulfils a primary need of all states. If order is not maintained, the process of nation-building will be based on only incomplete and insecure foundations. In this respect, it is surprising that the police have until recently either been overlooked or taken for granted, since they are commonly (if sometimes mistakenly) understood to provide the first line of defence against internal disorder. From a British viewpoint, such an oversight may seem justified. The proposition that the friendly, and familiar 'bobby' is somehow tarnished by politics, or (even more eccentrically) acts as an agent of the state would until recently have been dismissed as the fevered imaginings of the mad, bad and dangerous classes. Yet the attempt by Conservative governments since 1979 to redefine the relationship between state and society has led to a critical reappraisal of the role of the police. The heavy emphasis on social order which is characteristic of neo-Conservatism, together with its rejection of the post-war consensus, has generated a perception of the police at odds with the conventional view of them as disinterested arbiters of social conflict. The role of the police in upholding the *status quo* against the background of widely shared political values and rising material expectations was, for much of the period after 1945, conducive to a broadly harmonious relationship with the vast majority of the wider population. However, this is a different proposition in the changed ideological climate of Britain in the 1980s. The experience of continuing economic decline and mass unemployment, diminished life-chances and growing

1

disparities in material wealth have combined to make the policing of the new *status quo* much more controversial. In addition, the increased organisational capacity and seeming readiness of the police to engage in more aggressive forms of order-maintenance have generated doubts concerning their neutrality. In these circumstances, the idea that the police act in political ways to enforce government policies is no longer confined to the tributaries of radical opinion: it has flowed into the mainstream of British political debate.

This situation is by no means unique. In the contested political entity of Northern Ireland, the Royal Ulster Constabulary (RUC) has consistently been regarded by Irish Republicans as a repressive arm of the alien British state, whose purpose is to maintain the Unionist ascendancy. Moreover, where a dominant line of social cleavage is that of religous affiliation, the fact that the minority Catholic community is significantly under-represented in the ranks of the RUC is interpreted both by Nationalists and Republicans as *prima facie* evidence of discrimination and partisanship. The role of the RUC has become even more problematic since the signing of the Anglo–Irish Agreement in November 1985. In its wake, police officers have been subjected to intimidation and physical abuse by self-styled Protestant 'Loyalists', who regard the RUC's enforcement of the Agreement as an act of gross complicity in a process designed to undermine the Province's constitutional status.

The policing of public order in both Britain and Northern Ireland is discussed in this book. In addition, there are contributions on the Irish Republic, the USA, Israel, South Africa and China. In part, the choice has been based on the interests of the authors. Less prosaically, it has been governed by our concern to provide a breadth of comparison by including states at varying levels of development, with differing political structures and diverse ideological bases. Each chapter includes material on the size, composition and resources of the various police forces, although such data has proved more readily available in some cases than others. We have also tried to give a clear account of the formal structure of authority for the administration of the police in each case, and to provide a descriptive analysis of the relevant framework of public order law. The nature of police–military linkages is addressed, as are aspects of police militarisation. The mix of police and military can and does vary, not only across state boundaries but also within the same state over time. The police–military formula adopted in respect of domestic order-maintenance is one index of the nature of state–society relations. Emphasis on the military is (among other things) a signal of profound instability, whereas reliance upon the police suggests a more stable pattern of social relations. However, in the face of serious internal disorder a number of states have adopted the alternative of police militarisation as a means of either preventing or quelling disorder. This option may be preferred not only for tactical reasons but also because it enables states to sustain an image of civility for both their internal and external audiences. To illustrate public order policing in practice, each chapter cites a number of case studies that cover a wide range of situations and which disclose any apparent trends in the tactics and technologies of order-maintenance. Where possible, we have also produced evidence of public perceptions of the police, though the availability of such information varies considerably. Finally, each chapter analyses the police as a political institution so as to demonstrate the fact that they are not merely the dutiful and dispassionate enforcers of order, but policy actors with, (in some cases) decided views about the means they consider necessary to achieve social order. These items provide a common format for the book, with the authors lending particular emphases as they see fit.

The key concept of 'the state' which lies at the centre of this study is a contested one. In the Anglo–American world, the state only infrequently enters public debate. The legacy of liberal ideas in Britain and the USA has been a lasting one. By contrast, the continuing struggle for freedom in South Africa makes the state a more tangible entity, a prize that will symbolise the achievement of the oppressed. Similarly, the aspiration for a free and independent Palestine lends the idea of the state a more concrete reality as does the goal of Irish reunification. In China, the experience of revolution and the precepts of Chinese communism connote a markedly different relationship between state and society, with periodic outbursts of state-fomented disorder intended to purify and redirect the revolutionary creed. In short, the cultural and ideological values that form the bedrock of these countries crucially determine the nature and quality of state–society relations. Our major premise is that the condition of that relationship can be gauged by the nature and form of police–society relations as revealed in the realm of public order.

Just as states differ, so too do the police. The occasionally bewildering variety of police organisations within the seven countries considered did come as something of a surprise, not least in the case of Britain. Less surprising is the variation in the forms of police administration. Some (like South Africa) have a national police force which is administered by a single and centralised department of state. Others (like the USA) are characterised by a complex patchwork of forces, indicating a jealous regard for federal rights and resistance to centralised control. The primary responsibility for restoring internal order may be allocated to a functionally specialised unit, or it may be shared widely between a variety of forces, whose personnel are trained in the techniques of quelling disorder. Where external threats to the state combine with conflict founded upon internal divisions – as in Israel, South Africa and Northern Ireland – the linkages between the police and military are clearly evident, and the armed forces may emerge as the primary enforcers of order. In others such linkages are more discrete, and (as in Britain) police militarisation has become the preferred policy. Lines of control designed to secure the accountability of the police also differ and crucially influence the nexus between state, police and society.

'Public order' is itself an elusive concept. While each of the countries possesses a framework of public order law, the manner in which it is enforced varies not only between but also within states. Examples of such variations are perhaps most apparent in federal states like the USA, but they are no less evident in a unitary state like the UK. Differences in the way that outbreaks of disorder are dealt with exist not only between Northern Ireland and Britain, but also throughout Britain. The emphasis that is given to either preventive or suppressive strategies of public order policing takes its lead from the values of the prevailing regime. However, the police themselves can (and do) vary the manner in which they manage social conflicts. Their relative ability to exercise powers of discretion in choosing between alternative models of order-maintenance means that different styles of policing can co-exist within the same force, belying any simplistic assumptions about the 'national character' of any one police system. The exercise of discretionary powers also lends the police considerable political influence. The choices that police officers make in enforcing public order themselves affect the condition of state–society relations.

Nowhere are the police political innocents: to claim otherwise is disingenuous. By focusing on public order, policing is clearly revealed as a political activity. Recognition of this fact may be more palatable to the passive observer of events in South Africa or Northern Ireland, but it is no less true of Britain. Variations in the ways that order is maintained are not only instructive in themselves: setting their study in a comparative framework, provides insights into the relationship between state and society, and offers the opportunity to draw positive (and negative) lessons from the experience of others.

2 Great Britain

BACKGROUND

Public order policing in Britain has rapidly developed as a key issue on the contemporary political agenda. In the process, a number of seemingly inviolable features of both the police as an institution and policing as a set of functional activities have been challenged. The popular image of the British police as avuncular figures endowed with common sense and guided by the doctrine of minimum force now appears less persuasive. In the 1980s, police tactics during industrial disputes, at political demonstrations and during the course of violent street disorders in certain inner city areas, have damaged this sanguine portrait. Armed with new powers, possessing new equipment and co-ordinated on a national basis to combat disorder, they appear unfamiliar and discomfiting: less a part of society, more apart from it.

Yet the maintenance of public order, though essential, has always been a contestable activity: in Britain as elsewhere. As Reiner[1] observes, there has never been a 'Golden Age' of police–society relations. Episodic outbreaks of disorder have invariably raised doubts concerning the even-handedness of the police in dealing with those engaged in protest and dissent. The very creation of the 'New Police' in 1829 proved controversial, arousing the suspicions and hostility of rich and poor alike. The process by which they acquired legitimacy has been lengthy, and periodically turbulent. Indeed, the path to public acceptance was (and remains) uneven. But for much of the post-war period the police and policing policy have been relatively unproblematic. In part, this is explicable in terms of the prevailing bipartisanship that characterised inter-party debate about police matters. Until the 1980s, this debate was confined largely to the question of which of the two major parties, Conservative or Labour, was better able to increase manpower and improve the pay and conditions of service in order to prosecute the 'war against crime'. The terms of this debate tended to focus attention upon the police as crime-fighters to the relative neglect of (for example) measures making them answerable for their actions to the policed. However, the popular perception of the police as 'the men in the middle', uniformed but unarmed, has been crucial in winning and maintaining public consent. Moreover, their representation as the

6

'thin blue line' between order and anarchy seemed a durable meta-phor. Yet recent increases in police powers, the evolution of reactive or 'fire-brigade' policing, the adoption of unfamiliar crowd control equipment and tactics, the changes in public order legislation, in-stances of police violence, harassment and corruption, and evidence of racial prejudice in the country's largest force, the Metropolitan Police, have ensured that policing has become a live and salient issue in British politics.

Such developments have served not only to place a strain on police–society relations but they have also reawakened doubts about the nature of the British state. Changes in the nature of public order policing, set against the background of continuing economic decline and the occurrence of bitter industrial disputes and violent street disorders, have encouraged the view that Britain is becoming in-creasingly authoritarian. In some quarters, the police are now re-garded as a substitute for the continuing pursuit of collectivist and welfare-oriented policies, flourishing in an ideological climate that favours a conservative emphasis on political order at the expense of a liberal stress on rights. One casualty of the growth of this perception has been the post-war inter-party consensus about the police and policing. Its rupture is by no means confined to the order-maintaining function of the police, but extends to their mooted effectiveness in preventing and detecting ordinary crime. Recent reforms in police methods and organisation, including a heavy reliance on mobile patrol, are increasingly considered to be not only ineffective but counter-productive: by dramatising encounters between the police and public they have damaged the growth of police–community relations.

While the terms of the current debate may be new – between, for instance, 'hard' and 'soft' policing – the debate itself is not. In historical terms, its renewal may seem ironic. Peel's New Police were justified on a number of grounds, not least that they would both depoliticise and demilitarise the enforcement of law and order. Yet the police's newly acquired paramilitary capability has made explicit the inherent tension between order and liberty. Moreover, the in-creased readiness of the police to intervene publicly in this debate *is* novel and has contributed to the re-politicisation of policing.

STRUCTURE, ORGANISATION AND FINANCE

Numbers and Gender Composition

Since 1945, successive governments have both increased the size of the police establishment and transformed the organisation of the force into fewer and larger units. But assessing the numbers of police officers is not a straightforward exercise. Besides the regular police, the men and women in blue, there is a wide range of other forces that possess the executive powers of an ordinary constable, some of which are organised on an explicitly national basis. Moreover, the regular police have recruited an increasing number of civilians to undertake a variety of technical and clerical functions, thereby freeing uniformed officers from many routine and more specialised tasks. The regular force has itself become more specialised in a range of functions, not least that of order-maintenance. These and other developments, including the enhanced application of technology, have proved costly. Not only has the police budget grown, but it has in the recent past been sheltered from the exigencies of public expenditure cuts.

Over the past four decades, the number of British regular police forces has been reduced from 249 to 51: 43 in England and Wales and eight in Scotland. This trend towards fewer, larger forces was begun under the wartime Defence Regulations and accelerated by the Police Acts of 1946 and 1964, each of which empowered the Home Secretary to initiate compulsory amalgamations between forces. The final phase of reorganisation followed the reform of local government which was implemented in the mid-1970s. Throughout, the process has been justified on the ground of efficiency, although the development of larger units inevitably qualifies the idea of the police as a pre-eminently *local* force. The organisational distance of the police from the policed is further compounded by the existence in England and Wales of 10 (and in Scotland two) combined or joint forces, whose boundaries transcend single administrative counties.

Parallel with the accelerated restructuring of the police during the mid-1960s was a fundamental change in the organisation of policing, centred upon the concept of the 'Unit Beat'. Pioneered by an experiment in Aberdeen in the late 1940s, Unit Beat policing (UBP) was designed to achieve an efficient style of policing by marrying elements of old and new methods. It deployed resident area constables and motorised officers: the former anchored in local communities, intended to improve relations with the public; the latter providing fast response to incidents of crime and disorder. At station level, a

Table 2.1   Regular police in Britain: men and women 1960–84
(1960 = 100)

Year	Total	Index
1960	81 677	100
1965	94 771	116
1970	104 771	128
1975	119 514	146
1980	130 684	160
1984	134 248	164

Source: Calculated from the *Annual Reports* of Her Majesty's Inspectors of Constabulary for England and Wales and Scotland.

'collator' would assess information provided by the area constables to improve detection rates. This reform was described by the Chief Inspector of Constabulary as 'the biggest change in fundamental police operational methods since 1829'.[2] However, this mode of law enforcement has come to be regarded as 'fire-brigade' policing, minimising the familiar day-to-day contact between police and public.

During the early part of the war, the police were a reserved occupation, though as the manpower requirements of the armed forces grew it was progressively dereserved. Consequently the strength of the regular police fell from 57 102 in 1940 to 46 623 in 1945. The shortfall was made up by the creation of the Police War Reserve, a full-time body of paid temporary constables; the recruitment of full-time paid Special Constables; and the creation of the first Police Reserve, composed mainly of ex-policemen. The number of regular policewomen rose from 282 in 1940 to 418 in 1945; they were reinforced by the Women's Auxiliary Police Corps during the war.

Between 1946 and 1959, the total number of full-time regular police officers in Britain, men and women, rose from 54 382 to 81 889: this represented an improvement in police–population ratios from 1.56 per 1000 in England and Wales and 1.46 per 1000 in Scotland to 1.67 per 1000 throughout Britain. Using 1960 as the base year, aggregate figures for Britain at five yearly intervals are presented in Table 2.1. Police/population ratios have since risen consistently in both England and Wales and Scotland, though at differential

Table 2.2   Policewomen in Britain 1960–84 (1960 = 100)

Year	Total	Index
1960	2 553	100
1965	3 222	126
1970	3 975	156
1975	6 516	255
1980	11 201	439
1984	11 806	462

Sources: Calculated from the *Annual Reports* of Her Majesty's Inspectors of Constabulary for England and Wales and Scotland and the *Annual Reports* of the Commissioner for the Metropolis.

rates: from 1.68 to 2.43 per 1000 between 1960 and 1984 in England ane Wales; and from 1.70 to 2.60 per 1000 in Scotland over the same period.[3] While these figures conceal regional variations, the overall trend is clear: Britain has become more heavily policed.

Besides the growth in overall numbers, the gender composition of the regular police has been modified. While still overwhelmingly male, the number of policewomen has increased, in part because of the passage of equal pay and employment legislation in the mid-1970s. Between 1945 and 1959, the total number of full-time regular policewomen in Britain increased sixfold: from 434 to 2613. Since 1960, the figures at five-yearly intervals are shown in Table 2.2. The impact of the equality legislation is clear. Numbers have virtually doubled since 1975, so that the ratio of policewomen to policemen has continued to fall. In 1960 the ratio was 1:31, by 1975 it was 1:17 and by 1984 it had fallen to 1:10.

While women have entered the force in increasing numbers, there has been a conspicuous lack of success in attracting recruits from the ethnic minorities. The first non-White recruit to the Metropolitan Police (Met), Britain's largest force, joined in 1967. It was not until 1975 that the Met embarked on a campaign specifically designed to attract ethnic minorities. Its then Commissioner, Sir Robert Mark, signalled the purpose of the campaign thus:

> it is to be hoped that within the next few years the minorities will be represented in the . . . force in due proportion to their numbers

in the community. This is essential if [it] is to meet the challenge of policing London's increasingly multi-racial population.[4]

This goal has not been realised. In 1979, there were just 96 officers of 'New Commonwealth origin' in the Met; although this figure had risen to 232 in 1983, this was less than 1 per cent of the total force, whereas the proportion of non-Whites in the capital is equivalent to 11 per cent of the total adult population. Throughout Britain the picture is the same: less than 1 per cent of the total police strength is provided by non-Whites. Moreover, since the inner city riots of the early 1980s the position in London has further deteriorated. The poor quality of police – Black relations is reflected in the fact that applications from non-Whites to join the Met have fallen from 676 in 1982 to 400 in 1984: blue uniforms, white faces remains the rule.

One other trend of interest in the police's establishment is the growth in the number of civilian employees, which was fully endorsed by the 1967 report of the Police Advisory Board's Working Party on Manpower. Since 1960, the numbers of full-time civilians engaged in clerical and technical tasks has risen from 9358 to 32 441.[5] Using 1960 as our base index year, the growth of civilians at five-year intervals is: 1960, 100; 1965, 129; 1970, 218; 1975, 299; 1980, 323; 1984, 347.

Expenditure

The growth in the establishment of both officers and civilians, together with an increasing reliance on the application of technology, has inevitably led to rising police expenditure. Using 1967–68, the year of the Police Advisory Boards reports of Manpower, Efficiency and Equipment, as our base, net identifiable police expenditure (unadjusted) is presented in Table 2.3

Spending on the police in Britain appears under the general government heading of 'Law and Order and Protective Services' (LOPS), which also includes the penal system, law courts, civil defence, immigration and citizenship, fire service and community services. A recent study of LOPS spending[6] shows that it tripled in cost terms between 1963 and 1983, doubling its share of GDP to 2 per cent and increasing its share of public expenditure from 2.6 to 4 per cent. Over the same period, spending on the police increased on average by 5 per cent per annum in cost terms. The current Conservative government's stress on law and order is reflected by the fact that between 1979–83, while intent upon controlling public expenditure as

Table 2.3   Net identifiable police expenditure in Britain (£000) 1967–68 to
1983–84 (to nearest £000)

Financial year	England and Wales	Scotland	Total
1967–68	247 985	22 499	270 484
1968–69	259 149	24 019	283 168
1969–70	284 522	26 512	311 034
1970–71	333 278	31 819	365 097
1971–72	390 400	36 479	426 879
1972–73	425 800	42 413	468 213
1973–74	495 900	49 176	545 076
1974–75	640 300	62 528	702 828
1975–76	820 500	75 635	896 135
1976–77	989 844	95 460	1 085 304
1977–78	1 064 094	101 760	1 165 854
1978–79	1 177 994	118 177	1 296 171
1979–80	1 514 877	149 313	1 664 190
1980–81	1 805 420	179 563	1 984 983
1981–82	2 148 764	209 804	2 358 568
1982–83	2 364 710	230 200	2 594 910
1983–84	2 569 941	250 510	2 820 451

Source: *Annual Reports* of Her Majesty's Inspectors of Constabulary for
England and Wales and Scotland.

a whole, the police budget rose in cost terms by 5 per cent per
annum, compared with a rise of only 2 per cent in general government spending. In part, this was due to its electoral commitment in 1979
to improve police pay, which accounts for approximately 85 per cent
of the police budget, and also its traditionally heavy emphasis upon a
law and order platform. However, there has been relatively little
difference since 1964 between the ability of Labour and Conservative
governments to increase establishment levels. Between 1964 and
1970, under two Labour governments, there was a 14 per cent
increase; under the Labour Government of 1974–79 a 7 per cent
growth. The Conservative governments of 1970–74 and 1979–83
achieved establishment increases of 8 and 5 per cent respectively.
Paradoxically, the growth in both numbers and expenditure has
tended to have little impact on the effectiveness of the force as a law
enforcement agency: crime rates have risen while detection rates
have faltered.

A growing concern with police effectiveness has led the Home
Office to encourage all forces to adopt a new strategy, 'Policing by

Objectives', designed to improve performance levels. It represents the application to the police of the 'value for money' credo favoured by the Thatcher government and suggests a new era in police expenditure. For the first time since 1979 its LOPS budget for 1986–87 shows a reduction, while planned spending on the police has been increased below the anticipated inflation rate. To ensure compliance with the spending targets, the Home Office has assisted the Inspectorate of Constabulary in the development of a 'Financial Management Information System' which will be used to analyse spending at individual force levels. The apparent immunity from public expenditure cuts enjoyed by the police since 1979 seems thus to have been breached.

Other Forces

In discussing the British police, it is conventional to think of the 'thin blue line' of regular officers organised on a decentralised basis. While there have been periodic proposals for the creation of a national regular force, these have been rejected both by the police and successive governments. However, there *are* national police forces in Britain, plus a diverse range of other forces that give the police system as a whole a decidely patchwork character.

During the 1970s, the Home Office commissioned a now declassified study that identified 32 'other' forces ranging in size from the Ministry of Defence (MOD) Constabulary with (in 1977) over 5000 officers, to the Gloucester Park Constables with an establishment of two.[7] The three largest of these, the MOD police, the British Transport Police (BTP) and the UK Atomic Energy Authority Constabulary (AEA), each have their own Chief Constable, a national organisational structure, a distinctive line of ministerial responsibility and separate training establishment. Both the MOD and AEA police are issued with firearms which, in the latter case, extends to submachine guns when escorting fissile material to the reprocessing facilities at Sellafield. Until 1976, the AEA police were restricted in the use of their powers to within a 15-mile radius of atomic energy establishments. Following legislation introduced by the then Energy Secretary, Tony Benn, they are now able to exercise those powers in any place where it appears expedient to go to protect material or arrest a suspected nuclear criminal. The MOD police are limited to within a fifteen-mile radius of defence facilities and to personnel subject to the discipline of the three armed forces.

Nationally, the MOD police are divided into five areas, each under
the operational control of an Assistant Chief Constable, while the
BTP is organised into eleven territorial divisions. Since 1981, the
latter has possessed a dozen mobile patrol units covering London and
six other major cities that can be deployed to deal with 'situations
where public order is threatened'. Recent establishment figures for
the three forces are: MOD 3930, including 127 plain clothes officers;
BTP, 2154; UKAEA, 618. Thus, not only has the 'thin blue line'
thickened, it has been paralleled by a wide range of other forces –
public knowledge of which is, in some cases, rather scanty.

FORMAL STRUCTURE OF AUTHORITY

Tripartism

The regular police in Britain are governed by the terms of the Police
Act 1964. This describes the relationship between the three key
actors involved – central government (in England and Wales the
Home Office, in Scotland the Scottish Office); local government, in
the form of Police Authorities; and chief police officers. Formally,
the police are governed on a tripartite basis: yet the practical relationships within this framework are not as between equals.

Sections 4, 5 and 28 of the 1964 Act identify the respective
responsibilities of each of the actors. There are two important dimensions of the role of the Home and Scottish Secretaries who are
charged to 'promote the efficiency of the police'.[8] Until recently,
policing costs in Britain have been shared on a parity basis between
central and local government under grant arrangements first established in 1920. This provided the two central departments with a
powerful financial lever. Since April 1986, this lever has been strengthened; henceforth, central government is to provide 51 per cent of
policing costs, representing an enhanced shift to central control over
police funding.

The second dimension involves the Inspectorate of Constabulary.
Established in 1856, the Inspectorate is maintained by the Home
Office and visits each force on a regular basis to report on its
efficiency.[9] The financial contribution provided by the Home Office is
conditional upon the Inspectorate's view of force efficiency. If the
Home Secretary is dissatisfied with a particular force, he can with-
hold all or part of the grant provided by his department. In addition,
he can require a chief officer to retire in the interests of efficiency.

The powers of central government are extensive, and have been used to achieve uniformity and standardisation throughout the police service. The Home Office provides a wide range of services on a national basis, including police colleges and training centres, forensic science laboratories and research and development facilities. Though the authorised establishment for each force is formally determined by the three parties, the Home Secretary (advised by the Inspectorate) has the final say.

In operational terms, the chief officer is an autonomous agent. Though the Home Office periodically issues circulars to chief officers on aspects of force policy and efficiency, they possess only an advisory status. Neither the Home nor Scottish Secretary can instruct chief officers in 'the direction and control' of their forces. The same is true of Police Authorities. Additionally, this position is well established in law. British courts have emphasised that a chief officer is wholly independent of the executive arm of government and is answerable only to the law. The 1962 Royal Commission on the Police, which led to the 1964 Act, recognised that chief officers ought to be 'subject to more effective supervision', but insisted that their impartiality in law enforcement should not be compromised. Their consequent operational independence lies at the root of much current controversy, since it is increasingly perceived to qualify the meaning of police accountability. Though required by the Police Act to submit annual reports to the Home Secretary and the relevant Police Authority, in pre-operational terms the chief officer is inviolable. Furthermore, while a Police Authority can request other reports on specific events or incidents, the chief officer concerned can refer the request to the Home Secretary if he considers that it is not in the public interest, or unnecessary for the Authority's full exercise of its powers. The Home Secretary functions as the arbiter in such cases. While the Home Secretary is empowered to order an enquiry into any matter connected with the policing of any area, this power has tended to be used only sparingly; for instance, Douglas Hurd refused to establish enquiries into the street disorders in London and Birmingham during the autumn of 1985. Other powers enjoyed by the chief officer include the appointment, promotion and discipline of all officers to the rank of superintendent and the provision of mutual aid to another force at the request of another chief officer or if directed by the Home Secretary (see below).

The third set of actors in this triangular framework are the Police Authorities. In England and Wales, they consist of two-thirds local councillors and one-third unelected magistrates, charged by the 1964

Act 'to secure the maintenance of an adequate and efficient force for their area'. All but two of the 43 police forces have Authorities constituted in these terms. In London, however, the Home Secretary functions as the Police Authority for the Metropolitan Police while the Common Council of the City of London acts in this capacity for the City of London force. The Authorities are empowered to: appoint chief, deputy and assistant chief constables; require them to retire in the interests of efficiency; determine the number of officers of each rank; and provide and maintain buildings, equipment and vehicles required by the force. Yet *all* these powers are subject to the approval of the Home Secretary. Additionally, the Authorities oversee the investigation of complaints against their force's officers and as a whole functions as the disciplinary body for senior officers. Given the parity of police funding which existed until 1986 and the near parity that now prevails, it could be assumed that a Police Authority exerts an influence over its force commensurate with its financial responsibilities: this is not the case. The traditional implications of the maxim 'the power of the purse' do not apply to the police. What appears as a tripartite structure of police governance is in practice a bipartite system of control. Nowhere is this more apparent than in the context of public order policing.

In Scotland, the role of Police Authorities is essentially the same, with two important exceptions. First, the Authorities are composed entirely of councillors drawn from the eight regional tiers of government. Secondly, the Secretary of State is the responsible minister, but (according to a former Permanent Secretary to the Scottish Office) he is under no general duty to promote police efficiency, as is the case in England and Wales.[10] Despite such differences the weakest link in the structure of police administration is the Police Authority. Providing for an adequate and efficient force means, in practice, making men and material available to the chief officer, who uses his discretion in deploying them.

The introduction in 1986 of joint boards, composed of district councillors and unelected magistrates, to administer the police in six metropolitan areas of England has increased the powers of central government. The boards replace the previous Police Authorities which were formerly controlled by the majority party in the relevant administrative area. For the first three years, the budgets of the joint boards will be fixed by the Home Office. This represents enhanced financial control by central government over the policing of the most populous regions of England.

As neither servants of the Crown nor Police Authorities, all police officers enjoy an independence among public servants equalled only by judges. One important effect of this is to inure the police from Parliamentary accountability. While the generalised annual reports of the Chief Inspectors of Constabulary for England and Wales and Scotland, together with those of the Metropolitan Commissioner, are laid before Parliament, the more detailed reports on individual forces made by the Inspectorate are not. A distinction needs to be drawn between the provincial forces and the Metropolitan force in respect of Parliamentary accountability. In the latter case, as we have seen, the Home Secretary functions as its Police Authority: the Met's chief officer, the Commissioner, is accountable to him for force conduct, administration, policy and law enforcement. The extent to which the Home Secretary can intervene in operational matters is unclear, although his role does enable London's 92 MPs to ask Parliamentary Questions of him in respect of the force. It was not until 1983 that the House of Commons held what one MP described as the first full day's debate on the Met which, he estimated, allowed members to speak for approximately nine minutes each.

Unsatisfactory though this situation is, the position of MPs in relation to provincial forces is even less adequate. The implication that the Home Secretary is answerable to Parliament for them is uncertain. One observer notes that while prepared to answer questions on administrative matters concerning provincial police forces, successive Home Secretaries have 'shown a marked reluctance to answer [them] on police policy and law enforcement'.[11] This situation places the vast bulk of MPs at a real disadvantage in seeking to achieve accountability of their local forces. However, proponents of the *status quo* argue that the British police are fully accountable via the Police Authorities, disciplinary procedures, the complaints system and the law. Yet the weaknesses of the Police Authorities can be gauged from a brief overview of tripartism in relation to aspects of public order policing.

Tripartism in Practice

One of the implicit themes in the preceding discussion is that certain aspects of policing policy and administration display a trend towards centralisation. This carries profound implications for Police Authorities, the formal co-equals of central government, and chief officers. The constraints affecting the Authorities can be briefly indicated in relation to mutual aid, the role of the National Reporting Centre (NRC), and the acquisition of riot control equipment.

The system whereby local police forces are authorised to make standing arrangements to deal with public disorder is known in Britain as mutual aid. Originating in the late nineteenth century, mutual aid became generalised during the 1920s and was updated by the Police Act 1964. This authorised chief officers to provide men and material to any other force in need. It also empowered the Home Secretary to direct a chief officer to make such aid available if, in his view, it was required. During a national steel strike and street disorders in 1980, the mutual aid system was found wanting. This led the Home Office to conduct a review into the arrangements for 'handling spontaneous disorder' which resulted in improved and standardised arrangements for the co-ordinated mobility of officers trained in the techniques of order maintenance. Yet the Police Authorities were seemingly uninvolved in reforming the system which, *inter alia*, has had adverse financial implications for them. Under existing arrangements, where a chief officer provides aid to another force the Authority in receipt of that aid is expected to reimburse the donor Authority. If the relevant parties fail to agree upon the sums involved the Home Secretary acts as arbiter, fixing the amount according to a stipulated formula.[12] During the 1984–85 miners' dispute, a series of running battles was fought between Police Authorities and the Home Office over the costs incurred. The ability of chief officers to provide aid apparently regardless of cost, coupled with the Home Secretary's power to determine the basis upon which aid was made available, left the Authorities in a mire of confusion and put tripartism on the financial rack: 'The Home Secretary allowed [chief constables] to spend with immunity . . . police authorities have been shown to have no control over police expenditure for which they are responsible.'[13]

Mutual aid is normally provided at a local level between neighbouring forces to deal with short-term problems of crowd control. Occasionally, however, aid is needed on a scale deemed to require a national policing response. To this end, following an earlier miners' dispute that had exposed weaknesses in the police response to mass picketing (notably at Saltley coke depot), the National Reporting Centre was established in 1972.

Based at New Scotland Yard, the Centre is activated when, in the view of the leaders of the Association of Chief Police Officers (ACPO), police forces in a number of areas are likely to need aid to deal with major public order events. The NRC, which has no statutory basis, has been fully activated on at least five occasions including the inner city riots of 1981, the printworkers' dispute at Warrington in 1983 and the last miners' dispute. The actual chain of command via the Centre is a matter of some conjecture. According to a Home Office document issued during the miners' dispute, it is activated by the annually selected President of the ACPO in consultation with his colleagues and the Home Office. The President is assisted by a member of the Inspectorate and other ACPO members, and provides daily situation reports to the Home Secretary when the Centre is fully operational. The official view is that the NRC co-ordinates the deployment of officers, whereas critics regard its role as a controlling one – in effect, providing Britain with a *de facto* national riot police. It is unclear whether during the last miners' strike there was either executive direction by the Home Office over police deployment or that the Centre was instructing local forces on the policing of the dispute, thereby qualifying the operational autonomy of the aided chief officers. However, the frequency and stridency of Cabinet Ministers in extolling the 'right to work' of non-striking miners may have made the issuing of explicit instructions somewhat redundant.

While the relationship between the Home Office and the ACPO in relation to the NRC is opaque, the role of the Police Authorities *vis-à-vis* the Centre is transparent: it is non-existent. Yet the activation of the NRC to facilitate mutual aid throughout England and Wales (Scotland is not covered by the Centre) affects the Authorities in two important ways. First, the *aided* Authorities appear unable to exert control over the costs involved in receiving assistance; and secondly, the *aiding* Authorities find their force numbers depleted, thereby compromising their statutory duty to provide 'adequate and efficient' policing in their own areas.

The creation of the NRC, and its effects upon the mutual aid system, makes it clear that police forces in England and Wales possess the organisational capability to mobilise specially trained officers on a national basis to deal with outbreaks of disorder. Moreover, this capability appears to be governed on a bipartite not a tripartite basis, although the exact relationship between the Home Office and the ACPO exists in a twilight world of speculation, charge, counter-charge and denial. The directive role of central government is much more evident in relation to the acquisition of riot control equipment.

In his Annual Report for 1972–73, the Chief Inspector of Constabulary, commenting upon the enforced closure of Saltley coke depot by a mass picket, stated: 'If this type of activity persists, the police must and will improve their own flexibility and ability to maintain public order'. (Hence the creation of the NRC.) 'However', he continued, 'you may be assured that police officers will continue to do their duty by traditional methods and without special equipment, relying on experience, training and judgement and their customary good humour'. In the intervening period not only has a variety of forms of 'special equipment' been acquired, but they have become standard issue throughout Britain: for laughing and non-laughing policemen alike.

The most controversial items of riot control equipment are plastic bullets, even though they have not, as yet, been used on the British mainland. Officially styled as 'baton rounds', they have become a standard weapon in the armoury of the RUC in Northern Ireland since 1978, when they wholly replaced the rubber bullet, although they had been available to the army in the Province since 1974. In 1982, the Home Office announced that a supply of 3000 plastic bullets was to be made available to police forces in England and Wales. Following the announcement, the National Council for Civil Liberties (NCCL) conducted a survey to ascertain their distribution and the role of the Police Authorities in their acquisition. According to Spencer,[14] the extent of an Authority's involvement in their purchase depended upon the quality of its relationship with the relevant chief officer. Some Authorities deferred to their chief constables, viewing their acquisition as an operational matter, whereas others sought to influence the decision in a variety of ways. But initially it did appear that Authorities were able to exercise some discretion in both the purchase and the potential use of the weapon. However, there were two notional qualifications to be made. First, the statutory duty to provide mutual aid could compel an Authority to buy the bullets, otherwise it could be found wanting in its ability to supply assistance; secondly, the Home Office might take the view that an Authority which used its financial powers to prevent their purchase was failing in its obligation to provide an 'adequate and efficient' force.

Despite the apparent discretion available to Police Authorities, one or two anomalies did occur. For instance, the Chief Constable of the Greater Manchester Police, James Anderton, had his request to purchase the rounds vetoed by his Authority. To circumvent this opposition, he instead acquired them on permanent loan from the Metropolitan Police: a tactic that met with the full approval of the Home Secretary. In February 1986, the Chief Constable of the West

Midlands Constabulary, Geoffrey Dear, was denied his request to buy plastic bullets by his Authority. However, two months later he was able to acquire them when the Labour controlled Authority was replaced by a new joint board whose unelected magistrate members swung the vote in favour of purchase. Such anomalies are now unlikely to recur as a result of a decision made in May 1986 by the Home Secretary, Douglas Hurd. He announced that henceforth a force would be able to secure both CS gas and up to 1000 plastic bullets from a central store administered by the Inspectorate – notwithstanding the opposition of its Police Authority. The Authorities are thus unable to determine the forms of riot technology available to their police forces – even though the plastic bullet has been responsible for thirteen deaths in Northern Ireland, including those of six children.

The net effect of changes to the mutual aid system, the creation of the NRC and improved access to riot equipment by chief officers is the erosion of the role of the Police Authorities in the governance of the police. By degrees, tripartism has been diminished, to the heavy advantage of central government and chief officers.

POLICE–MILITARY RELATIONS

Order-maintenance Strategy

The Home Secretary's decision on plastic bullets and CS gas is one instance of the process of militarising the British police to deal with public disorder. Throughout, successive governments and police spokesmen have described this process as a reactive one. Developments in riot equipment, training and tactics are justified as responses to an escalating scale of violence on the part of marchers, demonstrators or strikers. The establishment of the NRC followed the ignominy experienced by the police in being overwhelmed by sheer numbers of pickets at Saltley. The use of riot shields at the Notting Hill Festival in 1977 was the result of the police having to defend themselves with dustbin lids at the same event a year earlier. Following the riots of 1980 and 1981, not only were mutual aid arrangements improved but a review of public order equipment was carried out by the Home Office. This resulted in the issue of new riot helmets, fire resistant clothing and three types of 'defensive' shield. Taken together, these developments have undoubtedly improved the ability and the preparedness of the police to quell various forms of disorder. They also threaten to impair the doctrine of minimum force – although the full effects of the changes in the style of public order policing were not evident until the 1984–85 miners' dispute, specifically at the Orgreave coking plant in Yorkshire.

The use of other than minimum force has not been uncharacteristic of Britain's colonial police. Indeed, it is arguable that recent methods of public order policing in Britain have incorporated tactics formerly tried and tested in the colonies. For instance, it seems more than coincidental that in the aftermath of the 1981 riots, senior officers from the Hong Kong police were invited to the Police Staff College to lecture to their British counterparts on crowd control techniques. More immediately, the police in Britain have drawn lessons from the experiences of the RUC in Northern Ireland, where rubber and plastic bullets and armoured vehicles have become orthodox methods of riot control.

Images of the British police bedecked with their new riot equipment do not square with the traditional picture of the 'bobby on the beat'; yet they are only the most graphic representation of recent changes to the force. The ability to acquire, interpret and exploit intelligence is no less relevant to the maintenance of order than more conventional forms of policing. The introduction by the Met of District Information Officers (DIOs) in 1982 is an expression of the need to gather information to head off potential disorder. Their role was defined by the Commissioner, Sir Kenneth Newman, as being 'conscious of tensions and undercurrents within communities which are likely to spill over into disorder'.[15] Rooted in the role of collator introduced in the 1960s the DIOs, by assessing information received from beat and patrol officers will, in Newman's view, enable local forces to take 'sensible' action designed to 'reduce friction and misunderstanding'. This innovation seems to be a lesson drawn from police practice in the USA, where emphasis has been given to the development of 'race sentiments barometers' that function as indicators of community tension.

Such preventive measures have not diminished the felt need of the police to create specialised mobile reserves to quell disorder where it occurs. Newman is sensitive to the problems created by the existence of such units: 'A delicate balance is to be struck between retaining an effective reserve for cases of sudden disorder and risking the alienation of significant parts of the community who see an uncaring anonymity or even veiled threat in the deployment of such forces'.

The balance can, according to the Commissioner, be maintained by 'increasing the level of local identification of such units in order to counteract negative impressions likely to be created by groups of unknown officers within a community'.[16] This seems unlikely. The nature of riot control equipment imparts a threatening anonymity to all officers, whether or not they are drawn from a local force. The creation of such reserves is of course an alternative to reliance upon the military to preserve or restore order. Yet the price has been the drift towards a paramilitary police force. Whether this is a pre-planned trend or a pragmatic response, the effects upon police–society relations will be qualitatively different from those that obtained in the more settled post-war decades.

The organisational forms through which the police maintain order are Police Support Units (PSUs), which are possessed by all forces in Britain. (In Scotland they are called Special Support Units.) They each consist of 23 divisionally based officers who are normally engaged in routine police work. In total there are, according to Kettle, 416 PSUs in England and Wales involving more than 13 000 officers.[17] In addition, the Met has other riot trained officers at its disposal, in the shape of the Special Patrol Group (SPG), and its version of PSUs, District Support Units (DSUs). The SPG has proved to be an especially controversial force. Formed in 1965, it was described by the then Commissioner as a 'highly mobile striking force' consisting of 204 men who were divided into six equal units which were based at 'strategic points' throughout London. The SPG swiftly acquired a reputation for violent public order policing, which culminated in the implication of a number of its officers in the death of a demonstrator (Blair Peach) during street disorders at Southall in 1979. Allegations of routine violence against the Group and the possession of a wide variety of unauthorised weapons by its personnel have led to demands by (among others) the Labour Party that it should be disbanded. Though the SPG still exists, its role was temporarily redefined. In 1983, the Met's Commissioner announced that the DSUs would in future provide the first and second wave response to disorder, with the Group relegated to a tertiary role in public order policing. However, this has since been superseded as the result of a recent review of public order policing undertaken by the Met.

The training received by the PSUs is governed by a manual, 'Public Order Tactical Options', devised by a working party of the Association of Chief Police Officers (ACPO) following the inner city riots of 1980–81.[18] This document, which has not been laid before Parliament or made available to Police Authorities, can be read in full only by officers of the rank of Assistant Chief Constable and above. It contains details of some 238 tactics and manoeuvres which are practised at special training centres possessed by a number of forces. (The Met's centre at Hounslow in west London is nicknamed 'Riot City'.) Four sections of the manual were disclosed during the trial of 14 miners accused of riot during the recent dispute. One of the sections describes how teams of officers equipped with shields, riot helmets and truncheons should form 'snatch squads':

> On command, the short shield officers run forward either through or around the flanks of long shield officers into the crowd for not more than 30 yards. They disperse the crowd and incapacitate missile throwers and ringleaders by striking in a controlled manner with batons about the arms and legs or torso so as not to cause serious injury.

The injunction to 'strike in a controlled manner' is, in effect, an invitation to inflict bodily harm, which to say the least is legally dubious. Moreover, in the heat of the moment at Orgreave, where these tactics were used for the first time in a major industrial dispute, it was evident to witnesses that the police involved did not restrict themselves to the bodies and limbs of the miners. Many of the strikers received head and neck injuries yet no police officers were charged as a result, whether on this occasion or elsewhere during the dispute.

Other sections of the manual advise that 'to use the show of force to the greatest advantage' officers should 'make a formidable appearance', while mounted police are instructed to advance in double rank at a 'fast walk or steady trot' so as to 'inspire fear created by the impetus of horses'. Officers are also recommended to beat their shields with their truncheons in a rhythmic fashion – a practice that was discontinued after widespread public protests. Such tactics are a far cry from the normality of mutual pushing and shoving that until recently characterised the pattern of police–picket relations.[19]

Another aspect of police militarisation is the issue and use of firearms. While the British police are popularly understood to be an unarmed force, the numbers of officers trained in the use of guns has grown. No figures are released about the number of police firearms that are on the streets each day, though certain specialised units are routinely armed. These include the Diplomatic and Royalty Protection Group; some Special Branch officers; members of the Anti-

Terrorist and Robbery Squads; certain SPG officers; plus members of elite firearms units like the Met's D11 squad, which is also responsible for firearms training within the force. As a result of a series of recent incidents involving police weapons that led to either the serious injury or death of a number of innocent people – including a five year old boy – training procedures have been overhauled and the Met has announced a reduction in the number of officers authorised to carry a firearm.

Police–military relations *per se* are codified in regulations known as 'Military Aid to the Civil Power'. The last occasion on which the military were deployed to restore order in Britain was in 1919 – during a police strike in Liverpool. However, since 1945 troops have been used on 36 occasions under the terms of 'Military Aid to the Civil Ministries' to maintain 'essential services' during the course of a variety of industrial disputes and states of emergency. Conspicuous evidence of police–military liaison has been provided during the course of incidents involving terrorists, most dramatically at the siege of the Iranian Embassy when units of the Special Air Services (SAS), supported by the police, stormed the building to release the hostages. In addition, since 1974 when the Met took over responsibility for its security, periodic anti-terrorist exercises involving both troops and police have been undertaken at Heathrow airport. Recently, police officers at Heathrow have been issued with the sub-machine guns acquired by the Met in 1984. Besides such overt evidence, police--military liaison is also close in the planning and implementation of security arrangements for major ceremonial occasions and other potential targets. This was given renewed emphasis after the Brighton bomb of 1984.

The need for information is a prime requisite in a strategy that seeks to prevent the occurrence of disorder. To this end, the police have developed increasingly sophisticated techniques to gather and store data. In 1970 the Police National Computer (PNC) was commissioned. Located at Hendon, it became fully operational four years later and provides immediate access to a wide range of information for all forces. In May 1985 written answers to a series of Parliamentary questions disclosed the extent of the computer's records: almost 5 million names listed on the criminal names index – equivalent to 1 in 11 of the total population; 3.5 million sets of fingerprints; over 35 million vehicle owners; and details of almost 350 000 suspect and stolen vehicles. The scale of these records, together with the fact that certain of them are encoded as of relevance to Special Branch, has provoked allegations that the PNC is a versatile and potentially sinister intelligence resource.

'Special Branch' is in one sense something of a misnomer. It is not a unified or national force although the Met's Special Branch does have national responsibilities in combatting Irish terrorism. Each force has its own Special Branch component, in total numbering 870 personnel in 1985, 379 of whom were attached to the Met. Their remit is to gather information about threats to public order, espionage, acts of terrorism, sabotage and the actions of individuals and groups deemed to be subversive. Each gathers its own information which can be disseminated to other Branches as the need arises. At the heart of this complex web of information (which includes the records held by the Met's 'C' Department, estimated to include details of 2 million individuals) is the relationship between Special Branch and Britain's security services, especially M15. Liaison between them is necessarily close since M15 operatives possess no executive powers. Search warrants are issued to Special Branch officers and all arrests are made by them.

The extent of information held in relation to 'public order' is not known: much seems to depend on the discretion of Special Branch. According to a former chief constable, his own component of his force displayed an insatiable appetite for information some of which was 'out-dated' and 'inessential'.[20] In 1985, a limited enquiry by the Home Affairs Select Committee into Special Branch, the first to be held in Britain, revealed a divide between the parties over its activities. The Committee's Conservative majority gave the force a clean bill of health in relation to its public order role, whereas the Labour members chose to emphasise the lack of scrutiny over the Branch and called for an independent inquiry into its records and practices.[21] Disclosures by a former employee of M15, Cathy Massiter, about the blanket surveillance engaged in by the intelligence services and the illegality of certain methods employed by both M15 and Special Branch officers, has done nothing to allay anxiety surrounding the domestic activities of those who have been described as 'the watchers'.

Public Order: the Legislative Context

In June 1979, two months after the street disorders in Southall, the newly elected Conservative government announced a review of public order law. During the review, a number of reports were published that were of direct relevance to it: 'The Law Relating to

Public Order' produced by the Home Affairs Select Committee; Lord Scarman's report on the Brixton disorders; and the English Law Commission's report, 'Offences Relating to Public Order'. The outcome of the review was the Public Order Bill 1982 which, in a second and revised form, was enacted in 1986 and has changed the law throughout Britain, with provisions made for the differences in common law in Scotland. Moreover, the Scottish Law Commission has yet to finish its review of the offence of 'mobbing and rioting', while a new system for regulating public processions was introduced north of the border by the Civic Government (Scotland) Act 1982. The legal framework of public order in Britain has thus undergone a number of important changes. Before turning to the proposed changes, a brief survey of current law is necessary.

Prior to the 1986 Act, public order offences in England and Wales – such as breach of the peace, riot, unlawful assembly and affray – depended on the common law and were not codified in any single statute. (In Scotland the common law public order offences are breach of the peace and mobbing and rioting.) In addition there is a body of statute law relevant to public order dating from the seventeenth century. The most important of these statutes is the much more recent Public Order Act 1936. This introduced the power to ban any procession which, in the view of a chief officer, is reasonably likely to lead to serious public disorder, together with a power to impose conditions on any march to prevent such disorder. Outside London, such a ban is imposed by the relevant local authority, with the consent of the Home Secretary. In the capital, the Commissioners of the Metropolitan and City of London forces are empowered to make a banning order if, like their provincial counterparts, they take the view that their power to impose conditions on any march are insufficient to prevent serious disorder. Such an order must (as elsewhere) be sanctioned by the Home Secretary. The number of banning orders in England and Wales between 1974 and 1984 is shown in Table 2.4.

Banning orders – which remain in force for up to three months – apply to all classes of processions and demonstrations (save those of a ceremonial or religious nature). The blanket nature of this power is intended to avoid allegations of specific bias against any group or organisation. Throughout England and Wales, a number of local Acts require the organisers of a procession to give the police advance notice of its date and route, while in Scotland written notice of almost all processions must be provided to the regional or islands councils at

Table 2.4   Banning orders in England and Wales 1974–84

Year	Number	Year	Number
1974	3	1980	6
1975	0	1981	42
1976	0	1982	13
1977	1	1983	9
1978	3	1984	11
1979	0		

Source: *Annual Reports* of Her Majesty's Inspectors of Constabulary for England and Wales.

least a week in advance. This procedure was introduced by the Civic Government Act 1982, and it enables the relevant chief officer to advise the appropriate council of the need to either impose conditions on the proposed march or to apply a banning order. The council does not require the consent of the Secretary of State to make such an order, though the Act does provide for an appeal against an order via judicial review.

The 1936 Act created a number of specific offences designed to deal with the menace created by the British Union of Fascists. These included a prohibition on the wearing of political uniforms in public and the organisation, training and control of private coercive forces. It also created the offence of 'threatening behaviour' and (by virtue of the Race Relations Act 1976) the offence of 'incitement to racial hatred' was inserted into its provisions. Other statutory offences relevant to public order are drawn from criminal law. These include obstructing the highway, obstructing a police constable, assaulting a police constable and criminal damage. In short, the variety of public order offences available to the police was extensive. For instance, up to the end of March 1985, of the 10 372 charges brought against miners in England and Wales during the 1984–85 dispute, more than half of the total were either common law or statutory public order offences. The same was true in Scotland where, like the rest of Britain, breach of the peace offences provided the single largest category. Yet the government, while acknowledging that there were 'no yawning gaps in the law', published its redrawn Public Order Bill in December 1985. The White Paper argued a need to 'extend and clarify' the law to enable the police 'to prevent disorder . . . before it occurs'. It continued: 'Once disorder has broken out the problem confronting the police is not a shortage of legal powers but . . . of enforcement.'

The 1986 Act draws together and redefines the common law offences of riot, rout, unlawful assembly and affray, making them statutory offences, and creates a controversial new offence of disorderly conduct. Described by the Home Secretary as 'a law against hooliganism', this offence does not involve a breach of the peace or a threat of violence. Even the government acknowledged that it was 'not easy to define', yet the lobby by the ACPO for its inclusion in the legislation was clearly persuasive. Its potential effects have been likened by Lord Scarman, among others, to those of the widely discredited and now repealed 'sus law': the discretionary enforcement of the latter was a source of simmering (and occasionally eruptive) discontent among ethnic communities.

The changes to the law will subject civil liberties in Britain even more to the operational discretion of the police. It proposes to introduce the seven-day advance notice provision for marches and processions that applies in Scotland and to retain the power to ban marches. However, it expands the criteria upon which a banning order can be made. Currently, the sole test is 'the risk of serious public disorder', but the new legislation increases police powers by proposing three additional tests: 'serious disruption to the life of the community', the need to prevent 'serious damage to property' and the 'intimidation of others'. Whereas in Scotland advance notice is given to local authorities, in England and Wales it will be given to the police who will then advise local authorities according to the expanded criteria. Decisions concerning the size and route of a proposed march or demonstration will also fall within the remit of the police, though the power to ban a march will remain with local authorities in the provinces and the Home Secretary in London. Moreover, these new police powers will also apply to static demonstrations and open-air assemblies which are of particular relevance to industrial disputes. What the Act fails to provide is a statutory right to engage in peaceful protest or assembly.

During its legislative passage, the Act revealed the extent to which the bipartisanship that previously typified attitudes to the police and policing had broken down. The Labour Opposition was wholly opposed to it on libertarian grounds and argued that the new laws would do nothing to prevent disorder – the government's primary justification for the changes. Moreover, Labour believed that their newly acquired powers would force the police to impose decisions that rested on political judgements, thereby threatening further to jeopardise police–community relations.

The divide between the parties was also evident in relation to the

Police and Criminal Evidence Act 1984 (PACE), which was implemented in full on 1 January 1986. Informed by the Criminal Justice (Scotland) Act 1980 and influenced more immediately by the Royal Commission on Criminal Procedure 1981, the Act seeks to achieve a balance between individual rights and the security of the community. To this end it introduced a range of new police powers and rights for suspects. However, the Labour Party announced its intention to repeal those powers which relate to stop and search, road checks, searches for evidence, arrest, detention, interrogation and finger-printing of suspects. The Act is accompanied by extensive codes of practice for the police and also introduced a new Police Complaints Authority. But whether the appropriate balance between individual and communal rights (itself a contestable distinction) has been struck is a moot point. Further, the duty solicitor scheme provided for by the Act is, according to a Law Society report, not available in 25 per cent of police stations in England and Wales. Although this is an unintended effect, it nevertheless impairs the civil rights of suspects.

The implications of PACE and the outcome of the changes to public order law are as yet impossible to assess. The impact of the Prevention of Terrorism Act 1974 – subsequently amended in 1976 and most recently in 1984 – is somewhat easier to gauge. It introduced to Britain emergency legislation that had long been a feature in Northern Ireland. It was in response to the Birmingham pub bombings by the IRA that Parliament rushed through, without a division, what the then Home Secretary described as the Act's 'draconian' measures. It banned the IRA and empowered the Home Secretary to ban any other organisation in the UK which appeared to him to be concerned with terrorism in Northern Ireland. (The Irish National Liberation Army was proscribed by this power in 1979.) It also empowered the Home Secretary and the Secretary of State for Northern Ireland to impose exclusion orders on persons suspected of terrorism (normally removing them from Britain to Northern Ireland if they are UK citizens, or to the Irish Republic if they are Irish citizens). Further, it extended police powers by enabling them to hold for questioning individuals suspected of terrorist connections for up to seven days.

Initially, the Act was renewed at six-monthly intervals but since its amendment in 1976 the renewal procedure takes place every 12 months via a Parliamentary debate and vote. Until 1982 the Act was renewed with all-Party agreement in the House of Commons, but in that year the Labour Opposition chose to abstain. This led the government to order a review into its operation, conducted by Lord Jellicoe, which eventually led to the 1984 version of the Act. This extended the powers of arrest and detention to include individuals suspected of international terrorism. The Labour party opposed the legislation throughout its passage, to no effect. Though measures are necessary to combat the indiscriminate nature of terrorism, the extensive executive powers provided by the Act cannot be challenged in the courts:

> vital features of the rule of law – the right to know the charges, the right to hear and challenge the evidence, the right to a fair hearing and the right of appeal – are abolished. The open decision of a court has been replaced by the secret decision of the police, civil servants and a Minister.[22]

Taken together, the existing law in relation to terrorism, the recent Police and Criminal Evidence Act and the changes to public order law represent a quantum leap in police powers, reinforcing the view that the British state is becoming increasingly authoritarian. The public order legislation will mean that the police, besides being charged with the duty to keep the peace, will be enabled to mediate the already constrained ability to engage in protest and dissent on a much wider front. The fact that the recent changes to the law in this sphere have been introduced by the Conservative government, in the face of principled Labour opposition, has served to accelerate the trend towards the politicisation of the British police. In this changed legislative context, the exercise of police discretion will be at a premium.

PUBLIC ORDER SITUATIONS

Besides these changes to the law, disquiet about police–society relations is apparent in the response to police behaviour at specific public order events. Before indicating, albeit briefly, an evident toughening in the style of public order policing, two points need to be made. First, the term 'public order event' covers a diverse range of situations which involve varying numbers of police officers. For example, in 1982 in the Metropolitan area there were 28 events requiring more than 1000 police: they included the Notting Hill Carnival, a National Front march, Trooping the Colour and the Falklands Thanksgiving Service. In addition there were 201 events involving over 100 officers, more than 1000 industrial disputes where the police 'maintained a presence', as they did at a further 444 sporting fixtures. Secondly, the vast majority of these events pass off without incident. The remarks made over a decade ago by a former Commissioner of the Metropolitan Police still largely apply: 'Most political demonstrations pose problems no worse than those arising from inconvenience to public and police'.[23] Yet in the intervening period the aggressive style of policing at certain public order events suggests a transformation in the readiness of the police to use other than minimum force.

Besides the weekly tests of strength at football matches, a litany of names chart the changes in police strategy: Saltley; Red Lion Square; Notting Hill; Lewisham; Grunwicks; Southall; St Paul's; Brixton; Toxteth; Warrington; Orgreave; Stonehenge; Handsworth; Broadwater Farm; Wapping: all are associated with the drama of order-maintenance and a toughened police response. Viewed from the perspective of the nineteenth and early twentieth centuries, when the deployment of troops led not infrequently to the deaths of protestors, recent changes in the style of public order policing may seem relatively trivial. But in the more immediate post-war context they amount to a sea-change in the policing of disorder. New forms of organisation, new equipment and a new readiness to deploy *de facto* riot squads trained in 'tactical options' indicates the deterioration in police–society relations and, perforce, the relationship between state and society. Lord Scarman, widely regarded as standing at the liberal pole of British politics, while emphasising preventive measures in his report on the Brixton disorders, also sanctioned the adoption by the police of what he chose to describe as 'a more positive, interventionist role in quelling disorder'.[24] However, he did recognise the implicit dangers involved:

> There should, I suggest, be no change in the basic approach of the British police to policing public disorder. It would be tragic if attempts . . . to bring the police and public closer together were to be accompanied by changes in the manner of policing disorder which served only to distance the police further from the public.[25]

While a number of Scarman's recommendations were implemented – including extended training for police recruits, the creation of statutory police–community liaison committees, and making racially discriminatory behaviour by police officers a disciplinary offence – his hope that traditional and new methods of public order policing could co-exist without adversely affecting police–society relations has proved to be overly sanguine. Evidence of breaches in this 'basic approach' can be instanced by the following examples.

In June 1985 a-500-strong hippy convoy of men, women and children attempted to celebrate the summer solstice in the vicinity of Stonehenge. A series of injunctions prevented them from entering the site of the ancient monument and the convoy was shepherded by the police into nearby Savernake forest. When they tried to leave, police blocked the exit roads and began to smash vehicle wind-screens. An eye-witness to what was dubbed 'the battle of the bean field', described the events thus:

> At ten past seven the battle began. In the next half-hour, whatever their plans and tactics, the police operation became a chaotic whirl of violence . . . basic rules of police behaviour were abandoned. The identification numbers of most officers were concealed by flame-proof overalls, in direct contradiction of Home Office undertakings. The guidance on the use of truncheons – to be used only as a last resort and only on arms and legs was abandoned . . . The command structure of the officers appeared to have disintegrated.[26]

Police officers, equipped in riot gear, were seen to commandeer vehicles which were used as battering-rams, while others systematically broke windscreens and smashed the hippies' possessions. In short, the police ran amok. Following the battle the area was sealed off and a police helicopter flew overhead to provide additional surveillance.

Earlier in 1985 evidence of police–military liaison was provided by the joint operation to remove 150 CND supporters from 'Rainbow Village' at the planned cruise missile site, RAF Molesworth in Cambridgeshire. The operation, later revealed to have been planned five months in advance, began at 11.30 p.m. on 5 February. It involved 1000 regular police, 600 Ministry of Defence police and 1500 Royal Engineers who, under the glare of arc-lights, erected a barbed wire around the base's seven-mile perimeter. The protestors were given an hour to leave or see their possessions and the makeshift 'Village' bulldozed away. Elsewhere, police officers set up road blocks in the area to prevent other CND supporters from entering the site. On the morning following the eviction the then Secretary of State for Defence, Michael Heseltine, arrived to survey the scene dressed in a flak jacket. Thereafter police issued vehicle identity discs to local residents to prevent 'unauthorised' vehicles from approaching the base.

On 1 March 1985 the former Home Secretary, Leon Brittan, visited Manchester University to address a meeting organised by Conservative students. According to an independent inquiry set up by the local and unofficial Police Monitoring Committee, a peaceful demonstration by 400 students was forcibly broken up by members of the Tactical Aid Group, Manchester Constabulary's equivalent of the SPG. Apparently, no warnings were issued before the police charge, which resulted in 40 injuries and 38 arrests. The inquiry, to which the police refused to furnish evidence, concluded that unnecessary force had been used in the operation to clear the immediate area. This seems small beer. More disturbing were subsequent allegations by two of the students. Having complained to the force about the injuries they had sustained at the hands of the police, they claim that thereafter they were subjected to harassment, threats and physical assaults by two as yet unidentified police officers

In September 1985, there were riots in Handsworth and Brixton as there had been in 1981. In October, there was another on the Broadwater Farm estate in the Tottenham district of London. In the latter case a police officer was hacked to death and firearms were used against the police for the first time during the course of post-war street disorder. In Handsworth, which 24 hours earlier had been enjoying a street carnival, the riot was triggered when police officers tried to arrest two men at the scene of a motoring offence. Within a matter of hours a full-scale riot took place. As a result, many shops were looted and burned out and two men died in the local post office which had been set on fire. The Brixton riot was precipitated by the accidental police shooting of Mrs Cherry Groce when armed officers entered her home in search of her son. The Tottenham riot came a day after a police raid on the home of Mrs Cynthia Jarrett, who collapsed and died while officers searched the premises for stolen property.

Each of these riots took place in inner city areas where concerted efforts had been made to foster communal involvement in local policing along the lines recommended by Scarman. All reflect the seemingly inherent fragility of police–community relations in areas afflicted by high unemployment, poor housing and a deteriorating infrastructure. But distinguishing between the immediate and under-lying causes of such disorders is a fraught and contestable matter. The extent to which styles of policing may have contributed is difficult to evaluate. The fact that the Home Secretary refused to set up official public inquiries into the riots has not helped to ascertain the reasons for their occurrence. The immediate response of the Metropolitan Commissioner to the riot at Broadwater Farm was forthright: 'I wish to put all people of London on notice that I will not shrink from using plastic bullets should I believe them a practical option for restoring peace.' The Home Secretary swiftly and fully endorsed the Commissioner's readiness to use plastic bullets where the 'police find themselves being attacked by petrol bombs'.[27] Yet the latter are now regarded by the police as an instrument of first resort on the part of rioters. If this is the case, then the use of plastic bullets to deal with riotous situations in Britain may become as familiar as in Northern Ireland. The implications for police–society relations and the danger of an escalation in the level of violence used by those who engage in street disorder makes any future decision by a chief officer to employ them a matter of fine calculation.

Though there were no public inquiries, a review of public order policing covering the period 1981–85 was conducted by the Met.[28] The review, though recommending a multi-agency approach to the prevention of disorder, is designed to improve the capability of the force to quell disorder. Among other things it recommends the issue of a rewritten public order manual; the organisation of an integrated and force-wide information system; the amalgamation of the SPG and DSUs into Territorial Support Groups to provide the first wave response to disorder, thereby contraverting an earlier decision to limit the public order role of the SPG; the development of new command structures to take effect in the event of a riot; the issue of long truncheons to all shield-trained officers to replace the standard truncheon; the acquisition of armoured vehicles; improved access to plastic bullets and CS gas, the first of which is identified as 'a realistic option in cases of serious disorder'; enhanced public order training procedures at both its own centre and at the Police Staff College; the review of weapons available to the police in the light of the use of firearms by rioters at Broadwater Farm; and an evaluation of water cannon and 'diversionary' tactics involving sound.

The next notch in the ratchet of public order policing is likely to be made by the use of plastic bullets, CS gas having been used for the first time during the urban riots in Liverpool in 1981. Moreover, the available evidence suggests that public opinion would support the firing of baton rounds and the use of other forms of riot technology.

PUBLIC PERCEPTIONS OF THE POLICE

The first systematic study of public opinion about the police was conducted in the Metropolitan area by Belson in 1972.[29] It showed that 96 per cent of adults in London were either 'very satisfied' or 'satisfied' with the force; 93 per cent 'liked' them; and 90 per cent trusted the police. Among the 13–20 year olds, opinions were also favourable though at slightly lower levels. In addition, 81 per cent of adults believed that public demonstrations were 'very well' controlled by the police, a view shared by 65 per cent in relation to crowd control at football matches, perhaps the most frequent contexts for disorder. However, opinions were not entirely uncritical. Belson noted specific criticisms relating to aspects of police behaviour, including rudeness; bad temper; bullying; the occasional over-use of force; and unfairness in dealing with demonstrators, the young and non-Whites (the latter view more common among the youth than the adult sample).

In the intervening period, support has remained high, though there is some evidence of slippage. For example, a 1980 poll placed police officers second to doctors in terms of honesty and ethical standards whereas they had fallen to sixth place in a similar survey conducted four years later. A 1981 poll showed that 90 per cent of the sample had either 'fair' or 'great confidence' in the police, while two years later the British Crime Survey indicated that those who agreed that the police 'did a good job' stood at 75 per cent. Also in 1983, a survey commissioned by the Met showed that this last figure had fallen slightly to 72 per cent among the whole sample, within the margin for error. But among the 16–34 year age band the figure was 65 per cent, while among non-Whites it was a mere 54 per cent.[30] This study followed the publication of the important report by the Policy Studies Institute[31] into the policing of London, which had been commissioned in 1976 by a former Metropolitan Commissioner. The report showed that while 79 per cent of Londoners believed the police to be 'fair and reasonable', 1 in 10 expressed a complete lack of confidence in them and almost half the sample held serious doubts about standards of police conduct. The survey also disclosed 'a serious lack of confidence in the police among substantial numbers of young people' and 'a disastrous lack of confidence among young people of West Indian origin'. The Commissioner acknowledged the scale of the problem in his annual report for 1983:

It is quite clear that in some quarters – in the hearts and minds of the Black adolescent for example – we have lost a great deal of our credibility. Unless the force continues and expands its real efforts to break the mutual mistrust, it is unlikely that Black youth will be sufficiently well-disposed . . . to take that positive step themselves.[32]

Newman, the author of the above comment, has sought to improve police–community relations in London by implementing what he describes as a 'preventive' model of policing involving a full commitment to the statutory consultative committees recommended by Scarman, the introduction of 'Neighbourhood Watch' schemes and a heavy emphasis upon police professionalism. This is presented as the preferred alternative to a 'crime control' model which incorporates assertive patrol activity, a prominent street-level police presence, abrasive street contact caused by an extensive use of stop and search powers, and a somewhat casual attitude to civil rights. Newman's aim is to promote the image of the force as a 'leading proponent of egalitarianism and human rights', and to this end he has presided over the formulation of a new code of conduct for his officers which, among other things, underlines the need for ethnically sensitive policing.

Newman's awareness that the crime control model carries with it 'the long term possibility of alienation of the community at large' does not appear to be shared by the general population. A survey conducted before the implementation of the Police and Criminal Evidence Act showed that a majority was in favour of extending police powers in ways consistent with this model.[33] For instance, 66 per cent believed the police should stop and search anyone they think suspicious; 61 per cent agreed that they should be able to fingerprint everyone in an area where a serious crime had been committed; and, – more pertinent for our purpose – 62 per cent thought the police should use plastic bullets, CS gas and water cannon against *potentially* violent demonstrators. In part, these figures suggest anxiety about growing crime rates and the decline in clear-up rates. They also imply that the general public is less concerned with the methods the police employ to solve crimes or restore order than with their effectiveness. In this sense, the premium which the police has traditionally paid to public consent has produced a handsome dividend. High and recurring levels of public support have created a congenial environment within which the acquisition (and prospective use) of new riot equipment seems to be generally acceptable. In no small measure this may be due to the recent attempts by the police to orchestrate public opinion and debate.

THE POLICE AS A POLITICAL INSTITUTION

Though in Britain there is a reluctance to admit to a connection between the police and politics – not least among the police themselves – policing is a political activity. The exercise of discretion, described by Newman as 'an art rather than a science', lies at the heart of this activity. Decisions concerning enforcement policies, police resources, organisation and administration are essentially matters of political choice.

The inventors of the British police idea sought to portray their charge neither as an agency of state nor government, but to align the fledgling force with the people as citizens in uniform. The image of the police as the men in the middle, mediating the line between state and society, lies at the root of the evolution of the British police. Its durability owes much to their self-presentation as neutral arbiters of conflict, qualified to perform this role through a rich mixture combining experience, expertise and good old fashioned common sense. But during the last two decades the claim to neutrality has been compromised as the police have undergone a process of politicisation.[34]

Public interventions into British politics, both on an individual and a collective basis, have become increasingly characteristic of the police. An early indication was the Police Federation's attempt in 1965 to mobilise public opinion in the 'fight against crime'.[35] Subsequent interventions included a televised critique of the criminal justice system by Robert Mark in 1973 and his much-publicised resignation over reforms to the police complaints procedure three years later. In 1975, the Police Superintendents' Association supported a law and order campaign launched by the Police Federation which it resurrected during the general election campaign of 1979. During 1977–78, concern over recruitment levels led the Federation to engage in a testy pay dispute with the Labour government, which responded by establishing an independent committee, chaired by Edmund Davies, that recommended a 40 per cent increase. The government, while accepting the increase, proposed to implement it in two equal stages, whereas the Conservative Opposition undertook to award it immediately and in full if elected. It was against the background of the dispute and a general deterioration in industrial relations that the election was fought: the parties in part clamouring for the vote by seeking to demonstrate their respective support for the renewed and police-led law and order campaign.

Conservative governments since 1979 have been willing partners in upholding the rule of law and enforcing order. Moreover, their electoral commitment of 1979 to 'spend more on fighting crime even while economising elsewhere' was fulfilled, as was the prompt award of the pay increase. As the self-regarding party of law and order, its ideological pessimism about human nature accords with dominant police attitudes towards the 'criminal classes'. An attitudinal affinity to the rule of law and the political necessity of aligning with public opinion provides much common ground between the police and the Thatcher government. The authoritarian populism of neo-Conservatism has proved to be a fertile soil for the police; their demands for increased resources, changes in public order law and enhanced powers have largely been met. While there is some compelling evidence to indicate that the British police display a strong preference for the Conservative Party,[36] to suggest that they are a monolithic bloc of Tories garbed, appropriately, in blue would be an over-simplification. Indeed, the relationship between the Police Federation and the Thatcher government has shown some signs of strain. At the 1985 annual conference of the Police Federation officers, unhappy over establishment levels, increased workloads created by the regulations governing the new powers provided by PACE and threatened stringencies in the police budget, barracked the then Home Secretary, Leon Brittan. However, the hostile reception accorded Brittan paled into insignificance in comparison with that given to the proposals of the Labour Party intended to achieve an improved system of police accountability.

The relationship between force effectiveness and public consent lies at the centre of the debate about the accountability of the British police. At the inter-party level the divide over this issue is apparent. The government has fully endorsed the implementation of Scarman's police–community liaison committees in the wake of the 1981 riots. Intended to breach the threatening divide between police and policed, notably in the inner cities, these statutory consultative bodies would, it believed, assist in the reconstruction of consent, help prevent crime and disorder and thereby contribute to the goal of police effectiveness. However, the committees leave undiminished the operational autonomy of chief officers and this has failed to satisfy the Labour

Party. Its 1983 general election manifesto proposed to 'create community police councils' which, in the spirit of Scarman, would 'provide an opportunity for open discussion between police and the community as to the quality and manner of police provision'. This much was uncontroversial. However, the manifesto also stated: 'We aim to create *elected* police authorities in all parts of the country, including London, with *statutory responsibility for the determination of police policy within their areas*' (our emphases). This commitment united both the government and police spokesmen in opposition.

For the Labour Party, the circle of effectiveness and consent was completed by democratic control of the police. The SDP–Liberal Alliance, while sharing the view that policing 'can only be effective if it is responsive', proposed in its manifesto to build on the Scarman-inspired reforms by supporting the local liaison committee's goal of involving 'local people in helping the police to do their jobs'. In addition, it advocated the introduction of a 'conciliation service' to 'enhance confidence in the police' and proposed to improve police accountability outside London 'by strengthening the community element on Police Authorities and encouraging community representation at the level of police divisions'. In respect of the Met, where the Home Secretary acts as the police authority, the Alliance proposed the interim establishment of a Select Committee, drawn from London MPs, to act as the forum for accountability. These ideas reflected the views of a former Chief Constable, John Alderson. He stood as a Liberal Parliamentary candidate at the 1983 general election and had long been a staunch and somewhat isolated police exponent of community policing.

The response by the Police Federation to the Labour Party's proposals was unequivocally hostile. This became apparent following a debate on the police at the Party's 1984 Annual Conference. Held against the background of the miners' strike, successive speakers roundly condemned 'police violence' and 'intimidation', demanding inquiries into police strategy and tactics and renewing the call for 'democratic control and accountability of the police'. The Federation's Chairman, Leslie Curtis, responded by wondering aloud if it was possible for the police to provide an equally loyal service for a future Labour, as opposed to Conservative Government. The Police Superintendents' Association, concerned at Curtis's implied partisanship, itself then entered the arena by reaffirming the loyalty of the police to all governments, stressing that the allegiance of the Force is to the Crown, not any one political party.

Since 1981, consultative committees modelled along Scarman's lines have spread throughout England and Wales, seeking to provide an intermediate buffer between local communities, the police and top-tier Police Authorities. But even these have been given a mixed reception by certain senior police officers. The Chief Constable of the Greater Manchester Police, James Anderton, has been especially critical. He regards the committees as a 'mistake', insisting that 'our results are still achieved through our own police-led contacts and not through politically formalised structures'. Anderton shares the view of the former Chief Constable of the West Midlands Constabulary, Sir Philip Knights, who considers that the police 'have to satisfy the electors far more than the party political machines . . . We have to take into account that the majority view in a political forum is very often that of only a minority of the electorate'.[37] Such sentiments are not confined to the upper echelons of the Force. Curtis – whose Federation broke with tradition in 1979 by reappointing as its Parliamentary adviser a Conservative backbencher rather than an MP from the Opposition benches – has decided views about the plans of the Labour Party to reform the mechanisms of accountability: 'The idea that the police will be more effective in the fight against crime when they are fully accountable to local politicians is frankly laughable'.

The populist view that the police must remain the servants of the people and not politicians eschews any mooted incursion of politics into policing. However, not all police officers share its naive confusion between politics and partisanship. Sir Kenneth Newman has recognised the distinction, insisting that it is 'foolish' to claim that policing is non-political. Unlike some of his peers, Newman welcomed the introduction of consultative committees. Together with the 'Neighbourhood Watch' scheme and a restated stress on professionalism they can, in his view, form the basis of a new contract between police and public and thereby restore the principle of policing by consent. But recent public order events in London and elsewhere, combined with the continuing antipathy of ethnic minorities towards the police, suggest that this contract is far from being fulfilled, whether by the police or sections of the public. The existence throughout Britain of unofficial 'police monitoring' committees that parallel the statutory committees is testimony to the continuing distrust felt by a number of communities towards the police.

The government's dismissal of these unofficial bodies and its support for the new *status quo* places a premium upon the ability of the consultative committees to incorporate local communities into a new framework of police–community relations. While they seem likely to find support among the vast body of senior police officers – not least because they leave unscathed the operational autonomy of the police – the debate about the nature and form of police accountability is far from over. The Labour Party's revised proposals will ensure that this issue remains high on the political agenda. While it proposes to drop its earlier commitment to provide Police Authorities with day-to-day operational control of their local forces, it still intends to create wholly elected Authorities with powers over force deployment, finance and training. It also intends to introduce a new and fully independent police complaints system, a reform that is also supported by the Police Federation. These and other proposals concerning police powers and public order law indicate the gulf that exists between the major parties over policing matters.

CONCLUSION

The rupture of the inter-party consensus over the police and policing in Britain mirrors the breakdown of the wider political consensus (commonly termed 'Butskellism') that characterised the terms of political and economic debate between 1945 and the mid-1970s. The shared commitment to full employment, rising public expenditure, a growing welfare ethos and a recognition of the legitimacy of trades unions as political actors, provided the cornerstones of a post-war settlement that promised the reconstruction of a more egalitarian society. In this context, public expectations of the police rested heavily on the principle of consent and the presumption that the body of the people were pacific and law-abiding.

In retrospect, this seems a sanguine view. Yet popular conceptions of the modern British state (influenced by the ideas of Keynes and Beveridge) were framed in terms of service and support: in so far as the state entered the popular consciousness, it tended to be perceived in benign terms as a guarantor of a caring social order. Similarly, the police themselves were viewed as the providers of a social service: familiarity with local social customs enabled them to exercise their discretionary powers in a friendly if paternal manner. The enforcement of 'the rule of law', which enjoyed a higher status than the state itself, was widely regarded as a technical matter, although reliant on the sense and sensibility of the police – themselves untainted by

politics. Moreover, the maintenance of order was commonly understood to be a matter of policing the margins of society while the broad
swathe of law-abiding people enjoyed the fruits of a growing economy.

However, the resurgence of ideological politics in Britain during
the mid-1970s, symbolised by the rejection of 'Butskellism', has both
transformed the condition of state–society relations and diminished
the quality of police–society relations. Far from policing the margins,
the police are now controlling large blocs of the population adversely
affected by a dogmatic assault on public expenditure. The pursuit of
egalitarianism has been jettisoned in favour of a set of political ideals
that makes a fetish of individualism and celebrates inequality. Protest
and dissent is criminalised by changes to public order law, while those
who fight back – like the striking miners – are labelled by the Prime
Minister as 'the enemy within'. The nature of recent industrial
disputes and the fragility of police relations with ethnic minorities are
represented as a challenge to the social order alleged to be far more
threatening than any that has emerged in the period since 1945.
Though there were outbreaks of disorder during the 1950s and 1960s
– race riots in the late 1950s, pitched battles between 'Mods' and
'Rockers' in the 1960s, or the anti-Vietnam protests later in the
decade – they were largely regarded as isolated episodes. By contrast, more recent disorders are constructed as symptoms of a trend
towards lawlessness, justifying a more aggressive response on the
part of a better resourced police force. In these circumstances, the
prior emphasis on policing by consent has been displaced by a stress
on police effectiveness. Against the background of continuing economic decline, the failed attempt to resolve Britain's economic problems has created not only mass unemployment on an unprecedented
scale but other forms of social discipline in the shape of new police
powers and a threateningly authoritarian framework of public order
law.

The emergence of the police and policing as an issue of mainstream
and not marginalised debate in post-war Britain is as unsurprising as
it is overdue. The focus on the principle of accountability is wholly
merited: it is intended to reconcile the demand for police effectiveness and the need for public consent. While the police can justifiably
claim to enjoy the broad and enduring support of a majority of the
British people, the extent of disaffection can no longer be ignored:
the thread of public consent has begun to unravel. Fewer people are
prepared to acquiesce in the claim that 'the police know best'. In this

environment, climbing inside the shell of 'professionalism' is an inadequate police response: not least because the police have behaved in decidedly 'unprofessional' ways in a variety of contexts. Moreover, the creation of half-way houses, in the form of statutory consultative committees, is unlikely to promote neighbourly relations between the police and those who feel policed-against.

Britain's much-vaunted liberality has been severely tested by the heavy emphasis on order and the perceived reduction in civil rights widely regarded as hallmarks of the Thatcher government. One legacy of neo-Conservatism is likely to be the overhaul of the tripartite arrangements devised in the more settled political climate of the 1960s. Besides growing demands for a codified Bill of Rights and freedom of information legislation, renewed proposals to redefine the structure of control over the police demonstrate the tension in the chain of relations between state and society in contemporary Britain. The replacement of existing structures with a system of accountability that places a positive and primary value on the role of ordinary people will both help to reintegrate the police with the wider community and contribute to a more stable relationship between state and society. Without such a reform, the British police run the increasing risk of being viewed more generally as a *force* rather than a *service*.

Notes

1. R. Reiner, *The Politics of the Police* (1985).
2. HM Inspector of Constabulary, *Annual Report 1967* (HC 272).
3. The ratios are based on authorised establishment figures.
4. Commissioner of the Metropolitan Police, *Annual Report 1975* (Cmnd 6496).
5. In addition, civilians are employed in clerical and technical posts on a part-time basis and in domestic work on both a full- and part-time basis. The figures also exclude police cadets and part-time Special Constables who, in 1984, numbered 16 056.
6. M. Joyce, *Spending on Law and Order: The Police Service in England and Wales* (London: National Institute of Economic and Social Research, 1985).
7. J.P. Miller and D.E. Luke, *Law Enforcement by Public Officials and Special Police Forces* (London: Home Office, 1977). This 4-volume study was declassified in 1980.
8. See S. Spencer, *Called to Account* (London: NCCL, 1985) and T. Jefferson and R. Grimshaw, *Controlling the Constable* (London: Muller, 1984). Both provide lucid accounts of the Act, especially in relation to the principle of tripartism.

9. With the exception of the Met, which has its own internal inspection procedures.
10. Sir William Fraser, *Postwar Police Developments: Restrospect and Reflections*, James Smart Lecture, Strathclyde Police Headquarters (1981).
11. R. Card, 'Police Accountability and Control Over the Police', *Bramshill Journal*, 1 (1979) 12.
12. There are three levels of financial aid: 'small', 'large scale' and 'major'. See S. Spencer, *Police Authorities During the Miners' Strike* (London: Cobden Trust, 1986) and B. Loveday, 'Central Co-ordination, Police Authorities and the Miners' Strike', *Political Quarterly*, 57 (1986) 60–73.
13. Spencer, *Police Authorities*, p. 26.
14. Spencer, *Called to Account*, pp. 67–70.
15. Commissioner of the Metropolitan Police, *Annual Report 1982* (Cmnd 8928).
16. *Annual Report 1982*.
17. M. Kettle, 'The National Reporting Centre and the 1984 Miners' Strike', in B. Fine and R. Millar (eds), *Policing the Miners' Strike* (1985) p. 30.
18. See *Observer*, 21 July 1985; additional information provided by a BBC documentary, *Brass Tacks*, broadcast on 17 July 1986.
19. See R. Geary, *Policing Industrial Disputes: 1893 to 1985* (1985) pp. 67–115.
20. J. Alderson, Evidence to the Home Affairs Select Committee Enquiry into Special Branch (HC 71-iii) 16 January 1985; reply to Q. 181.
21. Home Affairs Select Committee, *Special Branch* (HC 71) session 1984–85.
22. C. Scorer, S. Spencer and P. Hewitt, *The New Prevention of Terrorism Act* (London: NCCL, 1985) p. 7.
23. Sir Robert Mark, *The Metropolitan Police and Political Demonstrations*, Bramshill, Police Staff College Lecture (17 March, 1975).
24. Lord Scarman, *The Scarman Report: The Brixton Disorders 10–12 April 1981* (1982) p. 153.
25. *The Scarman Report*, p. 154.
26. *Observer*, 9 June 1985.
27. *Guardian*, 8 October 1985.
28. Metropolitan Police, *Public Order Review: Civil Disturbances 1981–1985* (London: July 1986).
29. W. Belson, *The Public and the Police* (London: Harper & Row, 1975).
30. NOP, *Residents' Views on Policing Needs and Priorities in Eight London Police Divisions: Summary Report* (London: NOP, 1983).
31. Policy Studies Institute, *Police and People in London* (1983).
32. Cmnd 9268, p. 15.
33. See *Sunday Times*, 8 January 1984.
34. For a more detailed account of this process of politicisation see Reiner, *The Politics of the Police*, pp. 61–82; and M. Kettle, 'The Politics of Policing and the Policing of Politics', in P. Hain (ed.), *Policing the Police* (1980) pp. 9–62.
35. The Police Federation represents officers from the rank of Constable to Chief Inspector; the Police Superintendents' Association represents Superintendents and Chief Superintendents; and the Association of

Chief Police Officers all ranks above Chief Superintendent. None are conventional trades unions and the police are prohibited by the Police Act 1964 from taking strike action. See R. Reiner, *The Blue-Coated Worker* (Cambridge: Cambridge University Press, 1978).

36. The relevant research is quoted in R. Reiner, 'The Politicisation of the Police in Britain', in M. Punch (ed.), *Control in the Police Organisation* (1983) p. 147.

37. *Observer*, 24 February 1985.

3 Northern Ireland

BACKGROUND

Since the creation of Northern Ireland as a separate political entity under the Government of Ireland Act 1920, a substantial minority of the population of Northern Ireland has continued to reject the legitimacy of partition, and consequently the legitimacy of Northern Ireland as a political entity within the UK. Indeed, the contested nature of Northern Ireland as a sub-state entity, both internally and externally, lies at the heart of the province's conflict.[1] This has had a fundamental impact on policing in Northern Ireland in all its aspects, though the vehemence of the Catholic minority's hostility towards the police has varied considerably since partition. At particular junctures the police have also come into conflict with the Protestant majority. Four principal phases in the development of policing in Northern Ireland can be identified: the plans made for the formation of the Royal Ulster Constabulary in 1922; the subordination in practice of policing to the political direction of the Unionist government from 1922; the attempt to civilianise policing after the dispatch of British troops to the province in August 1969; and finally (from 1976), the establishment of the doctrine of police primacy in relation to security. While the Anglo–Irish Agreement of November 1985 has had a considerable impact on Protestant perceptions of the position of the police, it has not as yet made any fundamental difference in practice to the role of the police, and even the more moderate political representatives of the Catholic minority have continued to decline to give unqualified support. Indeed, security policy is still an issue on which opinion in Northern Ireland remains largely polarised on sectarian lines.

Under the Government of Ireland Act 1920 it had originally been envisaged that the country's existing police force, the Royal Irish Constabulary (RIC), which was part of Ireland's separate civil administration under British rule, would simply be split into two parts to take account of the creation of new devolved authorities in Dublin and Belfast. However, when the British government was forced to enter into negotiations with Sinn Fein over the future political dispensation in the South due to continuing resistance to the constitutional proposals contained in the Government of Ireland Act, it became clear that the RIC would not survive the partition of Ireland. The actual decision to disband the RIC was made by the British government following the signature of the Anglo–Irish Treaty on 6 December 1921 by representatives of Sinn Fein and the British government, under which the Irish Free State was established as a self-governing dominion. Disbandment came into effect on 31 March 1922 in the South but was delayed to 31 May 1922 in the North to smooth the transition to the establishment of a new police force in Northern Ireland. The transfer to the Northern Ireland government of control of security and responsibility for law and order had been completed in December 1921 after the signature of the Treaty. Consequently, responsibility for the creation of a new force rested with the Northern Ireland government and the Minister of Home Affairs (Dawson Bates) in particular. In January 1922 he appointed a committee including policemen, civil servants, and politicians to advise him on the formation of the force under terms of reference that took account of existing security arrangements that had been established on an *ad hoc* basis to meet the unrest accompanying partition. The committee reported its recommendations to the Minister at the end of March 1922.

The main recommendations were that the new force should comprise an establishment of 3000, slightly larger than the existing establishment for the RIC in the six counties making up Northern Ireland, and that one-third of the force should be Catholic with the recruits being drawn from the RIC or from the civilian population if the quota could not be filled from the ranks of the RIC. The committee further recommended the recruitment of up to 1000 Protestants from the RIC, with the rest of the Protestant contingent being drawn from the Ulster Special Constabulary (USC). The USC was a recent creation with roots in the revival of the Ulster Volunteer Force (UVF) in 1920. Its establishment in the closing months of 1920 to assist the RIC in coping with unrest in Northern Ireland followed pressure on the British government from Unionist leaders to legitimise patrolling and other activities undertaken by the UVF to counter attacks by the Irish Republican Army (IRA) within the six counties. Although formally recruited independently of the UVF, the new force (organised in three sections as A, B, and C Specials) in practice drew most of its recruits from the existing UVF network and, like the UVF, was to all intents and purposes a wholly Protestant force. Legislation giving effect to the committee's principal recommendations was rushed through the Northern Ireland Parliament to prevent a hiatus between the disbandment of the RIC at the end of May and the establishment of its successor, which was named the Royal Ulster Constabulary (RUC) and formally came into existence under the Constabulary Act in June 1922. The organisation of the new force was on similar lines to that of the RIC.

Political controversy over the formation of the RUC centred mainly on the issue of its composition. In particular, there was strong Unionist opposition both to the Catholic quota and to the emphasis given to recruitment of former members of the RIC. This stemmed from Protestant suspicion of the RIC thanks to the predominance of Catholics in its ranks (approximately 80 per cent in Ireland as a whole) and to long-standing Unionist complaints about the force's effectiveness. Indeed, at first sight, it seems most surprising that the Unionist Government in Northern Ireland should have proposed such generous representation of the Catholic minority within the police. Michael Farrell in his book on the formation of the USC and the RUC describes the allocation of a substantial Catholic quota as 'an untypically conciliatory move'.[2] Part of the explanation was financial. The British government had made generous pension arrangements for members of the RIC after disbandment. Payment of the pensions was the responsibility of the new political authorities in Belfast and Dublin. Recruitment of former members of the RIC provided a means of reducing this burden in circumstances of considerable financial stringency. Farrell also suggests that Unionist overtures to Catholic businessmen in the North influenced the government's attitude towards the composition of the police.

In the event, political pressures on the Unionist government, the attitudes of Catholics towards the new state, and relations between Protestants and Catholics within the new police force ensured that the Catholic quota was never filled. For example, pressure on the Unionist government led to the lifting in August 1922 of the ban on policemen joining the Orange Order. In 1923 an Orange lodge specifically catering to police membership (the Sir Robert Peel Lodge) was established and received official encouragement. From a peak of 21.1 per cent early in 1923, the proportion of Catholics in the force stabilised at just over 17 per cent in the late 1920s.[3] By the onset of the Troubles of the late 1960s, the proportion was a little over 10 per cent. Nevertheless, the fact that the RUC never became a wholly Protestant force on the pattern of the USC remained a significant legacy of the proposals for the force's formation in 1922, and justifies its treatment as a separate phase from the parallel process that was turning the police into an armed wing of Unionism.

The principal mechanism in this process was the Civil Authorities (Special Powers) Act, which became law on 7 April 1922 even before the passage of the legislation establishing the RUC. The Act accorded sweeping emergency powers to the Minister of Home Affairs through the right to issue regulations under the Act. For example, from the outset, regulations were issued under the Act giving the security forces arbitrary powers of arrest and search. The Special Powers Act, as it was known colloquially, was modelled on UK legislation to meet the post-war emergency in Ireland (the Restoration of Order in Ireland Act 1920), the basis of what was, in effect, a martial law regime. By way of emphasising the special circumstances of its enactment, it was made a requirement of the first Special Powers Act that it be renewed annually by the Northern Ireland Parliament. This was done until 1928 when the Act was renewed for a further five years. In 1933 the Special Powers Act was enacted on a permanent basis; it was repealed after the imposition of direct rule on Northern Ireland in 1972. The disturbances that accompanied partition, with over 400 deaths from political violence between June 1920 and June 1922, provided the original justification for the emergency measures adopted under the Special Powers Act. However, political violence (notwithstanding IRA campaigns in the late 1930s and between 1956 and 1962) does not explain the Unionist government's continuing reliance on the Act after the ending of the Troubles of the early 1920s. That is to be found in the Act's role (through its use almost exclusively against Catholics) in the maintenance of a Protestant ascendancy within a nexus of dominant–subordinate relations. In this context, the restoration of order was understood in terms of the stability of such relations rather than of their supersession by the rule of law, and this explains the continued reliance on the Act through periods of tranquillity. It also provides much of the explanation for the survival of the USC in the form of the B Specials beyond the emergency in the 1920s.

Unsurprisingly, the repeal of the Special Powers Act and the disbandment of the B Specials occupied a central place in the demands of the civil rights movement in the 1960s, which challenged the continuance of the Protestant monopoly of political power within Northern Ireland. Given the brittle nature of the pattern of dominant–subordinate relations, it was also not surprising that despite the general commitment of the civil rights movement to non-violence the result of the challenge to the *status quo* in Northern Ireland was disorder. Among the main political casualties of the onset of the Troubles in 1968 and 1969 were the police. What the Cameron Commission (appointed in March 1969 to examine the causes of the onset of the Troubles in October 1968) described in its report of September 1969 as 'breakdown of discipline' and acts of 'misconduct' involving 'assault and battery', 'malicious damage to property', and 'the use of provocative sectarian and political slogans' by the police,[4] received wide coverage in Britain and abroad through the medium of television. Both the Cameron Commission and the Scarman Tribunal,[5] which had been appointed in August 1969 to inquire into the continuing disturbances in Northern Ireland, were also strongly critical of the sectarian nature and behaviour of the B Specials. The blow to the standing and status of both the RUC and the USC as the result of criticism of their handling of public disorder was enormous. Consequently, reform of policing formed one of the first objectives of intervention by the British government in the situation. At the time of the dispatch of British troops to aid the civil power in Northern Ireland in August 1969, the Home Secretary (James Callaghan) sent two mainland police officers (Robert Mark and Douglas Osmond) to Northern Ireland to act as observers and to report back to the British government on the state of the RUC. Their report identified major shortcomings in the functioning of the RUC and emphasised the need for reform. Mark was subsequently appointed to a committee under Lord Hunt to advise on the organisation of the police in the province.

The report of the Hunt Committee was published in October 1969. It based its recommendations on the need to end what it saw as the dual role of the police in Northern Ireland: on the one hand, performing 'all those duties normally associated in the public mind with police forces elsewhere in the United Kingdom', while, on the other, undertaking 'security duties of a military nature'.[6] The Committee recommended, among other things, the disbanding of the B Specials, the creation of a part-time reserve force to take over policing functions carried out by the USC, the disarming of the RUC, the establishment of a Police Authority to provide a buffer between the police and the Unionist government, the repeal of much of the Special Powers Act, and the introduction of a complaints system. Its proposals amounted to a far-reaching programme to civilianise policing in Northern Ireland in line with practices elsewhere in the UK. In effect, it represented the extension to Northern Ireland of the British state's liberal-democratic model of policing. There was a strong reaction to the Unionist government's acceptance of the Committee's main proposals, especially that to disband the B Specials, and publication of the Committee's report was greeted by serious rioting in Protestant areas of Belfast in which a sniper shot dead a RUC Constable, the first police fatality of the present Troubles.

In practice, the strategy of civilianisation was undermined by the continuing deterioration in the security situation, notwithstanding the RUC's relatively low profile in relation to political violence after the arrival of British troops. In particular, the disarming of the force proved temporary. Policemen were rearmed for their own protection early in 1971 after police fatalities in shooting incidents. The introduction of internment in August 1971 dealt a further blow to civilianisation, not merely because it reduced the acceptability of the RUC in Catholic areas but because the escalation of violence provoked by internment cast doubt on the relevance of the British model of policing in Northern Ireland's conditions of political instability. Internment damaged the RUC in two other ways as well. The poor intelligence provided by the RUC for the round-up of suspects on the introduction of internment led to widespread criticism of the police's competence, while members of the RUC's Special Branch, working alongside army officers, were caught up in the scandal over the officially authorised use of interrogation techniques involving the physical maltreatment of suspects.

With the imposition of direct rule from Westminster in March 1972, the British government assumed full responsibility for security in Northern Ireland. There was no immediate change in policing policy as a result. The role of the RUC in the combatting of political violence remained subordinate to that of the army. However, the refusal of any elements of the police to be drawn into Unionist opposition to the imposition of direct rule significantly enhanced the reputation of the RUC at an official level and helped to pave the way for later changes of policy that placed greater reliance on the RUC in the security field. The main aim of direct rule was to clear the way for a political settlement involving a radical restructuring of devolved government in Northern Ireland. This was achieved with the establishment of a power-sharing Executive comprising political representatives of both communities at the beginning of 1974. However, the power-sharing experiment collapsed within five months. It was followed by an attempt to establish the basis for devolved government involving both communities through the election of a constitutional convention in 1975. This initiative also failed, prompting a major change in the British government's approach to the conflict, with important implications for security policy.

The British government recognised that there was little likelihood of a political settlement in the near future, and that consequently there would need to be a more durable justification of security policy than as a short-term expedient to meet the immediate emergency. In particular, if Britain was to escape international criticism, the security policy would need to appear to be compatible with due process of law, or continue to be justified in terms of the existence of a grave emergency. The latter option was unattractive to the British government because it would have highlighted the failure of the government to achieve a political settlement, and because the government wished to take advantage of what it perceived as a widespread desire for a return to normality. This was the background to the adoption in late 1975 and in 1976 of a policy of police primacy, of Ulsterisation, and of criminalisation of political violence. The new strategy entailed a further expansion in the size of the RUC; its extensive re-equipping, amounting to partial remilitarisation of the police force; an end to detention without trial; and the phasing out of special category status for those convicted of terrorist offences. Despite setbacks to the strategy as a result of a scandal over interrogation techniques at the Castlereagh holding centre, disagreement between the army and the RUC over the policy of police primacy in 1979, and the challenge to the ending of special category status by the Republican hunger strikes of 1980 and 1981, the basic framework of security policy has remained unchanged since 1976.

However, the durability of present security policies is in doubt, most obviously because of the terms of the Anglo–Irish Agreement of November 1985. Under the Agreement, both the British and Irish governments agreed on 'a need for a programme of special measures in Northern Ireland to improve relations between the security forces and the community'.[7] The Agreement states that such a programme may include, among other things, new local consultative machinery, improvements in the complaints system, and action to increase the proportion of Catholics in the RUC. These commitments reflect the view put forward by the Irish government in the negotiations leading to the Agreement that action needs to be taken to end the alienation of the Catholic minority from the security forces and from the administration of justice. How far changes to meet these objectives will prove compatible with the existing framework of policy remains to be seen. Unionist opposition to the Anglo–Irish Agreement presents a challenge of a different kind to existing policies. In particular, in so far as Loyalist protest appears to threaten the reliance that the British government can place on locally recruited security forces to enforce any changes made under the Agreement, a threat is posed to the British government's perseverance with the policy of Ulsterisation of security or to the Anglo–Irish process itself.

STRUCTURE, ORGANISATION, AND FINANCE

Much of the present structure and organisation of policing in Northern Ireland dates back to 1970 when many of the reforms proposed by the Hunt Committee were implemented. One of the most important of these was the establishment of the Police Authority of Northern Ireland. Under the Police Act 1970, the Police Authority was charged with responsibility for determining the size and rank structure of the police force, for appointing the most senior police officers, for keeping itself informed of the handling of complaints against the police, and for equipping and financing the police service. The exercise of its principal powers remains subject to the approval, since the imposition of direct rule in 1972, of the Secretary of State for Northern Ireland, who also appoints the members of the Police Authority, subject to guidelines in the Police Act designed to ensure that membership constitutes a broad cross-section of Northern Ireland society. The original intention behind the creation of the Police Authority was to set up a body to whom the chief officer of the RUC (the name of which was changed from Inspector-General to Chief Constable in line with practice in the rest of the UK) would be responsible, while establishing the police force's autonomy from political pressures. This was to meet criticism both that too little supervision had been exercised over the actions of the Inspector-General and that the police had become identified politically as a tool of the Unionist government.

However, the Chief Constable's autonomy in respect of operational matters remains guaranteed by statute, and this has proved a significant limit on the supervision of policing by the Police Authority. In addition, the anxiety of its members to provide support for the RUC in the difficult circumstances the force faces and the unwillingness of the Social Democratic and Labour Party (SDLP), the major party of the Catholic minority, to accord recognition to the

RUC through participation in the Authority, have tended to undermine the credibility of the Authority as an effective overseer of the functioning of the police. In particular, the Authority attracted considerable criticism during the scandal over the maltreatment of suspects at Castlereagh holding centre in the late 1970s for failing to respond more vigorously to the evidence it received from its own doctors of police abuses in the course of interrogation. It was an issue that caused dissension within the Authority itself and led to the resignation of two of its members. In the mid-1980s there has been considerable speculation in the press that the government intends to change the basis on which the Authority is constituted, specifically to provide for the representation of political parties. There have also been suggestions that the Republic might play a role in a reconstituted Police Authority in the context of the Anglo–Irish process. Nothing has so far come of proposals of either kind. The former would require a change in the stance of the SDLP; the latter a change in the British government's position.

Full-time members of the RUC constitute the main body of police officers within Northern Ireland. They operate on a province-wide basis. At the end of 1985 they numbered 8259, slightly above the authorised establishment of 8250.[8] Figures for the years 1960–84 are given in Table 3.1. The most significant feature of these figures is the increase in the size of the force, first since the onset of the Troubles, and secondly since the adoption of the policy of police primacy in the mid-1970s. Another striking feature is the increase in the proportion of women in the RUC up to 1980. A factor limiting the role of women within the police is the RUC's policy that women police officers should not carry firearms; the policy has been challenged by a woman police reservist before the European Court of Justice on the grounds that the rule is contrary to European law prohibiting sex discrimination. The position of women within the RUC Reserve has been further aggravated by the insistence that all full-time members carry firearms. Consequently, there has been a decline in the number of women police reservists as the proportion of full-time officers within the Reserve has grown, as Table 3.2 shows. The RUC Reserve was established in 1970 in accordance with proposals of the Hunt Committee. It was set up to take over policing functions formerly carried out by the part-time B Specials (numbering approximately 8000 men prior to their disbandment), while the Ulster Defence Regiment (UDR) was established to assist the British Army in the security sphere. At the end of 1985 there were 2755 full-time and 1753

Table 3.1   Size and composition of the Royal Ulster Constabulary
1960–84

Year	RUC	Per 1000 population	Women (%)
1960	4205	2.96	1.17
1961	4120	2.89	1.33
1962	3601	2.51	1.75
1963	3379	2.34	1.86
1964	3270	2.24	1.74
1965	3375	2.30	1.84
1966	3298	2.22	1.73
1967	3183	2.13	1.85
1968	3216	2.14	1.55
1969	3044	2.01	1.94
1970	3809	2.50	2.57
1971	4086	2.66	3.52
1972	4257	2.76	4.20
1973	4391	2.84	4.99
1974	4565	2.95	6.18
1975	4902	3.19	7.20
1976	5253	3.42	8.41
1977	5692	3.70	9.70
1978	6110	3.97	10.07
1979	6614	4.29	10.22
1980	6935	4.48	10.25
1981	7334	4.69	9.71
1982	7718	4.92	9.08
1983	8003	5.09	8.34
1984	8127	5.15	7.87

Note: The RUC column represents actual numbers in police as of 31 December each year as supplied by the Ministry of Home Affairs for the years 1960–68 and the Northern Ireland Office for the years 1969–84. The figures supplied by the Ministry of Home Affairs include members of the Ulster Special Constabulary mobilised for duty with the RUC. The ratio of the force to population has been calculated from mid-year population estimates.

Source: *Northern Ireland Digest of Statistics*.

part-time members of the Reserve. The full-time members are employed on three-year contracts. Figures on the size and composition of the force between 1970 and 1984 are given in Table 3.2.

By international standards, the ratio of police to population of over 5 per 1000 is relatively high. It is even higher (approaching 7 per 1000) if full-time members of the Reserve are included in the calcula-

Table 3.2   Size and composition of the Royal Ulster Constabulary reserve
1970–84

Year	Size	Women (%)	Full-time (%)
1970	578	–	–
1971	1284	–	–
1972	2134	–	–
1973	2514	8.55	14.44
1974	3860	12.85	13.21
1975	4819	15.15	13.72
1976	4697	15.61	18.62
1977	4686	15.39	21.38
1978	4604	15.29	25.80
1979	4513	15.29	28.89
1980	4752	13.24	35.46
1981	4870	10.68	42.30
1982	4840	9.40	44.92
1983	4493	8.64	51.08
1984	4439	7.59	57.04

Source: *Northern Ireland Digest of Statistics.*

tion. The most obvious gap in official figures on the size and composition of the police is the absence of any breakdown of the RUC or
RUC Reserve in terms of religious affiliation. In reply to a Parliamentary question at the beginning of 1986, the Parliamentary
Under-Secretary of State for Northern Ireland (Nicholas Scott) indicated that Catholics constituted approximately 10 per cent of the
RUC and the RUC Reserve. This is slightly less than estimates of the
proportion of Catholics in the RUC at the onset of the Troubles in
1968 and 1969. More precise estimates than these are not available
from either official or unofficial sources. An SDLP policy document
on security published at the beginning of 1980 put the proportion of
Catholics in the RUC at that time at 6 per cent, while the Chief
Constable's 1984 Report recorded that there had been an increase in
the proportion of Catholics among new recruits, but gave no figures.
What is not in doubt, and continues to give rise to official expressions
of concern, is the very substantial under-representation in the police
of the Catholic minority, which constitutes approximately 40 per cent
of the population of Northern Ireland.

Net expenditure by the Police Authority up to 1985–86 is set out in
Table 3.3. Even allowing for inflation and the exclusion of figures for

Table 3.3   Net expenditure of the Police Authority of Northern Ireland
1970–71 to 1985–86

Year	Expenditure (£ million)	As % of public expenditure
1970–71[1]	7.8	–
1971–72	15.8	2.5
1972–73	19.2	2.6
1973–74	25.2	3.0
1974–75	36.2	3.0
1975–76	48.9	3.6
1976–77	62.2	3.8
1977–78	76.8	4.2
1978–79	92.7	4.3
1979–80	124.7	5.1
1980–81	159.0	5.5
1981–82	201.5	6.3
1982–83	217.9	6.3
1983–84	236.0	6.3
1984–85	257.5	6.4
1985–86	278.1	6.5

Note:
1   8 months.

Sources: Police Authority of Northern Ireland and *Government Expenditure White Papers*.

pensions from the first years of the operation of the Police Authority, it will be evident that there has been a very substantial increase in expenditure on the police. Salaries and wages of members of the RUC and RUC Reserve account for well over two-thirds of the Authority's expenditure. Their contribution to the increase in expenditure reflects not just the expansion in the size of the RUC and the increase in the full-time component of the RUC Reserve, but substantial improvements since 1970 in the pay of police officers. The present relatively high level of police salaries is reflected in large number of applications to join the RUC: for example, in 1985 there were 4648 applications, of which 390 were successful. The quality of applicants has led to the discontinuation of the RUC's Cadet scheme as no longer needed to furnish the force with suitable candidates. Equipping the police for its role in the security field in accordance with the policy of police primacy has also played an important part in the rise in expenditure. This has involved the partial remilitarisation of the police, the adoption of sophisticated technologies, and a large scale construction programme made necessary both by expansion and by the vulnerability of many older police stations to mortar attack.

The RUC is organised in eight departments designated by alphabetical symbols: A designates Administration, B Personnel, C Crimes, D Operations, E Intelligence and Special Branch, F Force Control and Information Centre, G Complaints and Discipline, and H Community Relations and Traffic. The primary tasks of the police are carried out through 12 divisions and 38 sub-divisions, which is how Northern Ireland has been divided up geographically for the purposes of policing since 1983, when the last changes were made in divisional boundaries and sub-divisional responsibilities, principally so as to place greater emphasis on local policing. A variety of special units has been established since 1970 to assist in the tasks of maintaining public order and of combatting terrorism. Particularly important are Headquarters Mobile Support Units and Divisional Mobile Support Units (DMSU), established in the early 1980s to provide mobile reserve forces used both in a counter-insurgency role and in riot situations. The use of DMSUs to enforce police policy on the re-routeing of parades by the Orange Order away from Catholic areas has placed these units at the centre of political controversy in the mid-1980s. In relation to terrorism, the activities of a special surveillance unit of the Special Branch (E4A) employing similar techniques to those of the Special Air Service (SAS), has been at the centre of the controversy over alleged 'shoot to kill' incidents in 1982. The forerunner of E4A was the Bessbrook Support Unit, which operated in south Armagh between April 1979 and April 1980 and pioneered the use of counter-insurgency techniques in the police. This militarisation of policing was the logical outcome of the pursuit of a policy of police primacy in the face of a continuing terrorist offensive that had blighted the hopes of a return to normality. It also provides the clearest evidence of the failure of civilianisation, the original aim of the organisational reforms initiated by the Hunt Committee.

FORMAL STRUCTURE OF AUTHORITY

Since the imposition of direct rule in March 1972, the British government has retained responsibility for security, including policing, and did so even during the short-lived experiment in power-sharing in the first half of 1974. Indeed, a feature of the various proposals the

British government has put forward for the re-establishment of devolved government in Northern Ireland since 1972 has been the exclusion of security from the powers recommended for devolution. The Police Authority, to which the Chief Constable is required under the Police Act to present an annual published account of the activities of the RUC, has the prime responsibility for supervising the functioning of the police, but it is not the only official agency monitoring the behaviour of the police. In 1977, an independent Police Complaints Board was established with responsibility for reviewing the handling of complaints against the police. Its members are appointed by the Secretary of State for Northern Ireland. The Board is notified of all complaints against police officers below the rank of Assistant Chief Constable. However, the double jeopardy rule, which exists to safeguard members of the police acquitted in the courts from being subject to disciplinary penalties for the same offences, has effectively limited the Board to the evaluation of minor disciplinary cases not involving the possibility of prosecution. In 1985, 2261 complaints were received by the Board, an increase of 268 over 1984.[9] Changes in the way complaints against the police are handled are presently under discussion. In April 1985 the Secretary of State for Northern Ireland issued a consultative paper setting out proposals for changes in the complaints procedure to take account of changes introduced in England and Wales under the Police and Criminal Evidence Act 1984. The main proposal was to replace the Police Complaints Board by a Police Complaints Commission with new and larger powers to supervise serious complaints. In addition, Article 6 of the Anglo–Irish Agreement lists both the Police Complaints Board and the Police Authority among bodies on the role and composition of which 'the Irish Government may put forward views and proposals' within the framework of the Anglo–Irish Conference.

Another body which has played an indirect role in monitoring the activities of the police is the Standing Advisory Commission on Human Rights. It was established in 1973 to advise the Secretary of State for Northern Ireland on the adequacy and effectiveness of anti-discrimination legislation. In practice (with official encouragement), it has also concerned itself with the functioning of emergency legislation and the operation of the security forces. In addition, a number of inquiries, such as that into police interrogation methods in 1979,[10] have scrutinised the actions of the police, as have a series of reviews of the operation of emergency legislation. This activity reflects the British government's concern that the enforcement of the law in

Northern Ireland should not be seen internationally to be in violation of basic human rights. The conflict in security policy between the protection of civil liberties and the perceived need to permit departures from normal procedures to contain political violence accounts in part for the contradictory perceptions of the police as shackled by political constraints in the war against terrorism on the one hand, and as operating a repressive security policy under the guise of normal policing on the other.

In the early years of the Troubles, the Special Powers Act remained in force. Indeed, the Act provided the legal basis for the introduction of internment in August 1971. Following the imposition of direct rule the British government appointed a committee under Lord Diplock to advise on changes in legal procedure so as to facilitate the prosecution of terrorist offences through the courts.[11] Its recommendations were put into effect by the Northern Ireland (Emergency Provisions) Act 1973, commonly referred to as the Emergency Provisions Act. The Act conferred on the police very wide powers of arrest and established non-jury courts with special rules of evidence to try terrorist offences. The rules governing the admissibility of confessions have proved particularly controversial, as has the non-jury nature of the courts, especially in cases involving the uncorroborated evidence of accomplices. This issue came to the fore in 1982 and 1983 when a series of trials involving hundreds of defendants were held based on the evidence of 'supergrasses' (as former members of Loyalist and Republican paramilitaries who turned informer were dubbed). However, the use of supergrasses as a systematic strategy to disable the paramilitaries was undermined by the acquittal on appeal of most of those initially convicted on supergrass evidence. The Emergency Provisions Act also provided for detention without trial, which replaced internment under the Special Powers Act. The last detainees held in terms of this provision were released in December 1975. Its continued use ran contrary to the adoption of the policy of criminalising political violence. However, the power to detain without trial remained in law and was included in the 1978 revision and consolidation of the Emergency Provisions Act. An official review of the operation of the Act published in 1984 recommended 'without qualification'[12] the repeal of this power, which has been kept in reserve by government in case of a dire emergency. Among other features of the 1978 Emergency Provisions Act are the listing of paramilitaries such as the Provisional IRA and the Ulster Volunteer Force as proscribed organisations, the conferral on the police of powers to fix the routes of funerals, and the outlawing of paramilitary uniforms and the wearing of hoods or masks.

The other main piece of emergency legislation is the Prevention of Terrorism (Temporary Provisions) Act. Passed originally in the wake of the Birmingham pub bombings in November 1974 in which 21 people died, the Act has been subject to regular renewal; it was redrawn in 1976. A new Act extending the scope of the legislation to meet the threat posed by international terrorism was passed in 1984 following a review of the operation of the 1976 Act by Lord Jellicoe. Because of their duplication of features of the Emergency Provisions Act, the relevance of the Acts to Northern Ireland has been limited to two aspects: the power to detain suspects for up to seven days, subject to Ministerial approval after 48 hours, and exclusion orders. Between 1975 and 1984 there were a total of 4360 detentions in Northern Ireland under the Acts with extensions beyond 48 hours granted in the case of 3087. 40 per cent of suspects were charged with some offence. This contrasts with the small number of those detained in Great Britain under the Acts who have been charged with any offence (7.8 per cent). Exclusion orders provide for the banning by executive decision of British and Irish citizens from either Great Britain or Northern Ireland (or both in the case of Irish citizens resident in the Republic) provided that they have not resided in the part of the UK from which they are being excluded for a period of more than three years. This extraordinary power of banishment, outwardly similar in some respects to Soviet internal exile, has principally been used to exclude Northern Ireland residents from Great Britain. For somewhat different reasons, it is resented by both communities in Northern Ireland.

POLICE–MILITARY RELATIONS

Since British troops were sent to Northern Ireland in August 1969 to aid the civil power, there has been a close working relationship between the police and the military. This is reflected institutionally at the top level in the Joint Security Committee. It originally consisted of the Northern Ireland Prime Minister, two of his Cabinet colleagues, a British government representative, the General Officer Commanding (GOC) of the Army in Northern Ireland, and the Chief Constable of the RUC. After the imposition of direct rule it was chaired by the Secretary of State for Northern Ireland, with British

Ministers taking over the positions previously occupied by the Northern Ireland politicians; it meets on a weekly basis. In addition, a second security committee attended by the GOC and the Chief Constable meets to discuss operational issues. In the first six years of the army's involvement in the Northern Ireland conflict, the Army was the dominant partner in combatting political violence, and this was formally reflected in the appointment of the GOC as Director of Operations. Throughout this period the RUC adopted a low profile under guidelines that emphasised that the police's primary duty was the preservation of life and the avoidance of confrontation. The Ulster Workers' Council strike in May 1974 (which brought down the power-sharing Executive established in January of that year) exposed the shortcomings in these arrangements. The Army's pre-occupation with terrorism as the main threat to law and order and uncertainty over its role in relation to lesser threats to public order (such as were posed by the erection of barricades to prevent people going to work during the strike), meant that there was little attempt made by the Army to stop unlawful action taken by Loyalist paramilitaries to enforce the strike. For its part, the RUC was reluctant to take action that could be interpreted as a violation of its guidelines to maintain a low profile. Poor communications and a lack of trust between the police and the Army added to the difficulties of the security forces during the strike. These problems were compounded by the reluctance of the British government (in the person of the Secretary of State for Northern Ireland, Merlyn Rees) to make a clear political commitment to sustain the power-sharing Executive by issuing direct instructions to the security forces to remove barricades, clear roads, and stop intimidation.

Following the failure of the power-sharing experiment in 1974 and of the 1975 Constitutional Convention, a review of security policy was carried out by a committee under a senior civil servant, John Bourne. The internal and confidential report of the Bourne committee, entitled 'The Way Ahead', emphasised the need to re-establish enforcement of the law by the police throughout Northern Ireland. Among members of the committee was the present Chief Constable, Sir John Hermon. The committee's report laid the basis of the adoption of the policy of police primacy. The new policy, which came into operation in 1976, placed the Army in a subordinate role to that of the police. The Chief Constable became the Director of Operations and meetings of the security committee dealing with operational matters were transferred to the headquarters of the RUC at Knock in

Belfast. Initially, there was little resistance to the policy of police primacy from the military. However (especially after the appointment of Lieutenant-General Timothy Creasey as GOC in Northern Ireland in 1977) Army unease over the implementation of the policy grew. Security policy was by no means the only source of conflict between the police and the military. Institutional rivalry, personality clashes between senior officers, and mistrust between the two organisations over the sharing of intelligence and the protection of sources also caused friction, as did specific incidents. An example was an episode in 1978 which led to the prosecution of members of an SAS patrol who shot an innocent 16 year old, John Boyle, in the course of staking-out an arms find. The troops were acquitted of the boy's murder, but the court case revealed the role played by mutual suspicion between the police and the Army in the tragedy, and itself contributed to recriminations between the two forces. However, such incidents were far from typical of the relationship between the police and Army.

The conflict over policy was of far greater importance. Its roots lay in different conceptions of the conflict. While the formal definition of the Army's role was that of providing military aid for the civil power, the military's dominant role in relation to security in the first years of the Troubles helped to ground the Army's conception of the conflict in a counter-insurgency model based on the British Army's experiences in places such as Cyprus and Aden. Such a model applied to Northern Ireland implied the existence of widespread disaffection in the nationalist community as support for the insurgency. It was an assumption that seemed to be amply borne out by the way the conflict developed after the introduction of internment. By contrast, the RUC approached the problem of terrorism from the perspective of law enforcement in a normal society, the more especially because any other approach evoked echoes of practices that had brought discredit on the police at the onset of the Troubles. For the RUC, police primacy and the policy of criminalisation went naturally together.

The decline in the level of political violence in 1977 and 1978 appeared to vindicate the shift in security policy, and to bear out hopes of a return to normality in a war-weary society. However, the Army remained sceptical of the progress claimed by the police; in particular, it continued to doubt whether the police were equipped, or had the experience, to meet the threat posed by the Provisional IRA through ordinary means of law enforcement. The Army's assessment was that the Provisional IRA was very far from being beaten despite optimistic assessments of the security situation emanating from the Northern Ireland Office and from the police. The Army's dissatisfaction with the policy of police primacy became particularly acute after 18 soldiers were killed in a Provisional IRA ambush at Warrenpoint in August 1979. In the aftermath of Warrenpoint, the Army pressed for a number of specific changes in security policy. These were permitting 'hot pursuit' across the border with the Republic of Ireland, the introduction of selective detention, direct communications with the Irish Army, and the appointment of a security supremo senior to both the GOC and the Chief Constable.[13] Only the fourth demand was acceded to, and that in a modified form. The government appointed a former head of the Secret Intelligence Service (M16), Sir Maurice Oldfield, as co-ordinator of security in Northern Ireland. His principal role was to improve liaison between the Army and the police, particularly in relation to the sharing of intelligence. The main innovation in security policy to which Oldfield contributed was the development of the supergrass strategy. However, there was a major change in the political context of security policy with the launch of new constitutional initiative by the Conservative government in October 1979. Despite this, there was no change in the policy of police primacy, although originally a policy of direct rule eschewing new initiatives had been seen as going hand in hand with police primacy.

While the evidence of the durability of the Provisional IRA's campaign of violence could not be ignored, the threat this posed was met through an evolution in the tactics of the police. In particular, the RUC adopted counter-insurgency techniques derived from the Army's experience and there was a mushrooming of special units within the force. However, the police did not adopt the ideology of counter-insurgency and remained formally wedded to the notion that political violence had to be combatted within the context of the impartial enforcement of the law. The emphasis that was being given in Great Britain to the development of special police units to meet any internal security threat on the British mainland helped to place these developments in the context of a philosophy of normal policing. The definition of the tasks expected of police throughout the UK was changing in response to the general threat that terrorism in a wider international context appeared to pose to society. One obvious reason why the British government insisted on the retention of the policy of police primacy was that the use of the Army rather than the police for combatting political violence tended to enhance the

Provisional IRA's legitimacy internationally, by projecting an image of the organisation as a guerrilla army fighting a war of national liberation. Another was the role played by the police in the policy of Ulsterisation that had brought a significant reduction in the numbers of troops from the British mainland committed to the province. (They fell to approximately 10 000 at the end of 1983 from over 17 000 at the end of 1973.)

The other main plank of Ulsterisation was the Ulster Defence Regiment (UDR). It had been established in 1970 to replace the discredited B Specials in the security sphere. Initially, it attracted significant numbers of Catholic recruits; however, as a result both of Catholic disaffection due to the introduction of internment and of intimidation by Republican paramilitaries, it soon developed into an almost wholly Protestant force with the proportion of Catholics in its ranks falling to under 3 per cent. About 40 per cent of its 7000 members are full-time. Serious crimes of a sectarian nature committed by a small number of its members, some infiltration of the force by members of Loyalist paramilitaries, and its reputation for the harassment of Catholics in the course of routine duties, have led to frequent calls for its disbandment by representatives of the Catholic community. In rural areas especially, the behaviour of members of the UDR at roadblocks towards ordinary members of the public, often Catholic neighbours whom they know personally, has generated immense resentment in the Catholic community. Its identification with Northern Ireland has meant that it has lacked the political protection afforded by Westminister to other units of the British Army that have become embroiled in controversy, making it a particular target of Catholic resentment over security measures affecting the community's daily life. The disbandment of the UDR was a major objective of the Irish government in the negotiations leading to the Anglo–Irish Agreement. A concession made by the British government at the time of the signing of the Agreement to meet the concern of the minority over the UDR was a declaration that in future UDR patrols would be accompanied by the police. To the embarrassment of both the British and Irish governments, this was contradicted by a memorandum issued by the Chief Constable of the RUC shortly afterwards. While reaffirming the police's commitment to extending their operations and, where possible, involving the police in Army patrols, the Chief Constable made it clear that this was an ongoing process and that the public must expect to continue to encounter Army patrols unaccompanied by the RUC. He declined to draw a distinction between the UDR and other Army units.[14] Nonetheless, a number of press reports, apparently based on police briefings[15] have suggested that the police do tend to view the UDR as a liability in the campaign to secure Catholic support for the security forces and would not resist its phasing out in the context of an expansion of the police's role.

PUBLIC ORDER SITUATIONS

The colloquial term 'the Troubles' itself provides the most appropriate definition of public order situations in the context of Northern Ireland, though a conventional definition of 'public order' might justify the inclusion of rare instances of minor crowd disorder that have occurred outside the context of sectarian conflict. However, these have had so little bearing on the generality of policy that they can be safely disregarded. Over 2500 people have died in the present Troubles. Details of fatalities between 1969 and 1985 are set out in Table 3.4; approximately 60 per cent of these deaths occurred in the five years between the introduction of internment in August 1971 and the formation of the 'Peace People' in August 1976. The period encompassed the imposition of direct rule from Westminster, the establishment of a power-sharing Executive, the Ulster Workers' Council strike that brought it down, two Provisional IRA ceasefires, and a campaign of random sectarian assassinations by Loyalist paramilitaries, partly, ironically, in response to the ceasefires because of the fears they inspired among Protestants of a deal between the British government and the IRA. Through the period of the Troubles as a whole, terrorism in the form of assassinations, attacks on the security forces, and bombings has been far and way the main cause of deaths.

An analysis by David Roche of the Irish Information Partnership of fatalities during the period from 1969 to the end of 1984 identified Republican paramilitaries as the agency responsible for the loss of life in 56 per cent of deaths, with Loyalist paramilitaries responsible in 26 per cent.[16] The same study put the numbers killed as a result of action by the security forces at 284, or 12 per cent of total deaths. Of these a high proportion – 161, or 57 per cent – were civilians who were not members of either Republican or Loyalist paramilitaries. The agency of the security forces responsible for the overwhelming majority of deaths, whether of innocent civilians or terrorists, was the

Table 3.4 Deaths in Northern Ireland arising out of the security situation 1969–85

Year	RUC	RUCR	Army	UDR	Civilians[1]	Total
1969	1	–	–	–	12	13
1970	2	–	–	–	23	25
1971	11	–	43	5	115	174
1972	14	3	103	26	321	467
1973	10	3	58	8	171	250
1974	12	3	28	7	166	216
1975	7	4	14	6	216	247
1976	13	10	14	15	245	297
1977	8	6	15	14	69	112
1978	4	6	14	7	50	81
1979	9	5	38	10	51	113
1980	3	6	8	9	50	76
1981	13	8	10	13	57	101
1982	8	4	21	7	57	97
1983	9	9	5	10	44	77
1984	7	2	9	10	36	64
1985	14	9	2	4	25	54
Totals	145	78	382	151	1708	2464

Note:
1 Including suspected terrorists.

Source: Chief Constable's *Annual Report 1985*.

British Army and approximately two-thirds of the deaths caused by the security forces in the period covered by Roche's study occurred prior to the adoption of the policy of police primacy in 1976.

A considerable number of the civilian deaths caused by the security forces occurred in the context of street disturbances, which constitute after terrorism the main source of deaths arising out of the Troubles. The most serious episode of this kind took place at the end of January 1972 on 'Bloody Sunday' when 13 unarmed demonstrators were killed when British paratroopers opened fire on an illegal civil rights march in the city of Londonderry. The pattern of street disturbances has varied considerably according to the political situation, though it has generally been related to the incidence of demonstrations. For example, during 1981 when 10 Republican prisoners died as a result of a hunger strike over demands to be recognised as political offenders through changes in the prison regime, there were a total of 1205 demonstrations between 1 March when the hunger strike began and

3 October when the protest ended. In that period, seven people were killed by plastic bullets fired by the security forces to quell disturbances. In the year as a whole, nearly 30 000 plastic bullets were fired by the security forces. There have been a total of 13 deaths as a result of the use of plastic bullets. They were first introduced in Northern Ireland in 1974 replacing rubber bullets as a riot control weapon; they were issued to the RUC in October 1978. There have been frequent calls for a ban on their use by nationalist politicians in Northern Ireland and internationally through resolutions of the European Parliament. Their use became a contentious issue among Unionists when a Loyalist demonstrator died as a result of being struck by a plastic bullet in disturbances in Portadown at the end of March 1986. A common justification of the weapon is that the security forces require it as a means of defending themselves against the use of petrol and acid bombs by rioters during disturbances.

Covert operations by the security forces account for an increasing proportion of deaths for which they are responsible. In fact, a general feature of the Northern Ireland conflict has been a shift away from the more overt forms of political violence to killings resulting from action directed at specific targets. Partly as a consequence, there has been a marked rise in the number of fatalities per violent incident, despite the fall in the annual toll of deaths from the Troubles. The targeting of the security forces by Republican paramilitaries is reflected in a rise in the numbers of members of the security forces killed as a proportion of total deaths. For example, deaths of members of the security forces were 54 per cent of total fatalities in 1985, compared to only 18 per cent in 1976. As a result of the policy of police primacy, an increasing proportion of these have been members of the RUC and the RUC Reserve. In the circumstances, the gathering of intelligence both by paramilitaries and by the security forces has loomed larger in the conflict.

With the establishment of special police units trained in counter-insurgency techniques, the RUC has become increasingly embroiled in controversial instances of covert action. Some of the most important incidents occurred towards the end of 1982. Three unarmed members of the Provisional IRA were shot dead by police at a checkpoint outside Lurgan in November 1982. In the same month, Michael Tighe, a youth without paramilitary connections, was shot dead by police at a stake-out of an arms find on a farm in county Armagh. In December 1982 two unarmed members of a Republican paramilitary organisation, the Irish National Liberation Army (INLA), were shot dead after police officers stopped their car on the outskirts of the city of Armagh. These incidents led to press speculation, partly encouraged by briefings journalists received, [17] that a 'shoot to kill' policy was in operation, although this was officially denied. Court cases in which the police officers involved in two of the cases were acquitted of murder, and the inquest into Tighe's death failed to dispel public disquiet over the circumstances of the shootings. As a result, the Deputy Chief Constable of Greater Manchester police, John Stalker, was appointed in May 1984 to conduct an inquiry into the incidents. By the time he was suspended from the inquiry in May 1986 over allegations concerning his conduct as a police officer in Manchester, it appeared that his findings might implicate senior officers of the RUC and perhaps others in authorising police action outside the law during the conduct of covert operations. That led to allegations that his suspension from the inquiry had been engineered to cover up the authorisation of illegal conduct. Much of Stalker's concern appears to have centred on the case of Michael Tighe, an incident with features in common with that of John Boyle, the boy killed in an SAS stake-out in 1978. One implication that might be drawn from the two cases is that the police's own involvement in counter-insurgency operations tends to blunt their capacity to insist that such operations are accountable to the ordinary law.

Although understandably the focus of most concern, deaths constitute only one dimension of the challenge to public order in Northern Ireland. Mass action at various junctures, such as the Ulster Workers' Council strike in 1974, has posed a considerable political challenge. Since the adoption of police primacy in 1976, the RUC has faced campaigns of political mobilisation involving mass action from both communities. On the nationalist side, the most important was the campaign in support of the Republican prisoners on hunger strike in 1980 and in 1981, while the 1977 Loyalist strike against security policy and protests in 1985 and 1986 over the re-routeing of Orange Order parades and over the Anglo–Irish Agreement have constituted the main campaigns among Unionists. Because of the involvement of the majority community and because of the RUC's past history of political subordination to Unionism and its largely Protestant composition, the latter have presented by far the greater challenge to the police. The indefinite general strike called by Ian Paisley in May 1977 provided an early test of the policy of police primacy. The effective handling of the strike, reflected in the clearing of barricades and action taken against intimidation, appeared in marked contrast to the passivity of the security forces in the face of similar tactics during the Ulster Workers' Council strike and provided an impressive demonstration of the RUC's reliability to enforce the law impartially.

The police's re-routeing of Orange Order parades away from Catholic areas became the pretext for serious disorder in the summer of 1985. Confrontation over the issue was foreshadowed by the Chief Constable's report for 1984 in which concern was expressed at the cost of policing parades, especially where parade organisers insisted that their supporters had a right to march through areas where changes in the composition of the population meant their presence was no longer welcome. Under Article 4, Paragraph 3 of the Public Order (Northern Ireland) Order 1981, the Secretary of State has powers based on information supplied to him by the police to ban parades, while the Chief Constable has powers under Article 4, Paragraph 1 to re-route or to impose other conditions on the holding of parades. During the 1985 marching season in which there were over 2000 parades, three parades were banned, while re-routeing or other conditions were imposed on parades on 22 occasions. Loyalist protest over the banning and re-routeing of parades centred on the issue of the Irish government's involvement in the decisions. Representations by the Irish government on behalf of nationalists living in areas affected by Orange Order parades led to allegations that decisions over parades had been taken at the behest of Dublin in the context of the Anglo–Irish process, allegations denied by the Chief Constable. The most serious clashes between police and Loyalists took place in Portadown in July and August 1985 when on successive occasions large crowds of rioting Loyalists attacked police units sent to the town to prevent Orangemen marching through a Catholic neighbourhood. In the aftermath of these attacks, a number of police officers were intimidated out of their homes in Protestant areas of the town.

After the signing of the Anglo–Irish Agreement on 15 November 1985, the issue of re-routeing became largely absorbed in wider Unionist protests over the Agreement itself. The initial protests against the Agreement were peaceful. In particular, a rally in Belfast at the end of November which was organised by the main Unionist parties and attracted a crowd of over 100 000 passed off without incident. However, in 1986 violence became a frequent feature of protests against the Agreement. For example, a protest march in January by Young Unionists to the headquarters of the Anglo–Irish secretariat at Maryfield House on the outskirts of Belfast ended in a riot in which 23 police officers were injured. After by-elections in 14 of Northern Ireland's 17 constituencies, staged as part of Unionist protest, demonstrated the strength of feeling against the Agreement in the Protestant community, the leaders of the two main Unionist parties called a one-day general strike on 3 March as part of their campaign to force the British government to abrogate (or at least to suspend) the Agreement. Contrary to the declared intentions of the two party leaders, the day was marked by serious violence, with Loyalist paramilitaries playing a leading role in enforcing the strike. Barricades were set up through much of the province blocking major thoroughfares, and there was widespread intimidation of those attempting to go to work. The RUC was strongly criticised both by nationalist politicians and by the small, non-sectarian Alliance Party for failing to take effective action to remove barricades or to prevent intimidation, while the Chief Constable issued a statement placing the blame on the Unionist leaders for failing to honour the commitments they had made on the conduct of the strike.

However, police restraint during the strike did little to temper Loyalist attacks on the RUC's conduct and the Loyalist response did not stop at verbal criticism. In the month following the strike on 3 March, there were a series of attacks on the homes of police officers in Protestant neighbourhoods, involving over 150 incidents of intimidation ranging from abuse and stone-throwing to petrol-bombings and shootings, with more than 30 police families being forced to move from their homes. The attacks on the homes of police officers were much more than just a reaction to what Loyalists chose to interpret as police support for the Anglo–Irish Agreement. They were also an attempt to play on the very evident strains in the lower ranks of the RUC and among reservists over the Agreement and to provoke a police revolt against the implementation of any measures under it. The death of Keith White on 14 April provided a fresh impetus for the attacks. He had been struck by a plastic bullet fired by police during disturbances that followed the banning of an Apprentice Boys' parade in Portadown at the end of March. In the same period, there was a spate of sectarian attacks on the homes of Catholics living in mixed areas. The attacks on the homes of police officers began to peter out in May. Fears of yet another confrontation between police and Loyalists at Portadown, on 12 July (the climax of the marching season) once again linked the issue of re-routing with that of the Anglo–Irish Agreement. In the event, confrontation was averted by the Chief Constable's permitting the Orange Order parade to take place along what was described as a compromise route. It was a compromise that angered both nationalists in Northern Ireland and the Irish government, as the new route still went through a Catholic area of the town. The recriminations over Hermon's decision highlighted the unresolved conflict between Nationalist expectations of the Anglo–Irish Agreement and the Chief Constable's insistence on his autonomy in relation to operational matters.

PUBLIC PERCEPTIONS OF THE POLICE

Notwithstanding the conflict between the police and Loyalists over the Anglo–Irish Agreement and other issues, both sides of the sectarian divide in Northern Ireland tend to view the RUC as a basically Protestant (or at least Unionist) institution, perceptions reinforced by the considerable emphasis that is placed within the force on loyalty to the Crown as part of the ethos of the organisation. This disposition is reflected in the attitudes of the main political parties towards the police. The Official Unionist Party, the party which represents a majority of Protestants, has been generally supportive of the police, and indeed has strongly criticised physical attacks on the force by hardline Loyalists. Like the Democratic Unionist Party (DUP) of Ian Paisley, it has pressed for the removal of political constraints on the police's operations against terrorists. It has supported measures such as detention without trial, the 'shoot to kill' policy, the supergrass strategy, and the use of plastic bullets against rioters, though the party's attitude on this issue has been tempered by incidents such as the death of Keith White. The attitude of the Democratic Unionist Party has been rather more inconsistent. While it has been even more strident than the Official Unionist Party in demanding greater police powers to tackle Republican terrorism and in pressing for the restoration of capital punishment, it has strongly objected to the use of emergency measures or tactics such as the supergrass strategy against Loyalist paramilitaries. At the same time, it has strongly attacked the qualified support given to the police by the SDLP. The DUP has frequently been at odds with the Chief Constable of the RUC while, like the extreme right in South Africa, cultivating support in the lower ranks of the force.

The Alliance Party struggling for votes across the sectarian divide has balanced its insistence on unequivocal support for the police by emphasising its opposition to measures violating the rule of law. The conflict between Loyalists and the police over the Anglo–Irish Agreement has allowed the party to advertise its backing for the police in a context unlikely to alienate any potential supporters. The qualified nature of the SDLP's support for the police is reflected in its refusal to encourage Catholics to join the RUC or to agree to the nomination of members of the party to the Police Authority. It limits its support for the police to the carefully contrived formula that its supporters should co-operate with the RUC in the impartial enforcement of the law. The SDLP has argued that a political settlement enjoying legitimacy across the sectarian divide remains a pre-condition for ending Catholic alienation from the administration of justice and from the security forces. The party has opposed the whole gamut of emergency security measures. Sinn Fein, the political wing of the Provisional IRA, is unremittingly hostile to the RUC, maintaining that it remains a sectarian and politically partisan police force. Sinn Fein policy is that the RUC should be disarmed and the UDR disbanded in the context of British withdrawal from Northern Ireland. It has always supported fully attacks on the police by the Provisional IRA.

The pattern of attitudes on policing and security policy among the political parties is broadly reflected in popular perceptions. Indeed, opinion poll surveys have confirmed the existence of very high levels of sectarian polarisation on the most contentious aspects of security policy. However, this degree of polarisation has not always been reflected in the responses to more general questions. An example is provided by an opinion survey on attitudes towards law and order carried out for the *Belfast Telegraph* in January 1985. The responses to a question on the fairness of the RUC are set out in Table 3.5. While they show a marked difference in the responses of Catholics compared to Protestants, Catholic opinion is shown to be almost equally divided on the issue. This would seem to offer some support for the RUC's claim that it receives much greater support in practice from Catholics than is reflected in the attitudes attributed to them by nationalist politicians. In November 1984, in response to Nationalist reaction to the British Prime Minister's rejection of the political options outlined in the *New Ireland Forum Report*,[18] the RUC reaffirmed its rejection of the thesis of Catholic alienation from the police.

The RUC's view of Catholic attitudes is based on its experience of policing Catholic areas. Although vigilantes have from time to time

Table 3.5   1985 opinion survey on attitudes towards the Royal Ulster
Constabulary

Question: 'How fair do you think the RUC is in the discharge of its duties
in Northern Ireland?'

Response	Catholics (%)	Protestants (%)
Very fair	4	37
Fair	43	59
Unfair	38	3
Very Unfair	15	1

Note:
Research conducted through a mailed survey of 1200 households between
7 and 28 January 1985, with 955 responding.

Source: *Belfast Telegraph*, 6 February 1985.

displaced the police in controlling ordinary crime in the more hardline nationalist areas, the RUC does appear to receive considerable
co-operation from Catholics in the investigation of crimes without a
paramilitary dimension. This instrumental support for the RUC
among Catholics is an important factor in underpinning the police's
conception of the Northern Ireland conflict. The weakness of the
RUC's claim to receive general cross-community support lies in its
failure to acknowledge the duality of its role as a civilian police force
on the one hand, and as the principal instrument of security policy on
the other. It can reasonably be surmised that the division of Catholic
opinion revealed by the *Belfast Telegraph* poll largely mirrors that
duality. While the results of opinion surveys need to be treated
cautiously because of their well-established tendency to overstate the
strength of moderate opinion, it is significant that the same *Belfast
Telegraph* poll revealed a considerably lower level of confidence
among Catholics in the legal system than in the police, reflecting in
particular the impact of changes in the legal system to facilitate the
prosecution of terrorists through the courts, and of the supergrass
strategy.

THE POLICE AS A POLITICAL INSTITUTION

The onset of the Troubles in 1968 and 1969 proved to be a watershed
in the history of policing in Northern Ireland. The RUC emerged

from the events of those years with its reputation severely tarnished. It was widely reviled as a sectarian police force that had contributed through indiscipline and partisanship to the disorder by which it had been overwhelmed. Consequently, reform of policing enjoyed a high priority at Westminster and there was little disposition within the force itself to resist change. The original basis of reform was civilianisation. While this initially enhanced the acceptability of the force in Catholic areas, that did not survive the introduction of internment in August 1971 and civilianisation consequently did little to restore the prestige of the RUC. The current high standing of the force owes much to the policy of police primacy introduced in 1976. Police primacy has transformed the RUC into a force recognised internationally for its role in combatting terrorism,[19] though at times its methods have prompted controversy. In particular, the scandal over police interrogation techniques in the late 1970s resulted in a decision by the US State Department in August 1979 to suspend the sales of handguns to the RUC in response to Congressional pressure that they were contrary to American policy to end the sale of arms to bodies or countries violating human rights.

Despite the fate of civilianisation, the reforms initiated as a result of the report of the Hunt Committee had a profound effect on the force that has endured. Two related aspects of the reforms, the emphasis on autonomy from political pressures and on professionalism, established deep roots within the RUC. In reaction to the disastrous consequences for the police of their political subordination to the Unionist government, a strongly anti-political ideology has been embraced by the upper ranks of the force. This has been reflected in the determination of successive Chief Constables to ensure that through the impartial enforcement of the law the force is able to fend off any demands that it be made more politically accountable for its actions. Distaste for political entanglements was a factor in the complicated Dowra affair, which led to a breach in relations between the RUC and the Garda Siochana in 1983.[20] In particular, the Chief Constable of the RUC, Sir John Hermon, was unwilling to assist an investigation by the Garda which he saw as related to party political manoeuvres in the South. Hermon has also been reluctant to meet Unionist politicians to discuss security policy, doing so only under the aegis of the Police Authority. Professionalisation of policing was welcomed as providing the means whereby the RUC could be insulated from social pressures of all kinds. The perception that the RUC was distancing itself from society was reflected in the creation in 1970 of a community relations branch as a separate, specialised unit within the force. The adoption of the policy of police primacy, greatly enhancing the status of the RUC as well as the scope of its operations, was partly a testament to the success of this model of policing.

The price the RUC has paid for autonomy and the relative social isolation resulting from professionalisation has been acceptance of legal constraints on police operations and of constant reviews of the functioning of emergency measures that have reflected the British government's concern that policing in Northern Ireland should be defensible internationally on human rights grounds. While senior officers of the RUC have for the most part appreciated the necessity for such constraints, they have given rise to a considerable measure of discontent in the lower ranks of the force. This has been most clearly reflected in statements from the Police Federation of Northern Ireland, which represents over 90 per cent of police officers in the province. On numerous occasions, spokesmen for the Federation have attacked what they have described as political obstacles in the way of police action to root out terrorism, echoing Unionist criticism of security policy while not actually sharing its political perspective. Paradoxically, the Federation has also been critical of the militarization of policing resulting from the policy of police primacy. For example, the chairman of the Federation (Alan Wright) has argued that the Army should be responsible for border security and for the conducting of counter-insurgency operations, as these are not properly speaking functions of a civilian police force. The Federation's concern to limit the role of the police stems from the very high rate of casualties among police officers since the adoption of police primacy, the highest in the world for a police force in terms of fatalities.[21] The intense pressure put on the police by Provisional IRA attacks has not been without result. Following the murder of three police officers in Newry in July 1986, bringing to 13 the number of police officers killed in acts of terrorism in the town in a period of 18 months, there was a resumption of Army patrols in Newry, the first for five years. Sinn Fein represented the killings and their impact on security policy as a defeat for the policy of Ulsterisation.[22]

In the 1980s the Police Federation has come into conflict on a number of occasions with the Chief Constable over these and other issues. At the end of 1981 a meeting of the central committee of the Police Federation narrowly carried a motion of no confidence in the Chief Constable, though this was later reversed. The antagonism towards Hermon reflected resentment on a range of internal issues, in addition to underlying discontent over security policy. In April 1986 the chairman of the Police Federation appealed to the Chief Constable not to attend meetings of the Intergovernmental Conference set up under the Anglo–Irish Agreement because of the Agreement's unpopularity among police officers and because of the effect of the role being played by the Chief Constable on public perceptions of the force's independence. Sir John Hermon strongly defended his participation in the Conference as solely motivated by policing considerations, including the improvement of cross-border security, while making it clear that the operational autonomy of the RUC remained guaranteed in the Agreement itself. In practice, both Hermon's stance on the issue of police supervision of UDR patrols and his handling of the re-routeing of parades during the summer of 1986 have demonstrated his commitment to maintaining the RUC's autonomy, and this seems likely to limit the flexibility with which the British government is able to respond to representations made by the Irish government over security policy through the Conference. Indeed, the pressures on the force place the Chief Constable in a very strong position to resist proposals for changes in security policy that fall short of changing the law itself. The Federation and the Chief Constable have also come into conflict over whether the Federation has any right to make pronouncements on policy matters under the rubric of representing the welfare of police officers.

The problem of cross-border security has also involved the Chief Constable in political controversy. Two aspects of the issue have proved particularly contentious, incursions into the Irish Republic by members of the RUC and RUC criticism of the performance of the Garda in securing its side of the border. The revelation that two members of E4A had crossed into the Republic in the course of their surveillance of two INLA suspects, subsequently shot dead in controversial circumstances by police inside Northern Ireland, came out in the course of the 1984 trial of a police officer in connection with the 1982 killings. The Chief Constable's assertion that the incursion was neither pre-planned nor deliberate provoked a protest from the Irish Prime Minister that Hermon's remarks pre-judged the inquiry into the episode that the British government had agreed to establish. Recriminations over the Garda's handling of cross-border security have been a more enduring and more serious source of friction in Anglo–Irish relations. The Chief Constable's involvement in the issue arose from remarks he made at an international conference of senior police officers in Texas in October 1985, less than a month before the signing of the Anglo–Irish Agreement. According to journalists at the conference, Sir John Hermon portrayed the South as a safe haven for terrorists, criticised the Garda as unhelpful with resources being diverted from the border to meet the drug problem in Dublin, and attacked the Republic's record on extradition. Despite the Chief Constable's insistence that his remarks had been misrepresented by the press, they were quickly taken up by the political parties in Northern Ireland to justify their respective positions on security policy and embarrassed both the British and Irish governments.

The Hermon affair, as it was dubbed, demonstrated the automatic disposition of both sides of the sectarian divide to regard the RUC as by inclination a Unionist force, despite the efforts made by the police to distance themselves from provincial political influences. This disposition exists not merely because of the composition of the force and its ethos or because of the RUC's past history. It is also partly a consequence of the fact that Catholics have tended to bear the brunt of action directed against terrorism or street disturbances that has involved abuses by the police of their powers. More fundamentally, it reflects calculations of how the force would behave in circumstances of a British withdrawal from Northern Ireland. However unlikely, the possibility of British withdrawal can never be ruled out entirely, given the clear distinction drawn politically and constitutionally between Northern Ireland and the rest of the UK, a distinction emphatically underlined by the terms of the Anglo–Irish Agreement. The role in which the RUC would be cast in such circumstances remains, and will continue to remain, a crucial obstacle to wholehearted nationalist approval of the force. It also places constraints on how far even the most hardline Loyalists are prepared to go in attacks on the police over their role in upholding the Anglo–Irish Agreement through simply enforcing the law. Partly for this reason, Loyalist pressure on the force seems unlikely to provoke a police revolt leading to the disintegration of the RUC.

Provided the British government takes care that any changes made in security policy to facilitate progress under the Anglo–Irish Agreement are achieved through legislation and not imposed through clumsy administrative measures likely to compromise its autonomy, it should be able to continue to rely on the RUC. However, the risks inherent in existing policies remain substantial, not least because of the danger of miscalculation by political forces in Northern Ireland. For the RUC, the previous policy of containment of violence within the context of direct rule, embodying a managerial approach to the conflict fitted far more readily the model of policing adopted by the force after 1970. What destroyed that policy as an option for the British government was the impact of the 1981 hunger strike on Catholic attitudes, reflected in the electoral advances made by Sinn Fein. The process of adjustment by the RUC to the new political context created by the Anglo–Irish Agreement has barely begun, though that is hardly surprising given the fragility of the Anglo–Irish process itself.

CONCLUSION

Policing formed a central issue at the onset of the Troubles in 1968 and 1969. It remains a central issue after almost 20 years of conflict. In that period, the RUC has been transformed from a force over-whelmed by unrest to a body that arguably constitutes the main barrier to chaos in Northern Ireland. Although political violence has declined from the levels reached in the early to mid-1970s, this has not been matched by any lessening of political polarisation within Northern Ireland. The improvement in the security situation, mea-sured by fatalities, is principally the result of a fall in the number of sectarian murders perpetrated by Loyalist paramilitaries. These kill-ings began to tail off sharply in 1977, partly as a result of a change in Protestant perceptions of British intentions following the adoption of the policy of direct rule and partly as a response to the activities of the 'Peace People'. The pursuit of Loyalist paramilitaries by the RUC, which resulted in the conviction of many of those responsible for the killings, has acted as a deterrent against any large scale resumption of such activities. Loyalist paramilitaries have generally preferred simply to busy themselves making preparations for dooms-day, as they have characterised the prospect of the forcible inte-gration of Northern Ireland into a united Ireland. In particular, they are reluctant to launch full scale operations in advance of a commit-ment to fight by the Unionist leaders themselves, given their experi-ence of repudiation by the politicians after the crises of the 1970s had passed. Nonetheless, the threat they continue to pose to law and order remains potent.

There has been much less (though there has been some) slackening in the campaign of violence by Republican paramilitaries. However, the nature of their campaign has changed with the commitment of the principal Republican paramilitary organisation, the Provisional IRA, to waging a long-term war of attrition. At the same time, the electoral successes of Sinn Fein have sustained the political impact of a lower level of violence. The extent of violence is not the only barrier to progress towards the civilianisation of policing in Northern Ireland.[23] The absence of any signs of a diminution of sectarian antagonisms has reinforced the British government's reliance on special measures in the field of security and the expansion in the scope of the RUC to maintain law and order in a divided society. Indeed, Protestant reaction to the Anglo–Irish Agreement has emphasised the fragility of the progress made to what has been described by British Ministers at various times as an acceptable level of violence. Any British government would be extremely reluctant to commit large numbers of British troops to Northern Ireland in any future crisis, given the degree of popular antipathy on the British mainland towards the warring factions in Northern Ireland and the probable international reaction. Consequently, the capacity of the RUC to sustain its dual role of fighting ordinary crime and of containing political violence remains crucial to the political future of the province. The targeting of police officers by the Provisional IRA and the campaign of intimidation against members of the RUC by Loyalists reflects the paramilitaries' recognition of the centrality of the RUC's position.

The fact that the RUC has so far stood up to the enormous pressures to which it has been subjected is testimony to the relative success of the model of policing that evolved during the 1970s. This involved the conscious distancing of the police from the norms of the divided society from which they were drawn through emphasis on professionalism and autonomy as the appropriate values of a modern police force. This distancing was made possible by the role of the British state both as a political force within the province that overarched sectarian divisions and as the guarantor of the framework within which the police operated. The image of the British state as a neutral umpire between the province's warring factions may be contested on the analytical ground that it is a leading party to the definition of Northern Ireland's constitutional status, the issue at the heart of both Unionist and nationalist discontent. Nonetheless, the political credibility of this perspective was important in establishing the notion of the impartial enforcement of the law as a goal of policing in Northern Ireland, free of the sectarian connotations that the maintenance of law and order had under Unionist governments.

The success of this process was placed in jeopardy not because of sectarian deviation from the norm of impartial law-enforcement by the police, but because of the gradual erosion of the credibility of Britain's role, largely as the result of the failure of successive British political initiatives. The British state came to appear less as a positive political force within the province standing above the centrifugal forces of sectarianism than as a weak intermediary lacking the authority of an umpire to secure the compliance of the contestants and too vulnerable to pressure to seem neutral.

For that reason, the Anglo–Irish Agreement is significant not just as a recognition that British policy in Northern Ireland needs the involvement and support of the Republic of Ireland, but (paradoxically) as a reassertion of British authority in the province. However, while the Anglo–Irish Agreement has ended the debilitating paralysis of British policy at a political level as well as eliciting a wide measure of international support, its implications for policing have been more problematic and not simply because Loyalist protest against the Agreement has put extra pressure on the RUC. In particular, as a result of the emphasis in the Agreement on the need to end Catholic alienation from the security forces, every policing decision of substance is likely to be scrutinised in the light of that objective and, if judged an advance or a setback, closely examined for its suspected political motivation. The controversy over the re-routeing of parades illustrates the process clearly, and points to the underlying danger that change effected through administrative fiat rather than law could politicise policing and undermine the credibility of the RUC's operational autonomy both inside and outside the force. At the same time, the political uncertainty arising out of the Agreement, including that over policing, has emphasised the essential nature of the contribution that the RUC as an institution makes to what stability exists in Northern Ireland.

There are few, if any, close analogies with Northern Ireland as a divided society elsewhere in the world. There are some similarities between the role Britain has played in establishing the political context of policing in Northern Ireland and that played by metropolitan authority in colonial situations characterised by deep cleavages of one kind and another. Shared features are the steps taken to insulate policing from local political pressures, the exclusion of the police from arrangements for the political accommodation of internal parties, and the tendency towards the militarisation of the police. However, the analogy is misleading in so far as it implies that decolonisation

– whether interpreted as an independent Northern Ireland or a united Ireland – constitutes a viable political option for British policy-makers in this case. An unusual feature of the Northern Ireland situation is the invitation that has been extended under an international treaty to a second state, the Republic of Ireland, to influence security policies in the province. The role of paramilitaries on both sides of the sectarian divide in Northern Ireland provides parallels between Northern Ireland and the cases of Cyprus and Lebanon, especially in the light of the importance of external parties. The breakdown of the state as a force overarching communal divisions in Cyprus and Lebanon resulted in partition in the former and chaos in the latter. On the basis of this analogy, failure of the British state to sustain the effective independence of the machinery it has created for governing Northern Ireland from domination by sectarian influences would point the province in the direction of repartition or civil war. The crucial role of the RUC within that machinery is a measure of the importance of policing in Northern Ireland.

Notes

1. On the contested nature of Northern Ireland as a political entity, see A. Guelke, 'International Legitimacy, Self-determination, and Northern Ireland', *Review of International Studies*, 11 (1985) 37–52.
2. M. Farrell, *Arming the Protestants: The Formation of the Ulster Special Constabulary and the Royal Ulster Constabulary 1920–27* (1983) p. 89.
3. Farrell, *Arming the Protestants*, p. 267.
4. *Disturbances in Northern Ireland: Report of the Commission appointed by the Governor of Northern Ireland (Cameron Report)* (Cmnd 532) (Belfast: HMSO, 1969) p. 73.
5. *Violence and Civil Disturbances in Northern Ireland in 1969: Report of the Tribunal of Inquiry* (Scarman Report) (Cmnd 566) (Belfast: HMSO, 1972).
6. *Report of the Advisory Committee on Police in Northern Ireland* (Hunt Report) (1969) p. 13.
7. *Agreement between the Government of the United Kingdom of Great Britain and Northern Ireland and the Government of the Republic of Ireland* (Cmnd 9657) (London: HMSO, 1985) p. 7.
8. *Chief Constable's Annual Report 1985* (Belfast: RUC, 1986) p. 41.
9. *Police Complaints Board for Northern Ireland: Annual Report 1985* (HC 385) Session 1985–86 (London: HMSO, 1986) p. 9.
10. *Report of the Committee of Inquiry into Police Interrogation Procedures in Northern Ireland* (Bennett Report) (Cmnd 7497) (London: HMSO, 1979).
11. *Report of the Commission to consider legal procedures to deal with*

terrorist activities in Northern Ireland (Diplock Report) (Cmnd 5185) (London: HMSO, 1972).

12. *Review of the Operation of the Northern Ireland (Emergency Provisions) Act 1978* (Baker Report) (Cmnd 9222) (London: HMSO, 1984) p. 71.

13. D. Hamill, *Pig in the Middle: The Army in Northern Ireland 1969–1985* (London: Methuen, 1986) p. 252.

14. Memorandum quoted in *Chief Constable's Annual Report 1985*, pp. 21–3.

15. See A. Pollak, 'Growing disillusionment over the UDR', *Irish Times*, 10 April 1985.

16. Calculated from D. Roche, 'Patterns of Violence in Northern Ireland in 1984', *Fortnight* (Belfast) 29 April–12 May 1985, p. 9.

17. See, for examples, J. Cusack, 'Policy on RUC tactics changed', *Irish Times*, 22 December 1982 and P. Bishop, 'Ulster calm credited to tougher tactics', *Observer*, 2 January 1983.

18. The options were a unitary state, federation, and joint authority. See *New Ireland Forum Report* (Dublin: The Stationery Office, 1984).

19. R.M. Pockrass, 'The Police Response to Terrorism: The Royal Ulster Constabulary' (1986), 143–57.

20. The Dowra affair concerned the circumstances in which a man due to give evidence in an assault case against a member of the Garda and brother-in-law of the Irish Minister of Justice had been prevented from doing so because of his arrest by the RUC in Northern Ireland.

21. *Belfast Telegraph*, 20 January 1983.

22. See, for example, the comments by Danny Morrison of Sinn Fein, *Irish Times*, 4 August 1986.

23. See R. Weitzer, 'Policing a Divided Society: Obstacles to Normalization in Northern Ireland' (1985), 41–55.

4 The Republic of Ireland

BACKGROUND

Ireland has been a sovereign state for less than 70 years. Much of its constitutional development has focused on the assertion of this sovereignty in the face of continuing economic and cultural influences emanating from its more powerful neighbour and erstwhile coloniser, Great Britain. As a leading writer on Irish politics has observed:

> When a national movement succeeds, people are very self-conscious about their statehood, however passive many of them may have been before. If the state is small and weak, anxiety about its continued existence and integrity is inevitably reflected in a heightened self-consciousness.[1]

Irish political culture bears many of the hallmarks of a newly-independent state that, having won its independence by force rather than consent, attaches an almost obsessive devotion to national symbols and jealously resists any encroachments on its right to make its own unfettered decisions. On the other hand, there was a remarkable degree of continuity from pre- to post-independent Ireland: a simple transfer of power not a revolution marked the birth of the new state. In the civil service, the judiciary, local government and in Parliamentary procedure itself, British patterns were almost instinctively followed. At the same time, however, as the young state developed (especially after the promulgation of a new constitution in 1937) conscious attempts were made to distance the Irish system from the British model. Irish was cultivated as the official language; a special role was accorded to the Catholic Church; the head of state became elective, and the upper house (Seanad) non-hereditary.

The functioning of the Irish state has displayed many of the characteristics of a traditional society: the emphasis on personal contacts and local roots. Being known, or carrying the 'right' family name, can be as important in political terms as experience. Irish society has remained stratified in economic terms: the gulf between rich and poor is wide by European standards. On the whole, however, this inequality is not perceived as being incompatible with the maintenance of democracy, whose main attributes are reckoned to be the right to vote in elections, freedom of speech, and the rule of law. Equality *per se* is not seen to be an essential feature of democracy.

Several writers have remarked, moreover, on the authoritarian strand in the political culture. This manifests itself in the deference accorded to the Church and, by extension, to priests, parents and teachers. It has been argued, quite plausibly, that authoritarian habits in government are accepted as part of the politico–cultural 'hangover' from the pre-independence period. Here, one is reminded of analogous patterns in other newly-independent states where the paternalism of the colonial regime is copied instinctively long after the metropolitan power has withdrawn. The cohabitation of authoritarian and democratic norms within the Irish state offers a paradox, but one that can be resolved[2] as a fruitful symbiosis wherein stern government has helped to defend and nurture Parliamentary democracy against the threat of violent subversion. There has been an acceptance, throughout the short life of the new state, that it needed to take extraordinary judicial and security measures against those who questioned its legitimacy. It has indeed been argued that during British rule in Ireland the scene was set for future challenges to governmental authority even after independence was achieved. In the nineteenth century, 'the state was widely perceived . . . as a mere relation of forces rather than a higher juridical or ethical entity. The extent to which it visibly rested on force undermined its claims to the monopoly of force, and its claim that violent resistance was illicit'.[3]

The partition of the island had given Nationalists 'half a loaf' – deemed, however, by most Irishmen to be better than no bread at all. The 'unfinished business' (that is the failure to achieve a 32 county Republic) in the years 1916–22 left an awkward legacy for public order in the new Free State. Attitudes towards the state as 'merely a relation of forces' were modified (but not expunged) by the establishment of the 26-county state. Neither it nor Northern Ireland had been brought into existence by the force of argument, but by the argument of force. It was not surprising, therefore, that the authorities in both parts of Ireland had to maintain control by force since, in both cases, there were groups willing (and able) to use violence against the two elected governments.

The emergence of the Free State in 1922 after a civil war that had been far bloodier than any preceding oppression was accompanied, remarkably it seems in retrospect, by the establishment of an unarmed police force, the Garda Siochana (colloquially referred to in Ireland as 'the Guards' rather than 'the police'). When one remembers that both the old Royal Irish Constabulary (RIC) and the new Royal Ulster Constabulary (RUC) in Northern Ireland were armed forces, the position of the Guards in the South was all the more noteworthy. There were other paradoxes that were happily resolved. The new force was not perceived as being merely the agents of the pro-Treaty government that ruled in Dublin from 1922 to 1932. By not being used as fighting men but simply as passive 'guards' (and mainly in the rural areas) they largely avoided the opprobrium of the anti-treaty segments of the population. The new force was placed under a Commissioner who was directly responsible to the Minister for Justice. Despite this apparently tight connection between the Garda Siochana and the government of the day, the transfer of power from pro-treaty to anti-treaty politicians in 1932 (with the election of the first Fianna Fail government), went smoothly with the Guards apparently finding no difficulty in maintaining a neutral stance.

Throughout its history, the Garda Siochana has had to face two potentially debilitating handicaps. First, the struggle for national independence and the incompleteness of the eventual settlement exposed the Guards to the accusation of being the supporters of a state whose legitimacy continued to be questioned, and whose opponents were prepared to use violence to press their case. While the scene of most of that violence has been Northern Ireland, the 'spillover effects' have been a major threat (arguably, the only significant threat) to public order in the Republic. Secondly, the decision to place the Garda Siochana under the Department of Justice, and make the Commissioner responsible to him and not to a police authority, has sometimes made it difficult for the Guards to maintain political neutrality, especially in cases where the government has sought to use them for party political advantage. Both these major themes will be addressed later in more detail.

STRUCTURE, ORGANISATION AND FINANCE

The Garda Siochana has always been a national police force headed by a Commissioner who is appointed by the Minister for Justice. Under the Commissioner there are two Deputy Commissioners and six Assistant Commissioners. The Dublin Metropolitan Area (DMA) comprises the city of Dublin, County Dublin and parts of County Meath, County Wicklow, and County Kildare. Outside the DMA, the country is covered by 18 divisions, all of which coincide with either counties or groups of counties. Each division is under a Chief Superintendent, while the DMA is under an Assistant Commissioner.

Until the 1960s, Ireland was so free from crime and problems of public order generally that authorised establishments for the Garda force were hardly ever reached. Both manpower levels and the number of police stations were actually reduced in the 1950s. Between 1951 and 1963, the Guards fell from 6904 to 6401, and Garda stations from 810 to 749. As the size of the force diminished, it came more under the influence of the Department of Justice.

During the 1960s, the founding generation of Guards retired or were serving in positions of leadership; unprecedented numbers of new recruits were coming into the force. Pressure quickly built up for better pay and conditions, which resulted in the Conroy Report (1970) making a number of recommendations based on a searching investigation of almost every aspect of the force's role and operations. The Report found that there was a serious problem of low morale in the force, but that pay and conditions were only part of the solution. The Report recommended better and longer training periods for Guards; more civilianisation to free uniformed men from clerical and vehicle maintenance duties; a research unit to plan better methods of coping with changing patterns of crime; and a re-examination of the relationship with the Department of Justice which the Report found to be 'unclear'. Very little progress has been made since the Report was published to implement its main concerns. In 1985, the training at the Templemore College (for Garda recruits) was still considered by many participants to be too brief and too militaristic. In 1980, the Ryan Report (on the Guards) noted that only 300 civilians were employed by the Garda Siochana in the whole country.

In response to the sudden increase in crime in the 1970s and the 'backwash effects' of the troubles in Northern Ireland, Garda Siochana manpower levels increased quite substantially. As of 1985, the Garda Siochana consisted of 11 380 officers, an increase of about 3000 in just ten years. As Table 4.1 shows, it was not until 1971 that the 1961 levels were again reached. However, in relation to the rest of Western Europe, the Republic is the most policed state with 2.89 policemen per 1000 population. In the British Isles, only Northern Ireland has more policemen; and even in 1971 the Republic had more policemen *per capita* than England, Scotland or Wales.

Surprisingly, perhaps, neither the calibre of recruits nor the struc-

Table 4.1   Actual Garda strength 1961–85

Year	Garda Strength	Gardai per 1000 population
1961	6612	2.34
1962	6531	2.31
1963	6401	2.24
1964	6452	2.25
1965	6568	2.28
1966	6545	2.27
1967	6536	2.25
1968	6546	2.24
1969	6543	2.23
1970	6532	2.21
1971	6612	2.21
1972	6961	2.31
1973	7794	2.53
1974	7990	2.56
1975	8419	2.64
1976	8449	2.61
1977	8485	2.59
1978	9182	2.77
1979	9396	2.78
1980	9693	2.85
1981	9722	2.82
1982	10 009	2.87
1983	10 869	3.09
1984	11 230	3.17
1985	11 380	3.20

Source: NESC, *The Criminal Justice System: Policy and Performance* (Dublin: The Stationery Office, 1984) pp. 211–3. Population figures on which the ratio is based are the United Nations annual mid-year estimates, published by the International Monetary Fund in *International Financial Statistics*.

ture of training has changed very much in the face of this rapid expansion, with the result that the effectiveness of the force has, in some respects, declined. In particular, the crime detection rate has dropped (from 50 per cent in 1974 to 32 per cent in 1983). Training and promotion procedures still fail to elicit the best talent available, and there has been a decline in morale, due partly to what is seen as 'political interference' by the Department of Justice – a long standing complaint but one which came dramatically to the fore in the early 1980s.

The 20 weeks spent at Templemore for training can be seen as inadequate in at least three respects. First, the course is militaristic, with a heavy emphasis on drill and physical fitness and little time being devoted to techniques for tackling urban crime or terrorism. Secondly, the training period is considered too short, with insufficient time for reflection. As one recruit put it, 'there isn't any time to think in Templemore and it doesn't in any way develop the individual. It crams in a lot of basic information and you have to learn a lot by heart'.[4] Thirdly, all recruits go in at one basic grade and promotion processes fail to identify leadership material until quite late in the career structure. There is no split-level entry system as exists in many West European countries, and which could be of value to the Garda Siochana where personnel and management skills are still very inadequate. There are 69 graduates in the Garda Siochana and 55 of these are at the basic Garda and sergeant grades.[5] Proposals for split-level entry or accelerated promotion in the force would probably meet some opposition from the two representative organisations, the Garda Representative Association (GRA) and the Association of Garda Sergeants and Inspectors (AGSI), since both are concerned that promotion opportunities are not curtailed for their members. However, both organisations recognise that the lack of management skills and rigid military style structure of the Garda Siochana are situations that cannot continue, and which in the long run will militate against good morale and high levels of efficiency.

The lack of training manifests itself in various ways that affect public attitudes towards the Guards: a vagueness about correct procedures to be followed, vital clues overlooked when investigating crimes, and a disregard of constitutional safeguards when suspects are being questioned. In response to a perceived need for better training, a Committee on Garda Training was established in 1985 – albeit 15 years after the Conroy Report had recommended such a step. How effective the Committee will be remains to be seen: it has little expertise from outside the Garda Siochana or Department of Justice, and no representatives from the GRA – a surprising omission in view of the GRA's long insistence on better training opportunities. Nevertheless, the Committee is a belated step in the right direction.

Adding to the structural problems of the Garda Siochana has been the proliferation of specialised units in response to what are seen as the problems of the day. Here the fact that the Department of Justice is the *de facto* police authority for the Garda Siochana can have deleterious effects on operational efficiency, since special units are sometimes established in response to problems that have become politically salient. Today, there is perhaps a problem of too much specialisation and the consequent danger of overlapping responsibilities.

The Security Task Force dates from ideas put forward by the Minister of Justice in 1976, which in turn were sparked by the Herrema kidnapping of 1975 when the Garda Siochana had to call on outside expertise to assist them. The main spur to the creation of such a force was the spate of armed robberies that afflicted the Republic in the 1970s. In 1980, two Guards were shot dead in County Roscommon: unarmed policemen facing armed robbers was becoming a disturbingly frequent occurrence. The Security Task Force consisted of about 60 men, of whom only 30 would be on duty at any one time; the Force made its first public appearance during the Pope's visit in 1979. After 1980, the Force became reorganised within all Garda divisions: about 18 detectives in each. More recently still, the Force has become absorbed into the Special Branch while still helping with normal detective work in the divisions. All detectives are armed as a matter of course and, on special assignments, they carry Israeli Uzi sub-machineguns. Training in the use of firearms, as with all training, is still rather rudimentary.

The Special Branch dates from 1924. Today, the branch concerns itself with groups on the political fringes and those linked with paramilitary organisations. In every Garda division an information collection system is based on informants whose reports are sent for central collection in Dublin. Known activists and suspect groups are kept under surveillance – especially in the larger cities – and a special fund rewards informers. Telephone tapping is one of the surveillance methods used, although this is much more closely supervised since the tapping and bugging scandals of 1983. Since 1983, all information is put on an IBM 4600 computer that is directly linked to every Garda division in the country. The new system (known as the National Communications Network) enables the Guards to make instant exchanges of information and check on vehicles or known criminals. The old card index system, used for decades by the Special Branch, is now redundant. Only senior officers with knowledge of special codes can gain access to the central data base.

The creation of special units within the Garda Siochana such as the Drugs Squad, Special Branch and Security Task Force carries with it inherent problems. First, for example, there has been some rivalry and jealousy between uniformed officers and plainclothes detectives – and this can cause inefficiency. Secondly, the special units tend to

Table 4.2　Expenditure on the Garda Siochana 1974–85

Year	Expenditure (IR£million)	Expenditure as % of total public expenditure
1974	23.9	
1975	54.1	
1976	59.5	
1977	63.8	
1978	73.7	
1979	94.4	
1980	119.5	1.4
1981	165.7	1.5
1982	186.7	1.5
1983	206.7	1.6
1984	224.0	1.6
1985	233.8	1.5

Source: NESC, The Criminal Justice System: Policy and Performance (Dublin: The Stationery Office, 1984) pp. 211–3; Revised Estimates for Public Services (Dublin: Stationery Office, 1985).

cream off some of the more talented officers, with a resulting loss of morale among 'men on the beat'.

The financing of the Garda Siochana comes under the estimates for the Department of Justice. As the force has increased in size its cost has increased even more dramatically. In Table 4.2, it can be seen that the cost of the force rose tenfold in the 10-year period 1974–84. Two points are worth making about Table 4.2. First, there is no evidence that expenditure on the Garda Siochana is affected by the political party that is in government. Fianna Fail was in power up until 1973, the Coalition until 1977, and then Fianna Fail until 1981. Secondly, the effects of inflation and the rising crime wave appear to be the main factors behind the steep rise in costs for the Garda Siochana in this period. If inflation is allowed for, it has been estimated that the rise in real terms of financing the Garda Siochana between 1961 and 1981 was a 250 per cent increase.[6] Moreover, as a proportion of all expenditure on the criminal justice system, the share attributable to the Garda Siochana actually fell, from 89 per cent in 1961 to 83 per cent in 1981, whereas prison costs jumped from 4 per cent to 13 per cent of total criminal justice costs in the same period. Overall, governments of both parties have spent much less on the Garda Siochana than its needs require, despite promises made by politicians, especially when in opposition. However the problems are not all financial: it is generally acknowledged within the force itself that lack of management skills is as serious as the lack of financial resources.

FORMAL STRUCTURE OF AUTHORITY

The Irish Republic is governed under the 1937 constitution (Bunreacht na hEireann) and its articles provide the most appropriate springboard for any discussion of the legislative context of policing and public order. The constitution is, among other things, a measure against which the laws of the state have to be judged; and it also contains basic rights that the state is bound to defend. Article 40 prevents any citizen being deprived of his liberty except 'in accordance with law' and Article 38 provides that no-one can be tried on a criminal charge except 'in due course of law'. However, although the constitution goes some way towards protecting the individual citizen's liberty, it does provide for restrictions on that liberty in the interests of the common good – and in particular when the security of the state is deemed to be under threat. Thus, in Articles 28 and 38, emergency legislation and special criminal courts can be introduced in the interests of public safety.

When governments passed legislation like the Offences Against the State Act 1939 and the Emergency Powers Act 1976, they were acting within the broad remit of the constitution. The 1939 Act declared a 'state of emergency' that lasted, in effect, until 1976 when it was rephrased (by the Oireachtas) as an emergency 'arising out of the situation in Northern Ireland'. Technically speaking, therefore, the Republic has tackled its public order problems with legislation dependent upon a 'state of emergency' for at least the last 40 years. Under the Offences Against the State Act, other provisions can be brought into effect by a simple resolution of the Oireachtas. For example, both the creation of the Special Criminal Court in 1972 and the introduction in 1976 of seven-day interrogation periods without a charge being necessary were products of enabling clauses in the 1939 Act.

The panoply of special powers available to members of the Garda Siochana, and in particular the notorious Section 30 (allowing seven-day detention without charge, later modified to 48 hours) gives the Republic some of the most draconian emergency laws in Western

Europe, even including in some respects those of Northern Ireland.[7]
It has to be understood, however, that the state has regarded its own
institutions as being under direct threat, even though the source of
the challenge is related to the situation in Northern Ireland. Hence
just prior to the discussion of the Emergency Powers Bill (in a
specially convened session in the middle of the summer recess in
1976) the Oireachtas passed a resolution stating that 'arising out of
the armed conflict now taking place in Northern Ireland a national
emergency exists affecting the vital interests of the state'. This formula replaced the one in 1939 when the emergency was deemed to
have arisen as a result of the outbreak of the Second World War. The
Emergency Powers Act was eventually passed on 15 October 1976. It
epitomises the extent to which the question of public order in the
Republic is caught in the 'backwash' of the violence in Northern
Ireland.

Essentially the Act provides for the arrest, custody and questioning
of persons suspected of certain offences. A member of the Garda
Siochana can stop, search, question, and arrest any person whom he
suspects of having committed, being in the act of committing or being
about to commit an offence specified under the Offences Against the
State Act 1939. The departure from common law practice lies in the
ability of the Guards to detain someone for a period of time without
charging them. Such legislation is obviously open to abuse by members of the Garda Siochana. A suspect might be intimidated into
making a statement in order to secure his freedom or, more generally, there is a danger that the power to detain without charge could
be used to 'screen' people. The Irish Council for Civil Liberties
(ICCL) has commented that:

> the detention power has quite often been used as a speculative or
> 'screening' device. In other words, the power has been used on
> some occasions to hold people whom the police believe to be in
> some general way associated with illegal organisations or involved
> with security offences, but whom they do not suspect for any
> particular offence. Such detention allows for finger-printing and
> photographing and thus builds up police files even if it does not
> contribute to a specific investigation.[8]

Another way in which the Act can be abused is to extend it beyond its
original purview. Offences outside those that pose a threat to 'national security' ought presumably to be dealt with under the normal
law and in the normal courts. Nevertheless cases have come to light
of the Emergency Powers Act being used to tackle ordinary crime.

The Special Criminal Court was established in 1972 also under the Offences Against the State Act 1939. The court consists of usually three judges and no jury. The Court is intended to deal with cases where a threat to the state is involved, and where there is reason to believe that normal jury trial would not suffice. Except for the lack of a jury the trial procedure is supposed to follow the normal pattern as far as possible. Even so, the Court did not succeed in obtaining many convictions against Irish Republican Army (IRA) suspects until the end of 1972 when the Dail passed another amendment to the 1939 Act. This placed the onus on the accused to repudiate any published allegation that he was a member of a proscribed organisation: failure to do so would constitute evidence of such membership. Thus if a senior Garda officer stated in court that a person was a member of the IRA the burden of refuting the accusation fell on the accused person. It has been estimated that of the 1500 people appearing before the Special Criminal court between 1972 and 1980 two-thirds were found guilty.[9] The extensive use of the Special Criminal Court has led to allegations that it has reached beyond the purely 'political' cases for which it was established but it should be noted that the distinction between political and non-political is not one that the Act itself recognises.[10]

The independence of the Garda Siochana and its accountability have been live issues ever since its establishment over 60 years ago. The relationship with the Department of Justice lies at the centre of this debate: to what extent do political influences affect Garda policy? How accountable are the Guards to the Government and to public opinion? The Conroy Report (1970) was clearly disturbed by the ambivalent character of the relationship between the Department and the Garda Siochana. The Report spoke of 'unclear definition of roles between the Department and the Garda Siochana', and urged that an examination be carried out by suitably qualified people into the 'role, organisation and personnel policy of the force and in particular its relationship with the Department of Justice'.

Very little happened during the 1970s, but the problems of accountability and autonomy did not go away. Most acutely the issue came before the public when the activities of the so-called 'Heavy Gang' (a number of Guards accused of maltreating persons in custody) in 1976 and 1977 did not result in a proper investigation. Although the O'Briain Report made recommendations for police interrogations, like many such reports it was little more than a sop to public opinion, and its advice was almost totally ignored. The price for such complacency was clearly paid by the Garda Siochana in the

Kerry Babies Case (1984) when interrogation procedures were once again in the limelight. The Kerry Babies case revealed the extent to which the O'Briain recommendations were desirable and could have been positively beneficial. The outline of the Kerry Babies case can be briefly summarised. In April 1984 a dead baby was found at Cahirciveen in south west Ireland. In their investigations the Guards came across Joanne Hayes a single woman who had been pregnant, was so no longer, and yet had no child. Under questioning she and members of her family confessed to being involved in the murder of this 'Cahirciveeen baby' when in fact Joanne had abandoned her own baby to die at the back of her house. The Guards accused Joanne of murdering both babies although blood tests later proved that she could not have been the mother of both. A tribunal was held under Judge Lynch to ascertain why Joanne had confessed to a murder she could not have committed; and why an internal Garda enquiry had failed to elicit the facts of this anomaly. Even the tribunal failed to come up with an answer to the central question of how a whole family had confessed to a murder it had not committed or even known about.[11]

The O'Briain Report had recommended, *inter alia*, that questioning should be by two Guards at any one time; that questioning should only in exceptional circumstances take place between midnight and 8 a.m.; and that when a person is questioned while under arrest there should be a 'custodial officer' responsible for that person's welfare while in custody. The *Sunday Independent* focused on the real issue to come out of the Kerry Babies case: 'However, the central question is whether we live in a state where the police force confessions. If we do, the law, the judicial system, the parliament are all corrupted by this.'[12]

In December 1984, the Oireachtas passed a resolution saying that the family's confession of a murder not committed by them constituted matters of 'urgent public importance', and yet the Lynch tribunal failed to get at the root of the matter, a failure that leaves the problem of the Garda Siochana's accountability as one of gravest for state–society relations in the Republic.

It was probably no coincidence that the Garda Complaints Bill 1985 came before the Dail in the wake of the Kerry Babies affair. The Bill established for the first time a tribunal to which complaints against individual members of the Garda Siochana could be brought. The ICCL, while welcoming the Bill as a first step in the right direction, had reservations about it: the right to silence for Guards is reduced; the tribunal is made up of government appointees; the investigation is carried out by other Garda officers thus compromising the tribunal's independence.[13]

POLICE–MILITARY RELATIONS

In the context of serious threats to public order emanating from the violence in Northern Ireland, it would be surprising if co-operation between the Army and the Garda Siochana had been anything but close. The Irish Army consists of about 15 000 soldiers and its role, for our purposes, can be divided into two parts: 'aiding the civil power' and 'defending the national territory'. In practice, of course, these two distinct roles may merge since incursions from Northern Ireland are often linked to criminal or subversive activities in the Republic.

In 1976, the Army was given, for the first time, the powers of arrest; but those arrested had to be handed over to the Garda Siochana within six hours. Even this extension of military powers into the area of policing aroused some public opposition in the Republic, since there were few safeguards for the person arrested and no formal complaints procedure.

Within the Army an elite corps, similar to the British Special Air Service (SAS), was created after the Herrema kidnapping in 1975. This group, of about 100 specially trained soldiers, in a sense mirrors the Special Task Force that was created within the Garda Siochana for much the same reasons. The 'Rangers' use special equipment, and have already proved their effectiveness in the Don Tidey kidnapping episode. More broadly the Army is now used, almost routinely, in cases where armed attack is either expected or possible. The Army thus provides guards for sensitive trials, escorts for cash movements, protection for banks, and bomb disposal expertise. The need for armed back-up for the Garda Siochana arises from the spate of armed robberies (especially bank raids) since 1970, and the concomitant increase in fatalities among the unarmed members of the Garda Siochana.

The principal arena for co-operation between the police and the military is along the border with Northern Ireland. Here the two roles of the Army merge. They are supporting the civil power and defending the national territory. In the 1970s, the Army would provide in a typical year 5500 checkpoint parties and 14 000 checkpoints in co-operation with the Guards. In an average year there would be about 600 requests for bomb disposal personnel to attend the scenes of suspect devices. In the 1980s, these levels of police–military liaison have increased dramatically: in 1982, for example, there were 21 000 military patrols provided for border checkpoints. At any one time there are about 2000 soldiers deployed in the border areas – about one-seventh of the entire Irish Army.

Communication between the Army and the Garda Siochana has improved over the past few years: radio contact has been much facilitated. Across the border, the RUC are both willing and able to inform the Irish security forces of incidents within minutes of their taking place, so that efforts on the southern side of the border can effectively complement the tactics in the North.

Police–military liaison in the Republic is now on a par with police–military liaison in the North. If anything, the Irish Army performs more policing functions than the Army in the North – for example, in relation to providing escorts for cash consignments. It can be argued, however, that this assistance is necessary because the Garda Siochana, unlike the RUC, is unarmed, and that the Army has in fact post-poned the need for the Garda Siochana to be routinely armed as a force. While the benefits are clear, the price to be paid for this liaison is the vagueness surrounding the legal rights of those detained or arrested by Army personnel. Happily, this has not been a major civil rights issue, and public opinion seems to be supportive of the role that the Army plays in keeping the Garda Siochana unarmed and therefore less of a paramilitary force than its counterpart in the North. The Army's participation in UN peacekeeping operations (made possible by Ireland's neutral status in international affairs) tends to enhance the position of the Irish Army in the eyes of the citizen. It is probably true, therefore, that co-operation between soldiers and Guards does the latter no harm in the eyes of public opinion.

PUBLIC ORDER SITUATIONS

The Republic of Ireland has been remarkably free of mass public disorder connected with industrial or political issues of the type seen so often elsewhere. The lack of public order problems and the low level of criminality up until the 1970s was the main reason why it was possible to reduce manpower levels in the 1950s and 1960s and helps to explain why the force has remained a generally unarmed one.

This relatively tranquil picture may require some explanation. Up until the late 1960s Ireland was an essentially rural society and an intensely religious one when considered in terms of attendance at church. Writers on Ireland, like Chubb, allude to the conservatism and deference found in Irish attitudes that manifested itself in respect for ecclesiastical authority – and, by extension, for authority generally. More pertinently, perhaps, emigration patterns up until the 1970s tended to siphon off some of the disaffected sections of the population who sought better economic opportunities in Britain and North America. However, when these avenues were closed by the recession of the 1970s, the Irish state had to face up to the challenge posed by demands for employment from ever-increasing numbers of school leavers (the Irish birthrate has been the highest in the European Economic Community for at least two decades).

Even so, when disorder came in the 1970s it took the form of reactive protests to events in Northern Ireland and not directly in response to shrinking economic opportunities in the Republic. A cynic might argue that the 'Northern question' has provided a safety valve for a variety of pent-up frustrations within the Republic's own socio-economic system. The two reactive protests that stand out are the demonstrations outside the British Embassy in Dublin in February 1972 and again in July 1981. The first of these was a response to the shooting dead of 13 civilians in Derry by the British Army, and culminated in the burning down of the Embassy building. The later protest was against the British government's refusal to concede any of the demands of the hunger strikers in Northern Ireland.

The riot outside the British Embassy on 20 July 1981 can be reckoned as the worst street violence in the Republic in the past 20 years. Its implications and aftermath are particularly relevant to any consideration of the relationship between the state, public order and the police. The National H-Blocks Committee had organised a march commencing in St Stephen's Green and then moving towards Merrion Road, where the British Embassy was located. *En route*, marchers threw missiles at a handful of Guards standing outside Leinster House and later at a group of about 40 Guards standing outside the US Embassy. At a point 200 yards from the British Embassy, a cordon of about 500 Guards (90 per cent of whom had been drafted in from outside Dublin) blocked the progress of the march. Most of the Guards were wearing helmets, visors and carrying short plastic shields: all had the regulation 15-inch truncheon. For about 20 minutes the cordon was subjected to a barrage of missiles: bottles, stones, iron railings, bricks and tools stolen from nearby gardens. An eyewitness said the 'air was thick with missiles'.[14] A Guard said afterwards that he had 'never seen a crowd so determined'. Realising that the tactic of waiting until the crowd ran out of missiles was not going to work, the cordon of Guards began a series of baton charges. At this moment, the Guards according to an eyewitness, seemed to have 'gone berserk'. Individuals were batoned to the ground, a German student had his leg broken, a journalist had his notebook taken, groups of people were beaten in corners and the doorways of houses where they vainly sought refuge. In the wake of the riot, there were clear cases of unprovoked brutality. Damage to property was extensive; 10 tonnes of debris were picked up from the streets; about a £1million worth of damage was done to buildings; 200 people were injured, 120 of them members of the Garda Siochana. At a press conference that evening the march organisers placed the blame for the violence on the Guards.[15]

The implications of the riot were several. First, the equipment of the Gardai had proved inadequate for this unprecedented violence: several helmets had been pierced by missiles. Shields were too short and leg injuries had resulted. Some Guards had no shields, and used bread trays from a nearby bakery to protect themselves. In the succeeding days of debate, a spokesman for the Garda Siochana said that the force had no CS gas, and no stocks of plastic bullets. Secondly, the tactics of the Guards came in for criticism; there were numerous allegations of unnecessary force. The static cordon was deemed inappropriate by some observers, and snatch squads to immobilise ringleaders were put forward as a more effective alternative. It emerged that training in techniques of riot control at Templemore was confined to a few lectures on crowd control. Thirdly, the advisability of allowing marches like this to take place at all came in for a lot of discussion. The government made its position on this quite clear, and said it saw no reason to ban a similar march that had been scheduled for the following Saturday. The Justice Minister said 'the Government's predisposition will not be to interfere with the right of peaceful protest'.[16] Fourthly, the government's attitude towards the riot itself was that it had damaged the cause it was alleged to be concerned about. The conduct of the Guards was pronounced as exemplary, although the Taoiseach's rationale for the actions of the Guards must have seemed rather esoteric to his listeners as he answered questions off-the-cuff from reporters. He alluded to his 'duty under international law to protect embassies', not to the state's duty to maintain domestic order. Finally, the riot raised the question of army intervention: in theory and in practice, the Guards could have called in the Army to 'aid the civil power'. Afterwards it emerged that 200 soldiers had been in readiness near the Embassy but were not in fact called upon by the Guards to assist. It is difficult to know what assistance they could have given, short of using live ammunition.

A second case which challenged public order is also illustrative and stands in contrast to that just described. The British businessman Don Tidey was kidnapped in south Dublin at 7.45 a.m. on 24 November 1983 as he was taking his daughter to school. The kidnap lasted for 22 days and culminated in a gun battle in a forested area of County Leitrim near the border with Northern Ireland. Unlike the British Embassy episode, the kidnap was treated as an act of terrorism and both the Army and the Guards were involved in the denouement of the three-week drama, with special units (the Rangers and the Special Task Force) playing prominent roles. During the period of the kidnap, roadblocks were set up in various parts of the Republic following tipoffs, and it was not until the end that the hunt switched to Leitrim after a man had been seen running across a field. About 1000 soldiers and hundreds of Guards concentrated their search in this area, assisted by helicopters. In the final shootout, Don Tidey was rescued but a soldier and a Garda recruit were killed. The recruit was the tenth Garda to be killed since 1970 and the twenty-sixth since the foundation of the state. It was, however, the first time the IRA had killed a soldier in the Republic during the Troubles. The jubilation of the government at the rescue of Don Tidey was overshadowed by the deaths of the two members of the security forces. Praise for the role of the Guards and soldiers began to wear a little thin as the terrorists themselves eluded capture, an innocent man was shot while going through a roadblock, and Dominic McGlinchey (wanted by the police in both parts of Ireland in connection with several serious crimes) came face to face with the Guards on three occasions but managed to give them the slip. The government felt vindicated in its policy of refusing a ransom for the return of Don Tidey (a demand for £5million had been made) since not only would other kidnappers be emboldened, but the IRA would be enriched, by such a payment. The Justice Minister defended the use of the Army in the search for Don Tidey, arguing that the 'Gardai are the security arm of the State to deal with crime whatever its nature. The Army are called in to aid the civil powers. They are constantly being called in in border areas'.[17] The Garda Siochana was clearly overstretched in the Don Tidey affair. The heavy involvement of raw recruits and the fact that many of them came in from the search in tears or suffering from shock indicated the extent to which every last man had been thrown into the hunt.

What both the Embassy riot and the kidnapping of Don Tidey illustrate is the desire of the state to distance itself from the physical force tradition of the IRA and its sympathisers. In both cases the Guards were involved in episodes that reflected the fragility of the state's authority and the thin shell of legitimacy that protects the state from its detractors.

PUBLIC PERCEPTIONS OF THE POLICE

In the last few years the public perception of the Garda Siochana has changed substantially. Whereas in the mid-1970s one could write of a society that was still broadly deferential to authority in the form of priests, parents and policemen; by the end of the 1980s public attitudes had become increasingly jaundiced by a series of episodes that were given ample publicity in the media and which raised considerable doubts as to whether the Garda Siochana was properly accountable. From 1972 onwards the Guards had won extra powers through the passage of emergency legislation, but the publicised abuses of these powers inevitably drove a wedge between the force and the community it endeavoured to serve. Lack of experience led to over-reactions at public demonstrations (the British Embassy riot); several cases of maltreatment of detainees during questioning came to light; there was evidence that the force had allowed itself to be used for party political purposes. But above all, there was concern about the ability of the Garda Siochana to investigate wrong doing within its own ranks. Even in the 'Heavy Gang' case (1976–77) the government enquiry avoided the main issues, and some of those involved were later promoted. Likewise in the 'fingerprint case' (1977–84) two Guards who tried to expose a deliberately falsified fingerprint identification were victimised within the force, and the officer most involved in the false identification was later promoted. We have already seen in the Kerry Babies case (1983–85) that a Garda enquiry failed to elicit the reasons why a person confessed to a murder she had not committed. It would be surprising if public confidence in the Garda Siochana had not been shaken by these and other disclosures.

At the same time, it has to be acknowledged that the pressures on the Gardai have also increased: crime has expanded more rapidly than the size of the force and morale within the ranks of the Garda Siochana has not been helped by the rigidity of promotion procedures and the tardiness of successive governments in responding to the need for reorganisation and better management techniques.

More detailed public attitudes towards the Garda Siochana can be seen from the Irish data made available from the recently published European Value Systems Study.[18] As is normal in other countries, older people have more faith in the police than younger people. In Ireland, while 86 per cent of respondents said they had either 'a great deal' or 'quite a lot' of confidence in the Gardai, the level of support drops to 81 per cent for the 18–24 age group but rises to 95 per cent for the over-65s. Variations among occupational groups are not marked, although the unemployed stand out as being the group most alienated from the Gardai – only 67 per cent saying that they have a great deal or quite a lot of confidence in the Gardai. Education, on the other hand, seems to have more of an impact on attitudes than occupational status. Those leaving school at 16 are less supportive (80 per cent saying a great deal or quite a lot of confidence), while the level of support from those staying on at school rises to 90 per cent. These variations have to be seen in the context of generally high levels of support for the Garda Siochana. Even in comparison with other 'national institutions', the Gardai come out ahead of the Church, the Army, the legal system, the civil service, Parliament and the educational system.[19]

THE POLICE AS A POLITICAL INSTITUTION

For reasons already given, the Garda Siochana have not escaped completely from the perils of politicisation. The fact that the force is responsible to (and its senior officers appointed by) the Minister for Justice places it in a vulnerable position. That is one theme that merits discussion: how far can the force operate without 'political interference'? Secondly, and consequentially, the two police representative bodies (the GRA and the AGSI) are more vocal (and possibly more influential) than their counterparts in Northern Ireland or Great Britain. What impact, then, do the representative associations have on the politics of policing?

The linkage between the Department of Justice and the Garda

Siochana attracted the attention of the Conroy Report in 1970. Thereafter, little has been done to define or refine the relationship more clearly. Nor has a civilian police authority been created that could stand between the Department and the Garda Siochana and act as a buffer. Given the volatility of party politics, with three general elections being held between 1980 and 1986, it would be surprising if the Garda Siochana had not become something of a 'political football'. Indeed, it has been a common complaint in the force that successive governments have been long on promises but short on action when it comes to the legal and organisational reforms that the Guards feel they need.

In 1982, a number of episodes that have now been fairly extensively researched[20] underlined the extent to which operational matters could become subject to political pressure. It has been claimed, for example, that the Minister for Justice actively sought the transfer of a Garda officer who tried to pursue an after-hours drinking case in the Minister's constituency. It is also alleged that the same Minister tried to get a Garda recruit through the Templemore college although he had failed, simply because the recruit was one of the Minister's constituents. The Minister is also alleged to have connived at the supply by the Gardai of a tape recorder so that one Government Minister could 'bug' a conversation with another, the tape then being transcribed by the Gardai. Two journalists had their telephones tapped under a Fianna Fail government, allegedly on grounds of national security but more probably because both were writing anti-Fianna Fail articles for their newspapers. The 'Dowra affair' was even more sinister. Here the Justice Minister's brother-in-law had been accused of assaulting a man. On the day that he was due to appear in court, the main prosecution witness was detained by the RUC and held for questioning at Gough barracks; the case was dismissed. The RUC have still not explained why the man was held at Gough for that day for questioning. There was strong suspicion that the Minister had succeeded in getting the RUC to co-operate on that day in order to protect one of his relatives. If the suspicions were ever substantiated, the political repercussions could be immense: for a Fianna Fail Minister to allow the RUC to have such a favour to hold over the Gardai and the Irish Government demonstrated an extraordinary lack of concern for the political consequences and extreme insensitivity to the traditions of his own party.[21]

When the Labour Fine Gael coalition took office in early 1983 a new Garda Commissioner was appointed, and many of the facts about the previous administration's interference with the Garda Siochana were confirmed. Inevitably, the outgoing government accused the Coalition of making capital out of these events, but even if this were true it would not, unfortunately, be the first time that an Irish government had done so.

It is worth remembering that the issue of 'political interference' really involves only senior members of the force. Rank-and-file Guards resent such interference, and both Garda representative organisations have called for a police authority to insulate the force from such intrusions. Since 1978 the AGSI have been calling for such an authority, and in the autumn of 1982 stated that there was now 'an urgent necessity for such an authority' (presumably a reflection of concern felt at some of the episodes already described above). There would be three advantages for the Garda Siochana from the establishment of such an authority: first, it would make the force less vulnerable to political interference; secondly, it would facilitate long-term planning; thirdly, it would define more clearly the hitherto rather vague relationship with the Department of Justice.

Obviously a great deal depends on the personalities of the key men involved in the relationship: the Minister and the Commissioner. Under the stewardship of Mr Noonan, for example, the Department of Justice had a high profile with the Minister frequently appearing on television with 'instant' solutions to the latest crime problem: joyriding in Dublin, drugs, bank robberies. In contrast, the then Garda Commissioner (a taciturn personality approaching retirement) preferred to run his force quietly without too much interference from outside. This meant that the initiative tended to swing towards the government whose constant innovations in the form of 'task forces' for every ill played havoc with the day-to-day operation of the Garda Siochana.

The strength of the GRA was seen recently in relation to the Garda Complaints Bill. At their 1986 annual conference in Limerick, delegates agreed to discuss proposals that required Guards to produce documents or answer questions in front of disciplinary hearings that related to their official duties. As a concession to the GRA the Justice Department agreed to set up a Disciplinary Appeals Board under a senior lawyer. Such a board would give the Garda Siochana a means of appealing against decisions that were viewed as too harsh. The GRA General Secretary said the new board was a major concession to the GRA and he said he could think of no other police force where policemen themselves had the level of input into disciplinary proceedings. 'It will guarantee fairness in the system', he said.

CONCLUSION

Like all new states, the Irish Republic has been jealous of its sovereignty and nervous of threats to its political institutions: the former have emanated from the island's proximity to Britain, and the latter from armed subversion within the state – and, more recently, from outside the state. In such circumstances, it was inevitable that governments of all political complexions should seek to bind the police force closely to themselves – hence the direct line of responsibility between the Garda Commissioner and the Minister for Justice.

We have also seen that the Garda Siochana has operated with the benefits of a 'state of emergency' for most of its history, an emergency first justified by the outbreak of the Second World War and then by the violence in Northern Ireland. Such legislation underlines the fragility of the new state's institutions, its vulnerability to events outside its jurisdiction, and its very genesis in the unstable compromise of partitioning the island, a compromise that left many scores to be settled and many aspirations unfulfilled. Emergency legislation can also become addictive, and there is a danger that a police force accustomed to it will become increasingly resistant to being weaned back onto 'normal' legal processes. At the moment the pressure, if anything, is towards obtaining more powers for the Garda Siochana, and further restricting the rights of the citizen. The maturity of the new state will be tested by the extent to which it can resist the temptation of 'short cuts' in the fight against crime and problems of public order.

The fact that the Garda Siochana has been so closely identified with the Department of Justice makes it surprising that the force's independence has been so well preserved – although much has turned on the personalities involved in the leading roles, and the nexus of political forces underpinning the government of the day. For some time, the Garda Siochana has wanted to free itself from political control – from party political control – and stand apart from the shifting fads of transient politicians. The idea of a Police Authority has long been on the political agenda, and often promised. To bring something about of this kind would help the Garda Siochana to shake up its management structure; it would free senior officers from the enervating influences of the government of the day; and it would be a demonstration of public confidence in the professionalism of the force. Above all, however, it would demonstrate the self-confidence of the state by cutting the umbilical cord that currently ties the Garda Siochana to the government. Such a change would not, of itself, restore the Guards to the status they have enjoyed in the past, but it would clear the way for other changes that are now overdue.

Notes

1. B. Chubb, *The Government and Politics of Ireland* (London: Longman, 1982) p. 9.
2. See D. Schmitt, *The Irony of Irish Democracy* (Farnborough: D.C. Heath, 1973).
3. C. Townshend, *Political Violence in Ireland* (Oxford: Clarendon Press, 1983) p. 412.
4. Quoted in C. Brady, 'Templemore ideal doesn't apply on the job', *Irish Times*, 7 November 1984.
5. *Irish Times*, 11 December 1985.
6. National Economic and Social Council, *The Criminal Justice System: Policy and Performance* (1980).
7. C. Brady writes (*Irish Times*, 26 September 1979), 'it is no exaggeration to say that the Garda Siochana have at their disposal now, more sweeping police powers than any force outside the Communist bloc, with the possible exception of certain turbulent African states'.
8. The Irish Council for Civil Liberties, *The Emergency Powers Act 1976: A Critique* (1977) p. 23.
9. T. Salmon, 'The Civil Power and Aiding the Civil Power', in J. Roach and J. Thomaneck (eds), *Police and Public Order in Europe* (1985) p. 80.
10. M. Robinson, 'Special Court Abuses', *Hibernia*, 6 December 1974.
11. *Report of the Committee to Recommend Certain Safeguards for Persons in Custody and for Members of An Garda Siochana* (1977).
12. *Sunday Independent*, 6 October 1984.
13. The Irish Council for Civil Liberties, *The Garda Siochana (Complaints Bill) 1985* (Dublin: ICCL, 16 October 1985).
14. *Irish Times*, 20 July 1981.
15. *Irish Times*, 20 July 1981.
16. *Irish Times*, 20 July 1981.
17. *Irish Times*, 17 December 1983.
18. M. Fogarty, L. Ryan and J. Lee, *Irish Values and Attitudes* (Dublin: Dominican Publications, 1984) *passim*.
19. Fogart, Ryan and Lee, *Irish Values and Attitudes*.
20. See J. Joyce and P. Murtagh, *The Boss* (1983).
21. Joyce and Murtagh, *The Boss*, p. 249.

5 The United States of America

BACKGROUND

The circumstances surrounding the birth of the US as an independent state at the end of the eighteenth century have left an indelible imprint on the relations between state and society ever since. In the first place, the concept of the state itself was deliberately dismantled by a federal constitution that was designed to entrench powers in the former 13 colonies and keep central government at arm's length. Secondly, the emphasis on individual initiative born in a pioneer society was reinforced further as entrepreneurial talent flourished in an expanding capitalist economy. As the new nation prospered in conditions of minimal state interference, this whole 'hands off' approach became a hallowed part of the citizens' attitude towards the state. An opinion survey in 1970 which suggested that the 'individual owed his first duty to the state' yielded a 68 per cent disagreement among American respondents compared with only 45 per cent in West Germany and 32 per cent in Italy.[1]

The phenomenal success of capitalism in the late nineteenth and early twentieth centuries inevitably produced wide disparities between rich and poor in American society, disparities that are today more pronounced than in other Western democracies such as West Germany and the UK. The achievement of high living standards by most Americans produced a predominantly middle class social structure. The relative affluence enjoyed by the bulk of the population became a self-validating support for the political and economic system: as a corollary, poverty came to be viewed as the fate of those who had failed, rather than as a fault of the system itself.

The political arena is singularly lacking in anti-regime ideologies. Both major parties are, ideologically speaking, mere commentaries on a broadly supported consensus, and both are 'catch-all' parties in that they garner votes from virtually all groups in society, with differences of emphasis only at the margins. Neither fascism nor socialism have taken root in a serious way, and (although a violent society) the USA has not been characterised by any domestic terrorism aimed at changing either the government or the constitutional system itself. It can be argued that the prevailing ideology is 'Americanism', a concept that has provided 'anti-Americanism' as a plausible antithesis in a way that 'anti-Italianism' or 'anti-Britishness' could not be.

The dominant ideology is faced with having to justify the persistence of serious economic inequalities. Thus the central tenet of the state's ideology is that there is equality of opportunity for all. Poverty is then explained as the failure to seize the opportunities on offer to everyone, opportunities whose credibility is daily demonstrated by an affluence that is widely available. The dominant ideology is reinforced by a judicial system that has increasingly reduced racial disadvantage, and discrimination based on gender. Access to the courts, equality before the law, availability of lawyers for all, freedom of speech and the right of protest are valuable ingredients in structuring a system that is apparently 'fair' and 'reasonable'. On the political side, this has been mirrored by reforms giving all citizens the vote, and the elimination of gerrymandered constituencies. The 'log cabin to White House' syndrome is constantly reaffirmed as Black mayors take over in the cities and Jesse Jackson runs for President.

Nevertheless, beneath the surface of 'equal opportunities' lies the gulf between rich and poor, a gulf that has not diminished in the past 30 years. Race is a badge of this relative deprivation, but not a certain indicator. While most Black people are poor, not all poor people are Black. In the context of public order problems, policing has to be seen as a function of the state's reluctance to upset the type of socioeconomic system described above. The function of policing must be to defend the dominant ideology against those who would benefit from its demise. The frustration that emanates from the dissonance between the state's proclaimed goals of equal opportunity and its tolerance of unequal achievement provide the raw material from which challenges to public order are fashioned.

STRUCTURE, ORGANISATION AND FINANCE

Policing in the USA today has firm roots in the colonial period when the law enforcement structure of the mother country was lifted, with little modification, and superimposed onto an essentially pioneer society. Constables enforced the law in the towns, and sheriffs took charge of policing the rural areas. Both types of office became elective after the Revolution. In the nineteenth century, as towns increased rapidly in size, constables became inadequate guardians of law and order; many cities began to organise their own police forces, although (at first) these merely supplemented during the day the functions performed by nightwatchmen in the hours of darkness. New York was the first city to amalgamate its nocturnal and daytime forces (1844) and Boston followed 10 years later. By the early years of this century, most cities had unified police forces whose chief officers were appointed by the mayor – or, in some cases, elected by the city's inhabitants.

Since 1945, the police forces of the USA have remained among the most decentralised and locally-based of any in the world. Five types of police agency can be identified: the federal system which includes officers attached to the Department of Justice (the Federal Bureau of Investigation), the Bureau of Internal Revenue (specialising in tax evasion), the United States Secret Service, the Drug Enforcement Administration, and the Postal Inspection Service; police forces and criminal investigation agencies established by each of the 50 states; sheriffs in 3000 counties and county police forces; police forces in about 1000 cities and 20 000 townships; and, finally, police forces based in 15 000 villages and boroughs, as well as special forces for Washington DC, for university campuses and for many tunnels, bridges, parks, and major installations. Today there are about 40 000 police forces in the country ranging in size from New York City's 30 000-strong Police Department down to one-man forces in many remote locations. 90 per cent of all municipalities with more than 2500 inhabitants have their own force, and 80 per cent of all forces employ fewer than 10 policemen. About 3000 forces are based on counties, 3000 in cities, and the remaining 33 000 are distributed throughout boroughs, towns and villages. The degree to which functional specialisation exists within police forces varies according to size. Members of small forces in rural locations fulfil a wide range of roles, while members of very large city forces are dispersed among several precincts and specialise narrowly in distinct areas of police work, such as traffic, narcotics, or community relations. The concept of local autonomy prevails, and tends to reinforce the structural decentralisation depicted here. A police officer's responsibility for enforcing law and order is normally confined to a specific territorial jurisdiction. However, these jurisdictions can often overlap as can be seen from a hypothetical example of a foreign professor visiting a university campus in Arizona. The professor goes one weekend to Nevada and brings back a woman whom he subsequently murders in his office. The case could then be investigated by the university campus police, the city police, the county sheriff, the FBI, the immigration authorities – and (if the woman was a drug user) the Drug Enforcement Administration. It need hardly be emphasised that such overlapping jurisdictions can lead to rivalries between forces, duplication of effort and ultimately a less efficient prosecution of the criminal.

Approximately half a million people work in the police forces of the USA either full-time or part-time. About 75 per cent of all employees work full time and 11 per cent are civilians. The distribution of police personnel across the USA is roughly correlated to population density. Thus the 'density of police per square mile' ranges from less than one in Alaska to 1278 in Manhattan. Across the entire nation, the number of police per 1000 population has increased steadily since the 1950s: from 1.6 in 1957 to 2.5 in 1977. This expansion mirrors a 436 per cent expansion in the crime rate in the same period: up from 1.1 crimes per 1000 population in 1957 to 5.9 per 1000 in 1980.

Due to difficulties in attracting recruits of the right calibre, many police departments are below their authorised strength. As in many other respects, each police force follows its own practice when selecting recruits. Normally, there is a written exam, age, health and height qualifications, and a physical fitness test. The background of shortlisted applicants is scrutinised for evidence of financial, educational or personal vulnerabilities that might make the person unsuitable for police service. Some forces require psychological testing. Training periods vary considerably: in 1970 a survey found a range between two and 40 weeks with the average being 10, but some forces have no training at all (believing that experience on the street is the best teacher), or postpone training until the recruit has had some weeks on patrol. The quality of the training varies enormously; there is little scope for refresher courses, and the emphasis is on policing in the locality, with a resulting variation of operational practices and standards across the country.

A major concern has been to attract sufficient numbers from ethnic minorities since it became apparent in the 1960s that the major urban riots were in part sparked off by tensions caused by predominantly White police forces patrolling the streets of the ghettoes. It became part of the received wisdom of the 1970s that a healthy ethnic mix in major city police forces would help both to defuse the accusations that the function of the police was to defend an economic system based on racial privilege, and to ensure that the Black community did not lay claim to economic equality in the way that it already had, in several Supreme Court rulings, been granted legal equality. As a result of sustained and conscious efforts to recruit from the ethnic minorities, the nation's police forces had by the 1980s begun to mirror the ethnic diversity of its population. In the early 1960s the proportion of Blacks employed as policemen was 3.5 per cent; by 1972 it was 7.5 per cent, by 1980 9.3 per cent and in 1983 13.1 per cent, roughly equivalent to the proportion of Blacks in the population. Similar progress has been made more recently with the recruitment of Hispanics.

During the 1970s, attention turned to the role of women in the workforce, and a number of Supreme Court cases threw a spotlight onto the issue of discrimination based on gender as, for example, in *Frontiero* v. *Richardson* (1973). At the same time, pressure from women's groups resulted in conscious attempts to raise female participation rates in the labour force; to promote the idea of equal pay for equal work; and to provide equal opportunities for recruitment and advancement. Employment practices in the police reflect this new concern. In the early 1960s just over 2 per cent of the country's police were female; by 1972 this figure had increased slightly to 2.6 per cent, but by 1983 it had reached 9.4 per cent.

Financing of the police is divided between the various levels of government that comprise the federal system in the USA. In 1981, policing cost $24.7 billion of which $15.3 billion was spent on local forces, $7.1 billion on state forces, and $2.3 billion at the federal level. Overall, policing is a small fraction of total public expenditure: about 1.5 per cent. In real terms, police costs grew by only 10 per cent between 1971 and 1979 while the cost of maintaining prisons grew by 29 per cent in the same period. It can be seen that the federal share of policing costs is relatively small; however, in the period 1968 – 80, the existence of the Law Enforcement Assistance Administration channelled extra funding from federal sources to (principally) the states and municipal police forces. The peak of this federal funding (much of which was devoted to 'hardware') came in 1975 with an overall grant of $850 million, but even then federal expenditure on policing never exceeded 5 per cent of the amounts spent by state and city administrations combined.

There are no standard conditions of service, remuneration, ranks, or uniform in the police forces of the USA. Wide differences exist in modes of operation, since these are essentially tailored to meet local conditions. To give an indication of the variety of structures that exist in American police forces, we look at two here: the New York Police Department (NYPD) and the Southampton Police Department in New York State. The NYPD is the largest police department in the USA. The Department is headed by the Police Commissioner who is appointed by the mayor. He is responsible for the administration and discipline of the department, and he is assisted by an Assistant Commissioner and a number of civilian aides who normally have had experience in uniform prior to their appointment. There are seven Deputy Commissioners who are responsible for discipline; organised crime; administration; legal matters; public information; trials; and community affairs. The NYPD is divided into six main units: Operations (covering most of the uniformed and detective services); Field Services (responsible for patrolling streets and parks and responding to emergency calls from the public); the Detective Bureau (sub-divided into five borough commands and specialising in three main types of crime: burglary, assaults, murder); the Special Operations Division (covering *inter alia* the Stake Out unit and Special Events Squad); the Traffic Division; and the Communications Division (responsible for providing a city-wide radio network on 37 separate channels). Male members of the force are required to wear a double action 0.38 revolver with a four-inch barrel (Colt or Smith and Wesson) while policewomen wear a similar weapon with a three-inch barrel. The current strength of the NYPD is about 30 000, and the population under its supervision about 8 million.

By contrast, the police department of Southampton (NY) has a force of 51 officers to cover a population of 30 000. The Chief of Police is assisted by a captain and the patrol strength is divided into four squads each commanded by a lieutenant aided by a sergeant. There are four detectives and a communications section. Each officer carries a 0.38 or 0.357 revolver and each patrol car is equipped with a shotgun.

FORMAL STRUCTURE OF AUTHORITY

The written constitution of the USA provides an appropriate point of departure for an examination of the legal framework governing the policing of public order. The broad rights contained in the constitution (and particularly in the first 10 amendments to it passed in 1791) have only slowly become diffused downwards into the statute books of the states, a process in which certain Supreme Court judgements have played a crucial role. The first amendment prohibits laws restricting religious freedom and freedom of speech; the fourth amendment covers search warrants; the fifth guarantees that no person shall be deprived 'of life, liberty or property without due process of law'; the sixth lays down the basic provisions for a fair trial; and the eighth prohibits any 'cruel or unusual punishments' (a phrase that has been used by those seeking to abolish capital punishment). The second amendment asserts the right of the people 'to keep and bear arms', which is the main constitutional obstacle to achieving greater gun control in the USA.

The control of public order has been the responsibility of the states and of local police forces and not (except in cases of serious urban rioting when federal help is sought) a matter for the federal government. The autonomy of local police forces has to some extent eroded by legal rulings at the level of the Supreme Court in the same way that civil rights generally have percolated downwards from norms set at the federal level. For example, the right of the police to stop people on the street and frisk them varied between states until 1968 when a Supreme Court ruling in *Terry* v. *Ohio* upheld the right of the police to frisk someone if they believed that the person was acting 'in a suspicious manner' and when they believed a crime had been or was likely to be committed.

Once a person has been arrested, he (or she) has a right to remain silent. Before a person can be interrogated he must be advised that he can remain silent, that anything he does say will be used in court, that he may have a lawyer present during questioning, and that if he cannot afford a lawyer one will be provided. These are the 'Miranda warnings' that originate in a Supreme Court ruling in *Miranda* v. *Arizona* (1966). In 1977, this ruling was refined to exclude the need for warnings to be given when a person goes voluntarily to a police station and is not prevented from leaving when he wishes to do so.

The police have the task of balancing the right of citizens to assemble peacefully against the need to keep the streets clear and protect people going about their lawful business. Police can intervene to disperse a crowd if it has assembled without a permit; when illegality is being urged by someone speaking in public; when an obstruction is occurring; or when people are behaving in an 'unruly' fashion. A riot is defined as a 'turbulent disturbance' of three or more people who are acting with the common intent of promoting violence terror or turbulent activity. The police have to distinguish between those participating in a riot and those who are present but not participating such as pressmen, shopkeepers protecting their premises, and persons driving through the riot area or merely watching the riot. In the 1960s, the police were sometimes criticised for attacking non-participants in civil disorder and the official investigation into the disturbances at the 1968 national Democratic convention in Chicago accused the police themselves of rioting.[2]

The strong distrust that Americans have of central government is enshrined in the constitution of 1787. Many governmental powers are given to the states, and the state constitutions reserve law enforcement for cities, towns and villages: hence the multiplicity of police forces in the USA. It is argued that local police forces deal most effectively with a community's particular needs; for this reason (among others) the extreme decentralisation and localised roots of police forces in the USA have never been seriously questioned. It has long been accepted that the best way to maintain the accountability of the police is to keep the lines between the local community and the police department as short as possible. In a federal system like the USA, there is a ready acceptance of the idea that local variations in the way the police operate are just as desirable as the legislative and judicial permutations that flow from the federal system itself. In most urban police departments the police chief is appointed by (and accountable to) the mayor. The voters in city elections are therefore, in part, judging a mayor on the way in which the city is policed. The lines of accountability are, however, rarely so clearcut in practice. There is a constant tension between the desire of the mayor to claim that the police are 'free from political interference' (i.e., acting as neutral law enforcers) and his need to demonstrate that the police are in fact accountable to the citizens via their elected officials.[3] The unfortunate legacy of the nineteenth century (when, in many American cities, the police were the objects of patronage and a means of party political harassment) has led in the twentieth century to a swing of the pendulum in the other direction. Now it has become more common for mayors to boast how autonomous their police departments are. However, the price to be paid for this autonomy (underwritten by a touching faith in the legal safeguards surrounding police conduct), is a lack of accountability and a reluctance in some cases of police departments to respond positively to public criticisms. This lack of accountability (coupled with a belief in the virtues of police autonomy) has been one ingredient in the persisting alienation of certain sections of the public from the police. These issues became particularly controversial in the 1960s when, in the face of wide-spread civil disorders, the police were involved in incidents where the issue of accountability became extremely relevant. Complaints against the police in such cases were met with denials, statements that such practices were necessary in the circumstances, or with a mayor stating that he could not interfere in police operational matters. If, for example, a Black teenager is shot dead by the police the question of accountability becomes almost philosophical. Is it the responsibility of the patrolman who fired the gun? The Police Chief under whose direction the policeman is acting, or the Mayor to whom the Police Chief is responsible? Is it the city council who are elected by the citizens to supervise all administration in the city, or is it the responsibility of the citizens themselves on whose behalf these functionaries are acting, and to whom they are ultimately answerable at election time? Attempts to appoint civilian review boards of some police forces have usually been resisted. American police forces prefer to root out 'rotten apples' themselves, adopt new tactics when they consider them necessary, and to use discretion in law enforcement practices based on their own local experience.

At the heart of local policing lies the belief that majority voting in the locality is the best way to achieve a truly responsive policing system. Arguably, however, it can be seen that the real test of a police force is not its sensitivity to majority opinion, but its readiness to uphold the rights of minorities (or even individuals) against the wishes of majority opinion in a city or a rural community. The close relationship between police chiefs and elected mayors in American cities makes it difficult for the former not to curry favour with what is perceived as the 'majority view' within his jurisdiction.[4] The responsibility of the police for protecting the right of a Black family to move into a predominantly White neighbourhood can strain mayor–police chief relations to breaking point. The police chief fears that his appointment could be terminated if he carries out policies that impinge directly on the interests of the mayor's political supporters: electoral considerations and impartial policing thus make awkward bedfellows. The strength of a mayor can be judged by the extent to which he is prepared to explain to his citizens why a police chief took a certain action that appeared to be against the interests of most of them. He may need to justify publicly the upholding of a wider constitutional right over the mere defending of sectional interests.

Pressure on the relationship between the police and city administrations is increased by the effectiveness of unionisation among the police. Since the 1970s unionisation has become more general so that rank and file officers are now able to make their views known on issues such as pay, conditions of service, internal discipline, and promotion. Police unions employ a variety of tactics to back up their demands: 'ticket blizzards' (clogging the court system with unmanageable numbers of parking prosecutions); 'blue flu' (mass stoppages on grounds of 'sickness'); and strikes. Police strikes are illegal in about 30 states but the use of the strike weapon enjoys greater support than hitherto among most police officers. Strikes are now more common and reflect a belief on the part of the police that their interests are equal in importance to those of the public. In Memphis in 1978, and in New Orleans the following year, for example, police strikes have lasted more than a week. The main grievance behind strikes has been pay, but the effectiveness of such industrial action has been vitiated by the willingness of neighbouring police forces (usually the state police) to 'cover' for striking policemen and thereby reduce the incidence of crime.

POLICE–MILITARY RELATIONS

As in other countries police forces in the USA are able to fall back on military help in situations of major civil unrest. On some occasions, the military have been called in to replace (rather than assist) the police in situations where the local police have been unwilling rather than unable to enforce the law, such as in upholding the rights of Blacks in the Southern states. The National Guard is the part of the US Army normally called upon to assist the police in major riot situations. It is organised at state level, composed of part-timers who undergo a minimum period of training, and is available for service in national or local emergencies. National Guard units are subject to the call of the State Governor except when ordered into service by the President of the USA. Equipment is supplied by the federal government and units must maintain certain standards to be federally recognised, 48 hours of drill, and two weeks training, are required each year, for which pay is received. Officers from the regular Army serve as instructors and inspectors for the National Guard. Experience has shown that the use of Army personnel in tense riot situations may be counter-productive, inasmuch as a lack of training in riot control techniques often results in panicky actions and unnecessary bloodshed.

The need to call in the National Guard has, however, been greatly reduced by the development within some police forces of quasi-military units. One of the enduring legacies of the 1960s was the creation of special units trained to deal with specific incidents of a potentially dangerous kind. The term usually applied to such units is Special Weapons and Tactics (SWAT) and by 1975 over 500 police forces had established SWAT units. Not all such units are, however, referred to as SWAT teams since errors made by such teams can tarnish by association: other acronyms have thus been used to describe the same phenomenon, such as STOP (special tactics and operations) in Massachusetts, and CDUs (civil disturbance units) in Washington, DC.

The idea of SWAT teams originated with an incident in Austin in 1966 when a sniper named Whitman killed 15 people from the vantage point of a 28-storey building, having killed his wife and mother the night before. The Los Angeles Police Department (LAPD) was the first to deploy SWAT teams, and to use that acronym. The mere threat of calling in a SWAT team has on occasion been a sufficient deterrent to end a potentially lethal situation. The circumstances envisaged for the use of SWAT teams include armed and barricaded suspects; hostages being held at gunpoint; snipers in buildings; a dangerous individual on the run; and occasionally in a pre-emptive role (as, for example, during the visit of VIPs). SWAT teams have to be highly trained and 'tend to wear military uniform, and body armour, carry automatic weapons, and are designed to deal with specific incidents'.[5] The successful SWAT operation is one during which the suspect is apprehended and hostages released without a shot being fired, and without injury to anyone.

PUBLIC ORDER SITUATIONS

The wide range of public order situations in the USA make it impossible to provide an overview of all relevant episodes of disorder in the past 30 or so years. However, a look at three cases can throw some light on the broader relationship between the state and the policing of public order. These cases are instructive at two levels: first, the role of the police during the riots suggests that their tactics may have exacerbated them, and their reliance on the National Guard underlined their inability to cope with major disorders. However, the tactics of the National Guard appear in some cases to have increased the death toll unnecessarily, but also to have quelled the riot by sheer force. The second level at which the cases are instructive concerns the mutual perceptions of the police and the participants in the riots. The cases selected here are the riots in Chicago in 1968, Detroit in 1967, and Miami in 1980. They are analogous to many of the other major disturbances that have taken place in American cities since the 1950s.

In August 1968, during the Democratic Convention in Chicago, a crowd of about 10 000 gathered in Lincoln Park. The composition of the crowd was heterogeneous: antiwar protesters, 'hippies', anarchists, Black activists and so on. The police stereotyping of the demonstration resulted in everyone in the area being liable to indiscriminate assault, irrespective of who they were and what they were doing. Most demonstrators were intent on a peaceful protest against the war policies of the government, although there was a broader undercurrent of protest against the 'system' itself, which Mayor Daley's Chicago seemed to epitomise. It was when the police started to clear Lincoln Park that the real violence began: the protestors were not blameless, but the amount of force used by the police was later characterised as a police 'riot'. Widespread attacks on bystanders, and on people trying to get away from the area, gave way later to attacks on pressmen, about 20 per cent of whom sustained direct assaults from the police; many film crews had their cameras wrecked or film destroyed. The Chicago episode encapsulates both the propensity of the police to act well outside the law, and their role as defenders of the 'system' against its detractors.

There may not be anything such as a 'typical' riot but Detroit, in particular, was one of the worst in terms of lives lost and damage to property sustained. It contains several features that are helpful when we come to consider the role of the police at the interface between society and the state. On Saturday 22 July 1967, Detroit police raided a number of illegal drinking dens. On Sunday morning, shortly after the Special Tactical Mobile Unit for the traditionally quiet period had been stood down, police raided their fifth bar. Out of 193 policemen patrolling Detroit at that time 46 were in the precinct where the bar was located, 82 people were arrested at what turned out to be a welcome home party for some returning Vietnam veterans. Being a warm night (the temperature the next day was to be 86 degrees) many people were still on the streets: soon a crowd of 200 people gathered. A rumour that police had used excessive force during the raids was now circulating. At dawn the police commissioner was informed of the deteriorating atmosphere. By 6 a.m. the number of police on duty had increased to 369 of whom only 43 were in the immediate riot area. By that time a crowd of several thousand had gathered: window smashing and looting were becoming fairly widespread. At 7.50 a.m. a police commando unit swept along 12th Street (the riot's epicentre) but was offered little resistance. Firemen began to fight fires and were not harassed by the crowd. By mid-morning a quarter of Detroit's police were on duty in the riot area. An atmosphere of near joviality seems to have attended the rioting at this stage. Looters seem to have been ignored by the police, and residents exchanged light hearted banter with police officers. Police were deployed in other sensitive parts of the city in case the fracas at 12th Street was simply a diversionary ploy. A Black congressman and several community workers entered the riot area in an attempt to defuse the situation. Their efforts proved futile, and the carefree mood persisted, with looters operating under the noses of the police and sharing jokes with them; both Black- and White-owned stores were targets. Police at the scene said afterwards that they had insufficient instructions. A squad of special police commandos with visors and bayonets fixed were deployed on a peaceful street but when their presence looked likely to attract a hostile crowd, they hastily withdrew. At this moment, a rumour that a man had been bayonetted by the police turned the mood of the crowd from hilarity to hostility. At around 1 p.m. bottles and stones were hurled at the police and now at firemen who were trying to extinguish several blazes. At 2 p.m. the Mayor met community and political leaders. A request for state police to be summoned produced 360 officers. A spirit of 'carefree nihilism' was taking hold. Rioting and destruction appeared to be becoming ends in themselves. In the evening, National Guardsmen were on the street having been summoned by Mayor Cavanaugh, who now imposed a 9 p.m. to 5 a.m. curfew. As darkness fell the first sniper fire was reported; and a 16 year old negro boy became the first gunshot victim of the riot. A 23 year old White woman was shot dead in her car at around midnight (ironically having just dropped off some Black friends at their home). The circumstances of other deaths were often disputed and sometimes the result of tragic error. A White man with a gun 'protecting his apartment block' was shot dead by police because they thought he was a sniper. A young man and a fireman were killed by falling power lines. By 2 a.m. on Monday, Detroit police were supplemented by 800 state police officers and 1200 National Guardsmen. Phone calls during the day to Washington, DC secured agreement from the Vice President, and then President Johnson himself, that federal troops be brought to the city.

During daylight hours on Monday, nine people were killed by gunshot in the city. A negro was shot dead in his garden after an argument with a White man. Two female bystanders were critically injured when stray police bullets (intended for fleeing looters) hit them instead. At 11.20 p.m. federal troops began to enter the city but added little to the effectiveness of the anti-riot operation. Some had travelled 200 miles, some had been 30 hours on duty without a break, few had had any riot training. Some of their attempts to control the riot ended in tragic farce. A Guardsman accidentally discharging his gun caused a nearby building to be sprayed with bullets when it was assumed that a sniper was firing from that location. The building was later stormed but found to be empty. When a supermarket guard summoned Guardsmen to arrest looters, they shot the guard in error. As normality returned, street lights were ordered to be turned on but Guardsmen not knowing of the order continued to shoot them out, with the result that a news reporter, thinking he was under fire from a sniper summoned help from the National Guard! Erratic firing of guns added to the tension and fear after the main rioting was over. The response of the National Guard became increasingly undisciplined. A man lighting a cigarette at a window attracted a hail of gunfire and a four year old child dropped dead at his side. A 51 year old White woman drawing back curtains to look at tanks in the streets was killed almost instantly as bullets hit the building.

During the whole riot period, 7200 people were arrested. Makeshift jails, buses sometimes being used, kept people cooped up for 30 hours or more. Some were incarcerated in an underground garage without toilet facilities. Of the 43 people killed during the riot, 33 were Blacks: 15 citizens, of whom four were White, one National Guardsman, one fireman, and a Black private guard, died as a result of gunshot wounds. Police killed 20 or 21 people, the National Guard killed seven (or nine), the Army one, and storeowners killed two; and four died in accidents. The total bill for damage came to $22 million. By Thursday 27 July most rioting had ceased. On 1 August the curfew was lifted, and the National Guard moved out.

The Detroit riot described above fits the pattern of 'general conditions' for a riot that have been suggested by Chikota and Moran.[6] They argue that a riot takes place when a number of specific contingencies are added to a background of general conditions, the latter being: a gap between Black and White economic living standards; channels of redress apparently closed to Blacks; a belief that rioting will change things; a breakdown of police–community contact; and the gathering of large numbers of people out of doors on a summer weekend. The contingent factors which decide that a riot will take place at a specific time and in a specific place include: rumours suggesting a riot is going to take place, a 'spark' event (an arrest or a rumour of police brutality), and a crowd gathered in one place (for whatever reason). Given this concatenation of events behind most urban riot situations, one can see immediately the potentially contradictory role of the police in both triggering and trying to control outbreaks of public disorder. If it is accepted that such disorders have their genesis in perceptions of relative deprivation on the part of urban Blacks, it is also easy to accept that the police may be cast in the role of defending this imbalance, since their duty to protect the property of middle class suburban Whites is an obvious block on the ambitions of the Black community to achieve social and economic change. When disorder breaks out it is often the police (in simply enforcing the law) who unwittingly incite retaliation on the part of urban Blacks, who in turn exploit the police action as a pretext for venting anger and frustration that has been long bottled up. The heart of the Detroit riot was the 12th Street area. This area was afflicted by problems that typified many in American cities at that time. The Black proportion of Detroit's population had increased from 30 to 40 per cent in less than a decade; the school system was severely overcrowded in Black neighbourhoods, and to reach the state (Michigan) average for class size 1650 extra teachers would have been needed; unionisation among White workers effectively closed off training and job opportunities for Blacks, with the result that unemployment in the 12th Street area was reckoned to be about 12–15 per cent (and over 40 per cent for those under 25). The more education a Black received, the greater the disparity between his income and the income of a White with similar education. These imbalances were mirrored in political institutions in the city: of nine council men one was Black, of seven school board members two were Black (although Black schoolchildren constituted 57 per cent of the city's total). Given these facts, the role of the police was clearly one of defending an inequitable economic system against the aspirations that that political system encouraged.

The 1970s were relatively peaceful in American cities: Blacks benefitted from legal reforms and economic expansion that was translated to some extent into political power. Several cities had Black mayors, and we have already noted that the country's police forces took on greater proportions of Black recruits.

When violence broke out in Miami in 1980 it was after 12 or so years of calm. The event that 'sparked' the Miami riot (in which 7 people died) was a jury verdict in which police officers were acquitted of the murder of a Black motorcyclist five months previously. The riot that followed can be usefully compared with that of Detroit and other cities in the 1960s. The Miami police kept a low profile at the start of the riot in the belief that the lessons of the 1960s had been that an excessive show of force by the police could actually exacerbate the situation. As the police chief remarked: 'If you stand there and make a confrontation you'll escalate it. It can easily get out of control.' The rioting in Miami displayed several features that enable it to be contrasted with the rioting of the 1960s. In the 1960s the riots were about better conditions; in Miami there was an intense hatred being displayed at having been cheated. In Miami, a long pattern of poor police–community relations had built up an image in people's minds as to how the police could be expected to behave in a given set of circumstances. The judicial system had, since the 1960s, been held up (rightly in many cases) as the avenue along which Blacks could obtain redress for past wrongs and obtain a better deal in the future. The Miami court verdict therefore came as the final straw. It added to a situation of intense frustration of an ethnic kind resulting from Cuban immigrants obtaining federal grants setting up new businesses and generally doing much better than the Blacks. This added insult to the past injuries – slavery, the Ku Klux Klan, segregation, and poverty – that the Black community had long been forced to suffer.

The riots of the 1960s were reckoned to have developed through a number of stages: a precipitating event, a verbal confrontation between police and Blacks, police over-reaction, an erosion of the authority of peaceful Black community leaders, a 'carnival' phase of rocks being thrown at cars, etc. and, finally, a 'war' phase with the National Guard being brought in and widespread looting and arson becoming ends in themselves. The Miami riot broke out at this fourth stage immediately, and stayed there for 30 hours. The riot was quelled by calling out (in order) off-duty policemen, police from neighbouring districts, and the National Guard. The worst of the trouble was over by the time the National Guard was deployed and only half were on duty at any one time. There were conscious efforts made to avoid their use in case they should exacerbate the bloodshed, as had happened in Detroit. Their main function in Miami seems to have been to 'consolidate and hold territory' won back from the rioters by the police. Their mere presence was normally sufficient to preserve the peace.

PUBLIC PERCEPTIONS OF THE POLICE

One of the aspects of their work which most worries American policemen is their relationship with the general public. The policeman is not regarded with respect or admiration, even by those sections of the public who benefit most from his services. To those sections of the public with whom the police come most frequently into contact, the men in uniform are regarded as rough, capricious, discriminatory and corrupt. These attitudes tend to feed the policeman's view of himself and the community he serves. It is thus less important that most Americans reportedly believe that the police do a good job than the fact that it appears to most policemen that the public views them with hostility. The low esteem in which the policeman's job is held affects recruitment. Police forces can rarely attract the calibre of personnel they need and thus the prestige of the police service remains low along with the quality of its recruitment.

Nationwide opinion surveys suggest that about two-thirds of Americans regard the police as doing 'a good job' at enforcing the law, and about the same proportion claim to have a 'great deal' of respect for the police. However, a substantial minority of respondents feel that the status of policemen is too low. A survey confined to Washington, DC, for example, found that two-thirds of those questioned thought the police should get more pay. In other city surveys majorities of respondents claim to be satisfied with police conduct and reject suggestions that the police act unfairly, illegally or brutally in their dealings with the public.[7]

However, these attitudes are not distributed evenly through the population: if they were there would be no police–community problem. Non-Whites are less supportive of the police than Whites. In the Washington, DC survey cited above only 18 per cent of White males agreed that 'you would need to replace at least half the police force to get a really good police force', while 40 per cent of other groups concurred with the same proposition. In surveys in Watts (Los Angeles) and in Detroit, Blacks of all economic levels alleged higher incidence of police discourtesy or brutality. In Watts, Blacks were more likely to have either witnessed or heard of police misconduct in the area. This disparity in attitudes between Blacks and Whites extends to almost the whole spectrum of police–community relations. Blacks feel that the police discriminate against them but Whites do not. Blacks feel that they need more police protection, but receive less, than Whites and it is true, statistically, that Blacks are proportionately more often the victims of crime than Whites.

Much of this data comes from the 1960s and is in a sense the bedrock of alienation from which much of the violence sprang in the later years of that decade. There have been two distinct reactions to perceptions of police–community friction. One has been to recruit more ethnic minority representatives into police departments; the other has been to establish 'community relations' as a specific function of police operations. The two responses are of course connected, in that improved relations between the police and the inhabitants of the ghettoes has made it easier to recruit Blacks (and Hispanics) into the country's police forces. For example, Black representation in US police forces rose from 7.5 per cent in 1972 to 13.1 per cent in 1983.

Recruiting more members of the ethnic minorities into the police has not been easy. First, traditional and mutually held suspicions between the police and the minorities have not been easily dissipated; and it has therefore been difficult for Blacks to come forward and risk cutting themselves off from family and kinsfolk. Secondly, even when such a step has been taken, the new Black recruit may encounter racist attitudes towards him from members of predominantly White police departments who have been slow to abandon illiberal views of ethnic minorities. Thirdly, educational qualifications have sometimes had to be waived or lowered in order to encourage Black recruitment, much to the detriment of the quality of the police force concerned. Finally, physical qualifications, height, eyesight, and so on tend to militate against the recruitment of Blacks, Hispanics and Orientals. Once within the police department, Blacks find promotion difficult and the stress of policing their own communities (with the accusations of 'uncle Tom' constantly taunting them) means that Blacks are more likely to be retired on ill-health grounds – physically and mentally torn apart by the strains of being fully accepted neither by their own communities nor by the police force itself. The participation of ethnic minorities in the police is one part of the effort to improve police–community relations; the other is the specific function of building bridges between the police force and the community. This work has long been considered the 'Cinderella' of police activities. Since it resembles social work, it is perceived as being outside 'proper' police functions (or, worse still, as the molly-coddling of people who will never appreciate what the police do because they are instinctively hostile to the law and order that the police seek to uphold). In some police forces, such community work is referred to as being that of the 'Commie relations unit'. It has been suggested that Black alienation from the police is less serious than it was, but that the differential perceptions between Black and White is still significant. Young Blacks are twice as unlikely as young Whites to rate police performance as 'good'.

Popular perceptions have to be balanced by police perceptions of their own role in relation to the public. Like policemen in most countries, the American police feel that they have to enforce unpopular laws in a society that is hostile to the standards that the law is trying to uphold and in a climate of opinion that places a high premium on toleration of deviancy. The policeman operates in a society that condones acute levels of relative deprivation, and yet has a tendency to seek society-based explanations for criminal behaviour. The obvious fact that the police tend to come into contact with the section of society (i.e., lawbreakers) least likely to be its biggest supporters, and with the victims of crime, means that the police view of human nature is inevitably all the more jaundiced. Because his job requires him to be conventional, the policeman is likely to have a conservative personality. As one writer has noted 'All a cop can swing in a milieu of marijuana smokers, interracial dates, and homosexuality, is the nightstick'.[8] Nonconformity is detested as much as criminality, and the two are often linked in the policeman's mind.

The police view of the disorders and riots of the kind discussed earlier is that they are caused by 'agitators' or 'communists' who lead people into creating disturbances. Often the legitimate right to protest is perceived as unlawful because it seeks to challenge a *status quo* within which the police themselves feel most comfortable and whose maintenance is their principal function. In dealing with crowd situations, the policeman tends to dehumanise the participating individuals, dismissing them as 'riff-raff', and failing to see them as citizens with specific constitutional rights and freedoms. Over-reaction by the police, or excessive displays of weaponry, can antagonise a crowd further, and it will begin to behave in a way that mirrors the police perception of it: a crowd can panic, act irrationally, and possibly become a real danger to the security of the police themselves. It is not surprising that some of the major disturbances of the 1960s were reckoned to have been started by police over-reactions to potentially innocuous incidents.

THE POLICE AS A POLITICAL INSTITUTION

We come finally to pose the question that has lain implicitly behind much of our analysis so far: the relationship between the police and the state. This question can be answered in a number of different ways. At the outset, we need to remind ourselves that the concept of the 'state' is not one readily intelligible to the mass of American citizens. The federal government is perceived as being distant, and rightly so. Most citizens identify with their locality (be it a city or a county), and the attempts by 'big' (i.e., federal) authorities to inter-fere with local autonomy are fiercely resisted. This instinct – crystal-lised in the division of powers between state governments and federal government – has influenced the structure of police forces and perceptions of their role. We have seen already the remarkably high degree of decentralisation and local roots that characterise police forces in the USA: efforts to amalgamate forces, to introduce com-mon standards of operation or modes of recruitment have been resisted, not only by the police themselves but by the citizens they serve. This resistance reflects a wider belief in the merits of keeping big government at arm's length and a faith in the ability of local opinion to be the best judge of local needs. Thus, at a very simple level, the structure of police forces in the USA is a mirror of the disintegrated political system, and a reinforcer of its emphasis on divergence. The local character of American police forces is entirely consistent with the local taxes, local laws, and local concerns that together constitute the environment in which most Americans live.

The police also reflect a widespread belief in individualism. Unlike his British or European counterpart, the American 'cop' does not rely on an abstract legal order to enforce his authority: quite remark-ably so, the personality of the individual policeman is paramount in his command of a situation. The remoteness of the 'state', the local roots of the police force itself, and the vagueness of constitutional guarantees all combine to place a premium on the ability of the man in uniform to use his discretion in a particular situation. By the same token, Americans do not expect very much from their policemen and are more tolerant of corruption or laziness than would be the case in, say, Britain. The belief that the policeman is 'only human' is very strong, whereas in Britain the expectation of 'superhuman' qualities in the police is still fairly widespread.

At yet another level, however, the police can be seen as the protectors of a social and economic structure within the 'shell' of the somewhat elusive state. If it is true that the USA is a country based not only on a liberal democratic ethos that proclaims equal rights for all but also on a free market economic system that distributes economic goods unequally, then it will not be surprising if the state itself suffers the consequences of this dissonance between political equality and economic inequality. The principal source of public disorder has, in fact, been a lack of congruence between economic reality and political myth.

By the end of the nineteenth century, the tradition of police repression against the labour movement had already become firmly established. In 1877, striking railroad workers were attacked by the police, with several fatalities resulting; in 1892, 8000 National Guardsmen were brought in to crush a strike in Pennsylvania; and, in the twentieth century, the pattern persisted with four carworkers being killed during a strike in 1932 at Dearborn, Michigan, by police armed with pistols and machine guns. The role of the police has remained virtually unchanged even though the specific contexts have more often been racial unrest and student protest. Whatever the context, however, the police find themselves standing at the intersection between the system and its detractors:

> Acting as a controlling radar calculated to keep a society within structural confines that tend to be somewhat narrower than its stated ideological commitments. Thus the police are the vehicle by which the limits, boundaries and permissibility of social tolerance are tested.[9]

The role of the police takes on an added racial dimension when one considers that the Black community has suffered most obviously (but not uniquely) from the frustrations that arise when the political promises are not matched by economic rewards. In housing, education, and employment, the Black community has experienced the kind of relative deprivation that has led it to perceive the police (notwithstanding Black recruitment to urban police forces) as representing a kind of 'occupation force' in the ghetto – or, as Eldridge Cleaver once called them, 'armed guardians of the social order'.

Whatever the issue may be that causes the problem of public order, the role of the police in the USA is to stand at the interface between society and the state and impose norms. The policeman is not a neutral arbiter backed up by an impartial legal system, although he may wish to be portrayed thus. He is an agent of a political system whose most glaring discontinuities are of an economic kind. He is the agent of a state whose most obvious characteristic is its diffuseness.

Notes

1. D. McKay, *American Politics and Society* (Oxford: Blackwell, 1983) p. 29.
2. P.C. Kratcoski and D.B. Walker, *Criminal Justice in America* (1978) pp. 116–19.
3. L. Ruchelman, *Police Politics: A Comparative Study of Three Cities* (1974) p. 99.
4. Ruchelman, *Police Politics*, passim 61.
5. F.E.C. Gregory, 'Changes in American Systems of Policing Since 1960', *Police Journal*, (1978) 357–65.
6. R.A. Chikota and M.C. Moran, *Riot in the Cities* (1968).
7. US Government, *Task Force Report: The Police* (1967) pp. 144–9.
8. Cited in M.R. Summers and T.E. Barth, *Law and Order in a Democratic Society* (1970) p. 69.
9. A. Niederhoffer and A.S. Blumberg (eds), *The Ambivalent Force* (1976) p. 12.

6 Israel

BACKGROUND

The external threat to Israel's existence as a state has been the dominant motif of Israeli life since the country's proclamation of independence on 14 May 1948. There have been five major wars with the country's Arab neighbours: the War of Independence between 1947 and 1949, the Suez campaign of 1956, the Six Day war in 1967, the Yom Kippur war in 1973, and Israel's intervention in the Lebanon between 1982 and 1985. Within Israel and the territories it has occupied since 1967, there have been considerable tensions between Jews and Arabs. Tensions have also arisen inside the Jewish community between Ashkenazim and Sephardim or Orientals or between ultra-orthodox religious elements and the more secular-inclined majority. Nonetheless, throughout the history of the state, internal divisions have been treated as wholly subordinate in importance to the wider Arab–Israeli conflict. Furthermore, the principal internal division (that between Jews and Arabs) has naturally tended to be seen as a by-product (if not a function) of the larger inter-state conflict. Thus, following a spate of terrorist murders within Israel in the summer of 1985, the country's response included a warning from the Chief of Staff of the Israel Defence Forces of possible military retaliation against Jordan on the presumption that those responsible for the outrages might have crossed the border from there. This overwhelming emphasis on the external dimension of the threat posed to Israel by political violence accounts in part for the extraordinary paradox that in a country obsessed by security, reflected in the widely quoted aphorism that 'an Israeli citizen is a soldier on eleven months' annual leave', the Israel Police should occupy a position more lowly than perhaps any of its counterparts in the Western world. Indeed, its low standing, and the relatively narrow conception of its functions, particularly prior to 1974, form the most striking features of the Israel Police.

From the outset, the Israel Police suffered from being the successor in institutional terms of the Palestine Police, which operated under the British Mandate from 1922 to 1948. It inherited not just the negative image of the Palestine Police among Jews by the end of the

Mandate, but also many of the shortcomings of the Palestine Police – undermanning, lack of finance, and high turnover. By contrast, the origins of the Israel Defence Forces (IDF) were rooted in the principal Jewish underground organisation, the Haganah, and consequently the IDF attracted all the legitimacy that went with the successful struggle for independence. Throughout its existence, the Palestine Police had to contend with riot and disorder. In the early years of the Mandate men recruited after the disbandment of the Royal Irish Constabulary (RIC) formed an important part of the force, but by the 1930s some 70 per cent of the force were local recruits, the majority of whom were Arabs. The Jewish community complained that Jews were under-represented in the force, a criticism that led to the establishment of the Jewish Settlement Police, which was partly financed by the Jewish Agency before its full integration into the Palestine Police. Infiltration of this force by the Haganah and, at the same time, the unreliability and defection of Arab members of the police following the Arab revolt of 1936, persuaded the British government of the necessity of increasing the British proportion of the Palestine Police. In practice, recruitment fell far short of the targets government laid down, while the quality of the new recruits was generally poor. Nonetheless, on the eve of Irgun's campaign of violence against British rule in Palestine in 1944, British officers constituted well over half of the Palestine Police, while Arabs formed just over 20 per cent of the force and Jews 13 per cent.

Even before the Irgun campaign got under way there had been ugly clashes between the Palestine Police and Jews protesting at arms searches conducted by British forces. Irgun terror, which made a particular target of the police, seriously aggravated relations between the police and the Jewish community. The official British response to the terror included collective punishments (imposed, for example, on a Jewish village accused of failing to co-operate with an investigation into the attempted assassination of the British High Commissioner), curfews, deportations, floggings, and executions of those convicted of serious crimes. Begin's account of the Irgun campaign contains allegations against the police of anti-Semitism, torture, and other misconduct.[1] There were serious episodes of police indiscipline; following the murder of four policemen in November 1946, members of the force had gone on a rampage damaging property and assaulting Jewish civilians. An even uglier police riot in Tel Aviv (resulting in the deaths of five civilians) followed Irgun's reprisal hanging of two British NCOs in July 1947. The police themselves suffered grievously.

In September 1947 11 policemen died and 53 were injured in an Irgun attack on a police station in Haifa.

The British announcement in November 1947 that it would withdraw its forces from Palestine by the middle of May 1948 prompted the first steps to establish the Israel Police in preparation for independence. Jewish members of the Palestine Police, numbering some 700, formed the core of the new force, supplemented by recruits from the underground movement. Despite a purge of those judged to have collaborated with the British and the infiltration by the underground of the Palestine Police, the new force found it difficult to shake off the stigma of association with the British regime under the Mandate. In organisational terms, too, the new force largely followed the model of policing under the Mandate, though divested of its militarised character. The British withdrawal had been accompanied not merely by the departure of British members of the Palestine Police (who had filled most of the higher positions within the force), but also by the destruction of files and the removal of equipment or its dumping at sea. The birth of the new state in conditions of war meant that policing was afforded a very low priority and that from the outset important issues of internal security, such as the threat posed by the existence of a hostile Arab minority within the state, were seen as a function of external defence. In particular, the organisation of security services with the task of gathering intelligence on internal and external threats to the state completely bypassed the police. The body responsible for counter-intelligence within Israel, the General Security Service or Sherut Bitahon Klali (best known by its Hebrew initials as Shin Bet) was made accountable from its inception to the Prime Minister's office, while the Arab minority within Israel was placed under military rule, which was to last from 1948 to 1966. The role of the police remained limited to fighting crime, regulating traffic, and controlling demonstrations, until 1974, when the Israel Police was formally accorded responsibility in the field of internal security.

STRUCTURE, ORGANISATION, AND FINANCE

Like the Palestine Police at the end of the Mandate period, the Israel Police is a highly centralised organisation. It is commanded by an Inspector-General with the rank of Commissioner, from headquarters in Jerusalem. For the purposes of ordinary policing the country is sub-divided (on a pattern similar to that of the Palestine Police) into four districts and 15 sub-districts covering both Israel proper and the occupied territories. Separated from the main body of the police force are the Border Police and the Civil Guard. The Border Police are a paramilitary organisation which was established in 1953 to guard the country's frontiers against guerrilla or terrorist incursions. The size of the force was 4218 in 1984. Its functions have expanded to include responsibility for the policing of harbours and airports and riot control – principally in the occupied territories, but also on occasion in Israel itself. Its militarised character has tended to set the Border Police apart from the rest of the police, and its reputation for the rough handling of demonstrations has made its use in this role controversial, particularly inside the 'Green Line' separating Israel from the occupied territories. For example, the use of a Border Police unit to quell disturbances on the Temple Mount in Jerusalem in January 1986, provoked by a challenge to the site's control by Moslem religious authorities, prompted adverse comment in the Israeli press and demands for the unit's removal from the Temple Mount. A notable feature of the Border Police is the high proportion of Arabs from the Druze community serving in its ranks. They constitute approximately a quarter of the force.

The Civil Guard was established as a volunteer force after the Yom Kippur war in 1973. It was created in response to fears of an increase in terrorist attacks on Israel. Its main functions are patrolling and the guarding of public buildings. It currently draws on some 50 000 part-time volunteers. Originally conceived as an anti-terrorist force, it has come to play an important role in the combating of ordinary crime, leading to demands from Arab citizens of Israel that they be permitted to join the force in their localities. These demands have embarrassed the Israeli government in view of its general policy of excluding Arabs (with the particular exception of the Druze community) from participation in the country's defence because of the security risk involved. There has also been controversy over the lack of experience of some of the volunteers, who include 16 and 17 year old high school students. Allegations by pupils from a school in Tel Aviv that indiscipline in the Civil Guard was rife and that patrols frequently assaulted innocent Arab bystanders created a scandal in 1984, and led to the closure of the base involved; the pupils had been required to volunteer for the force as part of their educational programme. Problems also arose over relations between the Civil Guard and the main body of the police force, which resented the

Table 6.1   Size and composition of the Israel Police

Year	Regular police	Ratio per 1000	Women (%)	Non-Jewish (%)
1948	1882	2.1	6	3.3
1952	5375	3.3	–	–
1956	5806	3.1	7.3	6.9
1960	5882	2.7	4.4	7.3
1961	5780	2.6	5.1	8.6
1962	5758	2.5	5.8	7.8
1963	5856	2.4	6.6	8.6
1964	6254	2.5	6.9	7.6
1965	6726	2.5	7.6	7.9
1966	7569	2.8	7.3	7.3
1967	8756	3.2	6.2	10.3
1968	9210	3.2	7.5	–
1969	9408	3.2	7.4	10.8
1970	9405	3.1	–	–
1971	9397	3.0	10.3	–
1972	9614	3.0	12.5	12.6
1973	10 005	3.0	14.6	12.9
1974	10 695	3.2	16.7	12.2
1975	12 302	3.5	16.2	11.3
1976	13 377	3.8	15.7	11.6
1977	14 023	3.8	–	–
1978	14 326	3.8	–	–
1979	16 456	4.3	–	–
1980	16 406	4.2	15.8	–
1981	16 841	4.2	16.0	–
1982	16 801	4.1	16.8	–
1983	18 851	4.6	15.4	–
1984	19 101	4.5	16.0	–

Note:
The Regular police column includes the Border Police. The figure given represents the size of the force at the end of the year cited.

Source: Annual Reports of the Israel Police and Ministry of Police (Jerusalem).

arrangement under which veteran Army officers assisted by some salaried staff commanded the Civil Guard with easier opportunities for promotion than existed within the regular police.

The numbers of regular police for the years 1960–84 and for selected years before 1960 are given in Table 6.1. The figures for the regular police include the Border Police but not the Civil Guard or civilian personnel employed by the Israel Police. Also excluded are auxiliary Arab policemen recruited for local duties within the occupied territories, many of whom were formerly members of the Jordanian Police. Actual numbers at the end of the year in question are given rather than the authorised size of the establishment, a higher figure rarely achieved in practice. Excluding the population of the occupied territories (as is the practice in the Annual Reports of the Israel Police), the number of regular police per 1000 of the population was 4.5 in 1984, a ratio that has risen substantially since independence. One in six Israeli citizens is an Arab, and by that criterion Israeli Arabs are under-represented in the police. In fact, the figures for the proportion of non-Jewish police in Table 6.1 understate their under-representation in relation to ordinary policing as the figures include members of the Druze community serving in the militarised Border Police. The position is even more stark if calculated on the basis that Arabs constitute 35 per cent of the population of Israel plus the occupied territories, though in this context the relatively small number of auxiliary Arab policemen serving in the occupied territories would have to be taken into account. Nonetheless, as compared to the 1950s and 1960s, there has been an increase in the proportion of Arab policemen within the force. There has also been a substantial increase in the number of women in the police since the 1967 war. They are mainly employed in non-operational positions or in traffic control. The increase in their numbers reflects the difficulties the police has encountered in attracting male recruits, rather than any commitment to enhance the status of women.

The poor public image of policing from the inception of the state meant that recruitment into the police was largely from lower socio-economic groups. In ethnic terms, this has led to a predominance of Orientals in the force, except in its higher ranks. In the early years of the state, particularly, the training provided by the police for new recruits functioned as an agency for the absorption of Orientals into Israeli society. The ethnic imbalance within the force has tended to reinforce its low status. Among the findings of a 1969 research project into the image of the Israel Police were that respondents of European or American backgrounds (that is to say, Ashkenazim) consistently had a lower opinion of the police than Orientals, as did the better educated and higher income groups.[2] In these circumstances, attracting recruits of a sufficiently high calibre has proved difficult. For example, in 1978 over 80 per cent of applicants for the police were rejected on the grounds of inadequate educational attainment, low IQ scores, or the possession of a criminal record.[3] Aggravating the manpower problem has been a very high level of resignations from the force, amounting to 18 per cent of the force per annum with a numerical turnover approaching 100 per cent every six years.[4] A major grievance of police officers who have resigned from the force has been pay. As no union or independent organisation of police officers, apart from a branch of the International Police Association, is permitted, agitation within the force over conditions of service is practically impossible. On a number of occasions wives of police officers have staged demonstrations to protest at their husbands' low pay; in November 1985 a number of police wives embarked on a hunger strike over the issue of pay outside the Prime Minister's office in Jerusalem. The protest resulted in a modest increase in salaries designed to bring police pay into line with Army rates of pay.

Reorganisation of the police has been quite frequent, reflecting concern both over the police's low standing and over public criticism of the effectiveness of the force, particularly as crime rates soared from the very low levels that prevailed in the 1950s and 1960s. Concern over rising crime and, in particular, the emergence of organised crime as a serious problem in the 1970s led to the establishment of the Commission to Examine the Topic of Crime in Israel by the Likud-led government elected in 1977. The government compared its initiative to President Johnson's establishment of a commission on law enforcement in the US in 1965. The report of the Shimron Commission was published in 1978. Its recommendations included the strengthening of the Bureau of Investigations; the creation under its aegis of several new operational units with the specific responsibility for combating organised crime, drug trafficking, fraud, and police misconduct and corruption; and the establishment of two high-level committees, a Cabinet Committee on Law Enforcement and the Central Committee for Integrated Operations Against Organised Crime, to co-ordinate the work of different ministries in what was grandiloquently called the 'war against crime'. The report also urged a number of measures (including the reintroduction of foot patrols) to increase the visibility of the police. To improve the enforcement of the traffic laws in the light of the country's very high accident rates, it recommended (among other steps) that the employment of students on a part-time basis for traffic control should cease.

However, the reforms initiated as a result of the Shimron Commission failed to allay public concern over crime. One factor contributing to this unease was gang warfare involving a series of car bombings that the police appeared impotent to prevent. Another was the easing of external pressures on Israel as a result of the peace treaty with Egypt in 1979, which prompted a greater emphasis on Israel's domestic ills. At the 1980 Independence Day celebrations, the Speaker of the Knesset declared that 'Israel needs not only safe borders, but also safe streets'.[5] Reflecting the higher priority the issue of policing was acquiring, the Israeli government appointed Herzl Shafir, a former Deputy Chief of Staff of the Israel Defence Forces, as the country's new Inspector-General in 1980. Significantly, Shafir was the first person to be appointed to this position from outside the ranks of the police. His appointment was widely welcomed as improving the police's standing; in the event, he was sacked by his civilian superior after only one year in office as a result of a row over the police's investigation of political corruption. Nonetheless, during his year as Inspector-General, Shafir carried out a thorough review of police operations and put together a five-year programme to improve the effectiveness of policing which became known as the Tirosh Plan (Tirosh being Hebrew for 'new wine'). The Plan, which was approved by the Cabinet, envisaged an expansion of the manpower of the Israel Police to over 20 000 officers by the end of 1984, greater use of computers, more routine rotation of personnel, radical changes in training, increased patrolling, and the opening of new police stations. As Table 6.1 shows, the first of these objectives was not achieved, though progress towards the target was made.

Restraint on public expenditure, especially in recent years, has proved a major obstacle to the implementation of reform. The police are financed out of central government revenue from the budget allocated to the Ministry of Police, with the exception of the financing of police units in the occupied territories, which comes out of the budget for the Ministry of Defence. The proportion of central government expenditure allocated to the Ministry of Police from 1960–61 to 1984–85 is contained in Table 6.2, and for the purposes of comparison the corresponding figures for the Ministry of Defence are also included. They reveal a predictable disparity in expenditure between the two ministries. The most striking features of these figures are not just the low level of expenditure on the police as a proportion of total spending, but the fact that, proportionately,

Table 6.2   Expenditure on the Ministries of Police and Defence as a percentage of total government expenditure

Year	Ministry of Police	Ministry of Defence
1960–61	2.24	17.57
1961–62	1.90	13.87
1962–63	1.94	16.56
1963–64	1.57	17.42
1964–65	1.83	20.46
1965–66	1.72	19.44
1966–67	1.83	19.50
1967–68	1.66	21.24
1968–69	1.59	25.51
1969–70	1.53	33.00
1970–71	1.30	33.33
1971–72	1.16	35.04
1972–73	1.00	27.33
1973–74	0.85	53.23
1974–75	0.92	40.05
1975–76	1.03	35.09
1976–77	0.92	35.05
1977–78	1.19	31.65
1978–79	1.29	26.59
1979–80	1.33	27.79
1980–81	1.29	28.65
1981–82	1.30	26.44
1982–83	1.32	24.76
1983–84	0.91	21.54
1984–85	0.88	17.03

Source: Calculated from figures for government expenditure supplied by the Ministry of Police (Jerusalem).

spending on the police has declined over the period since 1960–61 despite the increase in manpower and all the efforts made since 1977 to enhance the police's position.

FORMAL STRUCTURE OF AUTHORITY

Israel does not possess either a written constitution or a Bill of Rights. As in the UK, the legislature is the supreme law-making body. Under the proclamation of independence, a declaration was made that the laws as they existed in Palestine under the Mandate would remain in force, except in so far as they conflicted with the terms of the proclamation itself or with future legislation. The country's law today thus consists of an amalgam of Israeli statute and case law, Palestine Mandatory law, elements of English common law, and traces of Ottoman law. Within Israel, there are two principal systems of courts: religious courts, which have jurisdiction in relation to matters of personal status, such as marriage and divorce; and ordinary courts, which handle other civil matters and most criminal cases. There are three tiers to the ordinary court system: magistrates courts at the bottom, district courts, and the Israel Supreme Court, which both functions as a final court of appeal for the lower courts and, when constituted as the High Court of Justice, can grant redress in cases outside the jurisdiction of any other court or tribunal. In addition, there are a variety of special courts, subject to a measure of supervision by the ordinary courts. The most important of these are military courts, established in terms of the draconian Defence Emergency Regulations of 1945, brought in by the British in the closing years of the Mandate, or under special legislation such as the Prevention of Infiltration Act 1954.

Between 1948 and 1966 Arabs inside Israel were subjected to military rule under the emergency regulations. However, while the lifting of military rule considerably reduced the routine application of a whole panoply of restrictions over the lives of the Arab minority, the emergency regulations themselves remain in force and are invoked from time to time on security grounds. Under the regulations, it is possible for the Israeli government to declare any area of the country closed, to impose a military government, to proclaim curfews, to censor publications, to issue confinement orders, or to detain suspects without trial, among other measures. For example, during the 1967 war, military rule was reimposed in a number of Arab areas, while some villages were placed under curfew during the Land Day protest in 1976. In 1980, following a statement in support of the Palestine Liberation Organisation (PLO) by an Arab student organisation, the regulations were used to place a number of students under house arrest. This episode was followed by legislation making any public show of support for the PLO a criminal offence, punishable by up to three years in gaol.

The occupied territories (not including East Jerusalem which Israel annexed after the June 1967 war) remain under military rule, despite the establishment of so-called civil administration in the territories in November 1981. The legal system in the occupied territories is complex. For example, on the West Bank, Jordanian law and courts, subject to certain changes, continue to operate alongside military courts applying the emergency regulations and orders issued by the military command, which remains responsible for security. However, the Jewish settlers on the West Bank fall under the jurisdiction of ordinary Israeli law, giving rise to legal difficulties in cases involving disputes between the settlers and local residents denied access to the ordinary court system in Israel. The settlers may also be brought before military courts in the occupied territories, as in fact occurred with the trial in 1976 of Rabbi Levinger on charges of breaching public order and insulting an Army officer, a case that precipitated fierce controversy in Israel, including a debate in the Knesset.

Defence against external attack constitutes Israel's major justification for the most drastic measures it employs against Palestinians, such as deportation and collective punishment, including the demolition of the homes of political offenders. Generally speaking, the Israel Defence Forces are responsible for their implementation. Consequently, both within the occupied territories and in relation to the policing of Arab dissent more widely, the police tend to play a relatively minor and subsidiary role. For example, the 1975 Annual Report of the Israel Police described the two main objectives of police operations in the occupied territories as being 'to prevent the organising of cells for hostile activity against the administration, like distribution of leaflets, daubing hostile slogans on walls, trade strikes, or demonstrations', and, secondly, 'to prevent the smuggling of stolen property from Israel into the administered areas'.[6]

Politically, the Inspector-General is responsible to the Minister of Police, who is a member of the Cabinet. In 1977, after Likud's election victory, responsibility for the police was transferred to the Minister of the Interior. However, with the formation of the National Unity Government following the 1984 general election, the position of Minister of Police was re-established. In 1974, the police were given responsibility for internal security, a potentially far-reaching enlargement of the police's functions. However, as a 1983 study of the Israel Police noted, 'neither the Israeli government nor the Israeli police adjusted to the implication of the force's change of mandate'.[7] In particular, the role of the police's Special Duties Division, which is the principal police agency in the security field, remains subordinate to that of the General Security Service, Shin Bet. As the Israel Police's representative in the US candidly explained in an interview in 1980, 'to prevent anything like [a bomb] you need intelligence. This part of the job, as it concerns terrorism, is not in the hands of the police'.[8]

The Bureau for the Commissioner for Control and Public Complaints is the police body responsible for handling complaints against
the force. Established in 1973, it investigates approximately 3000
cases a year. A measure of supervision over the functioning of the
Ministry of Police is also provided by the office of the State
Comptroller, which oversees the whole range of government institutions. In 1971, the State Comptroller was given authority to consider
individual petitions and to act as an Ombudsman in relation to
departments of government. Reports of the State Comptroller have
frequently been critical of the functioning of the police. In 1980, the
State Comptroller criticised the absence of an overall conceptual
framework for the work of the police, and the lack of a plan for
providing the force with the resources it needed to achieve its aims.
In 1986, the State Comptroller complained of serious negligence by
the police in their handling of complaints against individual police
officers, particularly in relation to accusations of brutality.

POLICE–MILITARY RELATIONS

In status, the Israel Police has been described as the step-brother of
the Israel Defence Forces, a description that in reality understates
the contrast between the low standing of the police and the enormous
prestige the military has acquired in a state perpetually under siege
since independence. The huge disparity between the two institutions
– not just in size and budget, but also in terms of political influence –
constitutes the most important determinant of police–military relations. In particular, the subordinate position of the police has limited
the possibility of rivalry between the two institutions in the handling
of internal conflict (as has occurred, for example, at various times in
Northern Ireland). However, the desire to emulate the position of
the military has influenced the Israel Police and has been reflected in
the police's determination to retain responsibility for the paramilitary
Border Police. One of the many objectives of the 1980 Tirosh Plan
was to enhance co-operation between the police and the community
on the model of the close ties that have been established between the
Israel Defence Forces and Israeli society.

The principal area in which controversy has arisen over police
–military relations has been the policing of the West Bank. In 1980, a
group of Israeli academics from law faculties in Jerusalem and Tel
Aviv petitioned the Attorney General to investigate charges that acts
of violence by Jewish settlers against Arabs in the occupied territories

were going unpunished. Following this petition and other protests about the wave of vigilante violence sweeping the West Bank, the Attorney General appointed his deputy, Judith Karp, to head a commission of inquiry into settler violence and the police's failure to apprehend or prosecute those responsible. A report on the situation was submitted to the government in May 1982. After the government failed to act on her report, Karp resigned from the commission in April 1983. As a result of continuing public pressure on the government over the issue, portions of what became known as the Karp Report were released in February 1984.[9] It was fiercely critical of the police, presenting a picture of them as incompetent in their handling of investigations – or, at worst, indifferent towards settler crimes against Arabs. Serious omissions by the police, such as the failure even to have a report of a case involving the fatal shooting of a girl in a refugee camp, are mentioned among the report's catalogue. But most revealing of all was the light the report cast on relations between the police and the military in the occupied territories.

A major part of the police's defence of their actions in the occupied territories was their subordination to military authority. For example, when a police officer was questioned by the commission on his failure to investigate harassment of an Arab shopkeeper in Hebron by Jewish settlers, he produced a letter from the military governor of Hebron ordering the police not to investigate the case. This was by no means an isolated episode. In March 1982, after the commission had been established, a telegram was sent from the military commander of the West Bank to local police stations informing them that incidents involving the shooting of Arabs by settlers should be dealt with by the Military Police and not by the Israel Police. The implication was that the settlers should be treated as soldiers rather than civilians. Some sort of justification for such treatment could be found in the fact that the settlers carried Army weapons and served as reserve soldiers in their own settlements. While this particular order was rescinded before it came to the Attorney General's attention, it bore out the police's general contention that they came under pressure from the military not to follow up cases involving the settlers. A further reason for the reluctance of the police to investigate crimes by the settlers against the Arab population was that behind the military stood a Likud-led government strongly committed to the settlement of the West Bank as part of the land of Israel. How far the police could be blamed for their omissions in these circumstances became a matter of debate in Israel when the Karp Report was published.

Many of the most serious acts of violence against Arabs in the occupied territories (including the bomb attacks on three Palestinian mayors in June 1980) were carried out by an underground organisation formed by Gush Emunim settlers. In July 1985, 18 members of the organisation received prison sentences after their conviction in a Jerusalem court on terrorist charges. However, they were apprehended not as a result of any police investigation but thanks to infiltration of the underground by Shin Bet and action by Shin Bet agents that led to members of the underground being caught redhanded planting bombs on five buses in East Jerusalem in April 1984. At their trial, attorneys for the accused put forward the sensational defence that Shin Bet had discovered the identities of those involved in the underground shortly after the attack on the Palestinian mayors, but had failed to make any arrests because of high level political and military support for the actions of the underground. After a review of volumes of classified Shin Bet documents, this line of defence was rejected by the Israeli Supreme Court. Any political protection the underground might have received appears to have ended when Yitzhak Shamir succeeded Menachem Begin as Prime Minister in 1983.

PUBLIC ORDER SITUATIONS

In the case of Israel, it is necessary to distinguish not merely between the different forms that threats to public order take but also their sources, for threats emanating from the subordinate Arab population are generally handled quite differently from those originating in the dominant Jewish community. A feature of the dominant community is its high level of political mobilisation, which has been reflected in a level of participation in demonstrations approaching a quarter of the country's population. Indeed, Israel has been described as 'the most protest-oriented country in the western world'.[10] Under laws inherited from the British Mandate, all public demonstrations involving more than 50 participants or with political speakers require a permit from the police. This licencing system allows the police to impose conditions on the holding of demonstrations in relation to the location, stewarding, and nature of the protest, and thus to ensure that demonstrators adhere to ground rules laid down by the police. The outright denial of a permit, preventing the holding of a legal demonstration, is rare. Further, the police generally exercise considerable restraint in their handling of unlicenced demonstrations, even when they are held in breach of the law. In particular, religious groups rarely seek permission for the holding of demonstrations. According to a study of public protest in Israel by Professor Lehman-Wilzig, participant violence occurred in 10 per cent of over 1200 demonstrations in the 1970s.

Political divisions involving the main parties, the ethnic cleavage between Ashkenazim and the Oriental majority, and the division between ultra-orthodox and secular Jews have provided the principal sources of contention within the Jewish community. In 1952, the issue of whether Israel should accept reparations from the West German government gave rise to serious unrest, culminating in a demonstration outside the Knesset in which the windows of the Parliament building were broken and over 100 policemen injured. The threat of an invasion of the Knesset itself by the mob led the Speaker to order a recess, in which the Prime Minister (David Ben-Gurion) called in the Army to disperse the demonstration and restore order. 30 years later, controversy prompted by Israel's invasion of Lebanon in June 1982 and by the massacres of Palestinian civilians in refugee camps outside Beirut in September 1982 gave rise to a large number of demonstrations in Israel. A protest demonstration in Tel Aviv shortly after the massacres attracted a crowd variously estimated at between 100 000 and 350 000, the largest in the country's history. Despite the high degree of political polarisation generated by events in Lebanon within Israel, almost all protest passed off peacefully. The main exception was an incident in February 1983 in which a hand grenade was tossed into a group of Peace Now demonstrators in Jerusalem. One person was killed in this attack.

The ethnic cleavage was the source of serious unrest in 1959 and 1971. The disturbances in 1959 were sparked off by an incident in Wadi Salib, a poor and almost wholly Oriental suburb of Haifa. Called to deal with a brawl in a bar, the police shot and wounded a Moroccan involved in the trouble who resisted arrest. A rumour that the Moroccan had died in the shooting prompted a large and angry crowd of Moroccan immigrants to gather outside Wadi Salib's police station. An attempt by the police to disperse the crowd led to extensive rioting. The episode shocked the political establishment and a commission was appointed to investigate its causes, bringing to light widespread Oriental resentment over discrimination and the privileged position of Ashkenazim. The unrest in 1971 arose out of the activities of the Black Panthers, a small radical movement formed largely by young Oriental Jews unable to find jobs as a result of brushes with the law. Early in that year, the Black Panthers applied to the police to stage a demonstration in Jerusalem. They were refused a permit and on the eve of their proposed demonstration several were taken into custody by the police. Despite the ban and the arrests, the demonstration went ahead with some 400 participants, passing off relatively peacefully. However, a further demonstration in May 1971 in the centre of Jerusalem degenerated into a riot lasting several hours in which three Molotov cocktails were thrown. Although briefly boosted by the notoriety they acquired as a result, the Black Panthers went into decline after the government took steps to tackle some of the grievances among Orientals that they had brought to light.

Religious issues have been by far the most consistent and frequent cause of disturbances within the Jewish community in Israel. They have acquired especial prominence in the 1980s – indeed, at times, the confrontation between the ultra-orthodox and the rest of society has escalated to a point where Israelis have ranked its importance above that with the Arab world in opinion surveys. Further, the manner in which the police have handled protests by the ultra-orthodox has attracted more criticism than practically any other aspect of the police's duties. There are two main factions among the ultra-orthodox, those that accept the legitimacy of the state of Israel and participate in its institutions, and a much smaller and more radical faction which refuses to recognise the state's authority. The former are represented politically through the religious parties, principally the National Religious Party and Agudat Yisrael, attracting between 10 and 15 per cent of the vote in national elections. The latter are centred on the Neturei Karta (Guardians of the City), a group of several hundred families concentrated in a small area of Jerusalem.

Securing Jewish conformity with the Halakha (Judaic religious law) constitutes the principal outward objective of the ultra-orthodox. Two factors have assisted the ultra-orthodox in pressing their case: the pivotal position of the religious parties within Israel's political system, and the ambivalent attitude of many non-orthodox Israelis towards the demands of the ultra-orthodox, which arises from the contribution of religion towards the forging of Jewish identity and its place in their heritage. Both factors have affected the police's handling of disturbances arising out of direct action taken by the ultra-orthodox; direct action has long been a favoured tactic when other means have failed to ensure compliance with the Halakha. In the 1950s and 1960s, an issue at the forefront of ultra-orthodox protests was the dissection of bodies for medical research. Despite a number of attempts by the government to achieve a compromise that would satisfy the ultra-orthodox, by 1962 protest had escalated into violent clashes between the police and the ultra-orthodox outside hospital gates. A further governmental inquiry into the issue leading to legislation restricting the circumstances in which dissections could take place still failed to end the protests, and police protection had to be given to doctors singled out by the ultra-orthodox. However, in spite of numerous attacks on doctors and their homes, prosecution of ultra-orthodox assailants very rarely occurred.

Since 1977 there has been an intensification of conflict over religious issues. In 1980 and 1981 serious violence erupted over a motorway which skirted religious suburbs of Jerusalem. The ultra-orthodox objected to the fact that the residents of Ramot used the motorway on the Sabbath; in October and November 1980 ultra-orthodox demonstrators stoned vehicles using the motorway on the Sabbath in defiance of their wishes. While the police took action to stop the stoning, no arrests were made in spite of damage to several passing vehicles. The demonstrations continued into 1981. Following a day of stone-throwing on the Ramot road in March, a riot erupted in the Mea Shearim, one of the religious suburbs, in which 10 police officers were seriously injured. After written orders had been issued by the Inspector-General of the Israel Police, a police operation was mounted by regular police and a Border Police unit to search Toldot Aharon Yeshiva, a religious school of the Neturei Karta in the Mea Shearim. Violent resistance to the operation prompted a violent over-reaction from the police. In response, the ultra-orthodox staged a massive demonstration in the centre of Jerusalem and appealed to the religious leader of the Druze community to make representations to the Inspector-General over the use of the Border Police, apparently with some success.

In 1981 and 1984, ultra-orthodox objections to archaelogical excavations in the city of Jerusalem gave rise to violent incidents, while their objections to 'immodest' attire has been a frequent cause of minor disturbances. In the summer of 1986, a campaign was mounted by the ultra-orthodox against advertisements for swim wear on bus shelters, in which a large number of shelters were destroyed. In response, a group calling itself Terror Against The Ultra-Orthodox daubed swastikas on Tel Aviv's main synagogue and ransacked two religious schools. Part of the explanation for this violent reaction is to be found in the police's unwillingness to take strong action against breaches of the law by the ultra-orthodox. A 1983 study of the police's handling of religious protests in Israel concluded that the police assumed 'the role of mediator of rights rather than enforcer of law'[11] when responding to actions by the ultra-orthodox in respect of the Halakha.

While divisions within the Jewish community have a high profile in Israeli life, none has ever presented as serious a threat to public order as those arising from the Arab–Israeli conflict. In the first two decades of Israel's existence, infiltration across the country's borders by guerrillas recruited from Palestinian refugees living outside Israel constituted the main threat to Israel in this context, for (prior to 1967) the Arabs within Israel remained relatively quiescent, with few incidences of mass action in Arab areas of the country. However, since the 1967 war there has been a radicalisation of the Israeli Arab population as a result of contact with their fellow Palestinians in the occupied territories, and in response to land expropriations. It has been reflected in high levels of political mobilisation, including participation in demonstrations. Veiled threats by government ministers of the mass expulsion of Israeli Arabs have failed to deter their protests, which have frequently led to violent confrontations between demonstrators and the Israel Defence Forces or the Border Police.

Some of the most serious clashes occurred on 30 March 1976, the day of a general strike amongst Israeli Arabs to protest against land expropriations in the Galilee and Negev. The 'Day of the Land' was widely observed in Arab areas of Israel, with the shutting of shops and offices in Arab towns and villages and the staging of a large number of demonstrations, in the course of which six demonstrators were shot dead by members of the Israel Defence Forces, four in a village placed under curfew by the military authorities. This example illustrates the principal differences between the handling of demonstrations originating in the subordinate community and the treatment accorded protest inside the Jewish community. They are the regular use of the military or paramilitary organisations such as the Border Police and the Green Patrol[12] rather than the ordinary police to quell disturbances, and the frequent resort to firearms to disperse demonstrations, with consequent fatalities.

In the occupied territories themselves, where there has been much less readiness among the Arab population to accommodate to Israeli rule, violence has become endemic, though it has varied in intensity over the years. A period of relative quiescence lasting up to the end of 1973 followed the initial resistance to the imposition of Israeli rule in 1968 and 1969. Between November 1975 and April 1976, a wave of unrest engulfed the West Bank, initially partly in response to international support for the PLO at the United Nations and later in reaction to the activities of Gush Emunim, which was pressing for the incorporation of the West Bank into Israel as Judea and Samaria. This culminated in the election of a number of radical mayors supportive of the PLO in local elections on the West Bank. Likud's election victory in 1977 and the support the new government gave to Jewish settlements throughout the West Bank led to a process of creeping annexation which gave rise to further conflict. Widespread demonstrations, in which six Arabs were shot dead, followed the dismissal of three radical mayors and their replacement by Israeli Army officers in March 1982. A pattern of violence in which demonstrations by the local population or attacks on the security forces ranging from stone-throwing to petrol-bombing are followed by punitive measures by the military authorities, leading to further disturbances, has become established. Increasingly, too, the settlers have become embroiled in the violence and a number of 'tit-for-tat' killings have occurred, though with many more deaths among the local Arab population than among the settlers. As the Karp Report showed, the ordinary police have been notably ineffective in curbing settler violence against Arabs. A further cause of disturbances in recent years has been the activities of Rabbi Kahane's Kach Party, which advocates the expulsion of Arabs from both Israel and the occupied territories, and which has sought to provoke confrontation by the staging of marches through Arab villages.

Although violence from the occupied territories has occasionally spilled over into violence in Israel itself, Palestinian terrorism originating outside of territory controlled by Israel still constitutes far and away the main source of political violence in terms of fatalities in Israel. Almost all the most serious incidences of terrorism (such as the attack on Maalot in May 1974 in which 20 schoolchildren died, the attack on the Savoy Hotel in Tel Aviv in March 1975 in which 18 people died, and the landing by 11 members of Al Fatah south of Haifa in March 1978 which led to the deaths of 35 Israelis) were the result of armed incursions by Palestinians across the country's international borders. This partly accounts for the emphasis that continues to be placed on the external dimension of security, and for the tendency to treat threats to public order originating from the Arab population of Israel and the occupied territories in this wider context, thus limiting the role of civilian policing.

PUBLIC PERCEPTIONS OF THE POLICE

A common feature of divided societies – especially those in which it is possible to draw a clear distinction between dominant and subordinate communities – is the polarisation of attitudes towards the police, as the cases of Northern Ireland and South Africa in this book show. Typically, the dominant community looks on the police as the guarantor of its position, while the subordinate community tends to see the police as the agents of their oppression by the dominant community. This factor has proved of relatively minor importance in shaping popular perceptions of the Israel Police, especially those of the dominant community. In part, this reflects the limited role played by the police in relation to the maintenance of internal security, notwithstanding the enlargement of the police's mandate in 1974. In part, it also reflects the marginal position of the Arab minority within Israel politically, geographically, and economically, as a consequence of which the minority is not seen as posing a serious challenge to the position of the dominant community in a domestic context. This view might change if Israel annexed the occupied territories, but that would require a more fundamental change in the dominant community's conception of the boundaries of Israel than the Right has hitherto been able to bring about through advancing the notion of the land of Israel, incorporating Judea and Samaria.

In the early years of the state the principal factors affecting the dominant community's perceptions of the police were the Israel Police's inheritance of the negative image of the Palestine Police and the often unpleasant memories that immigrants brought with them of policing in the countries they had left. Enforcement of the law tended to be associated in many people's minds with oppression. Whereas the state of Israel enjoyed enormous prestige as the guardian of the community, the status of the law remained low. In an interview with the writer Amos Oz in November 1981, a Jewish former member of the Palestine Police recalled his idealistic expectation that the establishment of the state of Israel would do away with the need for a police force altogether.[13] This legacy continues to affect attitudes towards the police, and it is still the case that the state has greater legitimacy than the law, the reverse of the situation that prevails, for example, in Britain. In particular, the law tends to be seen as negotiable, especially in relation to minor infractions. This attitude is well described by Amos Elon:

> Few Israelis respond to police orders in the streets without pro-longed argument. Few will docilely accept a traffic ticket for jay-walking, speeding, or driving through a red light, without an intense effort to dissuade the issuing officer from writing out his form, or without, at least, an attempt to bargain over the para-graph he has chosen to describe the contravention, which may call for a higher fine than another paragraph on his list. Bribes are rare and likely to be ineffective; persistent argument, whether reason-able or not, is more often crowned with success.[14]

Elon partly attributes what he describes as the proverbial timidity of the police to their unease in practising a traditionally un-Jewish profession. The fact that involvement in minor traffic violations forms a very common type of contact between the public and the police has tended to reinforce the low standing accorded to much of police work. The composition of the force (especially the prevalence of Orientals in the lower ranks) is another factor that has tended to underline the low status of the police. Opinion surveys have also indicated that the public has little confidence that the police perform their primary function of fighting crime effectively. A victimisation survey carried out with the co-operation of the police in 1979 re-vealed that many Israelis were reluctant to report crimes to the police. 57 per cent of the victims of theft, and 38 per cent of assault victims, failed to file complaints.

While the role the police play in the maintenance of internal security necessarily looms much larger in the daily lives of Arabs in Israel and the occupied territories than it does in the experiences of the dominant community, the limited role and the subordinate posi-tion of the police in the security field have tended to deflect Palesti-nian criticism of Israeli policies away from the police as an institution. Although members of the Israel Police frequently appear in accounts of the violation of human rights in Israel and the occupied territories (such as the torture of suspects during interrogation, the harassment of civilians at roadblocks, and the use of excessive force against demonstrators) the police's involvement in such activities has tended to be less conspicuous than those of other institutions, such as the Israel Defence Forces and Shin Bet. For example, a scandal over the deaths of two bus hijackers in 1984 while they were in the custody of Shin Bet led to the resignation of the head of Shin Bet in June 1986. Shin Bet was also at the centre of allegations by Amnesty International in 1986 of the maltreatment of suspects in the occupied territories. In general, however, the variety of institutions involved in the control of the Arab minority has made it more productive for critics of Israeli policy to focus on particular practices that violate human rights than to single out the operations of a particular institution. For instance, *The Sunday Times*'s 1977 *exposé* of Israel's use of torture named four different institutions (one of which was the Special Duties Division of the Israel Police) as implicated in the maltreatment of prisoners.

In his defence of police operations on the West Bank following the publication of the Karp Report in 1984, Commander Karty of the Israel Police emphasised the difficulties his force encountered in policing a 'hostile and disaffected Arab population', and contrasted the situation on the West Bank with that in Israel inside the Green Line. However, while there have been attacks on police stations in the occupied territories, there appears to be little opposition to routine activities of the police or to the police as such, judging by accounts of investigations of ordinary crime within the Arab population in the occupied territories. A 1980 survey of Israeli Arab opinion revealed a higher level of satisfaction with the functioning of the legal system (58 per cent) than with the operation of Israeli democracy (37 per cent). The absence of specific studies or opinion surveys of Arab attitudes towards the police makes it hazardous to generalise further on the feelings of the subordinate community about the Israel Police.

THE POLICE AS A POLITICAL INSTITUTION

The fact that the Israel Police was seen as the successor of the Palestine Police was the most important determinant of its place within the political system after independence. Israel's first Minister of the Interior successfully resisted the inclusion of the police in his Ministry on the grounds that the police's association with the Mandate would adversely affect the image of his department, and ensured that the police remained the responsibility of a separate Ministry. From the outset, too, the negative image the police inherited from the Mandate placed the position of Minister of Police at the bottom of the political pecking order within the Cabinet. The first Minister of

Police was Behor Shitrit, at independence a member of the small Sephardic Party and the only Oriental to be given a Cabinet post. During Israel's first decade he remained the only Oriental in the Cabinet. He held the post of Minister of Police for almost 19 years. His two successors as Minister of Police were also Orientals, leading the Israeli sociologist, Sammy Smooha, to characterise the position of Minister of Police as an 'Oriental benign quota'.[15] It was an arrangement that did little to enhance the status of either the Ministry of Police or of Oriental Jews. On the contrary, it tended to confirm the low political standing of both.

The pattern was broken by Likud's election victory in 1977. Under Likud, the Ministry of Police was absorbed into the Ministry of the Interior, with the post of Minister of Police disappearing and the Minister of the Interior assuming political responsibility for the police in Cabinet. It was argued in favour of the change that the existence of an independent Cabinet agency had worked to the disadvantage of the police because the Minister of Police had been an isolated figure in Cabinet with little political influence. The Prime Minister (Menachem Begin) advanced the argument that the post of Minister of Police was characteristic of totalitarian regimes; a different explanation of the change was that the enlargement of the mandate of the Ministry of the Interior had been a political concession that the leader of the National Religious Party and Minister of the Interior (Yosuf Burg) had wrung from Begin in the bargaining over the formation of a new coalition. In short, according to the critics, empire-building by Burg was the main reason for the change. The new arrangement lasted seven years. After the 1984 general election and the establishment of a national unity government that included Labour and Likud, the Ministry of Police was re-established as an independent Cabinet agency. However, there was a change from past practice. The post of Minister of Police was filled by a leading figure in the Labour Party, and former Chief of Staff, Haim Bar-Lev.

The influence of the political system on police operations has taken a variety of forms. In a study of demonstrations in Israel between 1950 and 1980 Professor Lehman-Wilzig concluded that the police's handling of demonstrations by the ultra-orthodox varied according to the composition of government. The enforcement of the law was most lenient when both the National Religious Party and Agudat Yisrael were part of the government, slightly less so when only the National Religious Party was in government, and most stringent in the two years when neither party had a place in government. The effect of the 1977 transfer of the police to the Ministry of the Interior, a portfolio held by the National Religious Party, was to make the police more tolerant than ever of religious demonstrations. Apart from such generalised influences, there have been specific instances of political interference in the conduct of police investigations. The most notable was the Afarsek (rotten peach) affair, which led to Shafir's dismissal as Inspector-General of the Israel Police at the start of 1981. The origin of the affair was a police raid on the offices of the Ministry of Religious Affairs in August 1980, a raid prompted by allegations made by the Ministry's former Director-General against the Minister of Religious Affairs, Aharon Abuhatzeira. Shafir had authorised the raid after obtaining permission from the Attorney-General's office but provided no advance notification of the raid to his political superior, the Minister of the Interior, because he feared that Burg would attempt to obstruct the investigation of fraud on the part of a fellow member of the National Religious Party.

Shafir's fears on this score were soon to be confirmed. Shortly after the police raid Burg demanded that the investigation be suspended until after the country's general election in 1981. (Burg's public admission that he had made this demand followed his dismissal of Shafir.) Burg alleged that Shafir attempted to blackmail him by assembling the so-called Afarsek file on financial irregularities in the Ministry of the Interior implicating the National Religious Party in further wrong-doing. Shafir denied the allegation of blackmail, but refused to show Burg the file. On 1 January 1981, Burg dismissed Shafir from his position as Inspector-General of the Israel Police. His explanation of the dismissal, which centred on Shafir's refusal to submit to civilian control and his insensitivity to civil rights in the conduct of police investigations, contained a further list of complaints against the former Inspector-General, including giving false information to the press to get testimony from a witness and secretly recording a meeting in the Ministry of the Interior. Burg's conduct contrasted sharply with that of Shlomo Hillel, the Minister of Police in the previous government, who had refused to interfere with police investigations of political corruption, despite the damage to his party in the period just before the 1977 general election. In 1985, the police's investigation of allegations of land fraud on the West Bank (entailing the questioning of the Deputy Minister of Defence) brought protests from Likud prompting charges in the Israeli press of political interference with the investigation.

The political outlook of the police themselves has not been an issue in Israel, with the exception of a short-lived controversy over a special unit of the Border Police established in 1977 at Kiryat Arba. Although the ostensible basis of recruitment to the unit was residential, the consequence of basing it at Kiryat Arba (a Jewish settlement on the West Bank which Gush Emunim had established) was a unit made up exclusively of adherents of the pro-settlement movement. The issue prompted a debate in the Knesset. Although the government successfully defended its establishment of the unit in the Knesset debate, the danger that the unit might function as Gush Emunim's private army in the end persuaded the government to accede to demands for the unit's disbandment.

CONCLUSION

References to the Israel Police as an institution in general studies of the politics of Israel are sparse, to say the least, although particular episodes such as the Wadi Salib riots or the Afarsek affair have attracted passing mention. In addition, there are very few specific studies of the force outside the pages of specialist police journals. Indeed, as significant a feature of the Israel Police as its relatively low status is its low profile, both within Israel and externally. At first sight, this seems most surprising. Israel (including the occupied territories) has many of the features of deeply divided societies, such as Northern Ireland and South Africa, in which controversy over the role of the police constitutes a central aspect of the conflict between dominant and subordinate communities. In short, why has the Israel Police escaped the kind of criticism, described elsewhere in this book, that both the South African Police and the Royal Ulster Constabulary have attracted?

The simplest explanation is the limited role played by the Israel Police in the field of security. Restricting the police's involvement in this field has the very considerable advantage that ordinary policing of the subordinate community, such as the investigation of non-political crime, is not compromised by hostility towards the police's security role. However, there is little evidence that this factor has influenced government policy on the role of the police, while the police themselves have sought to enlarge their security functions as a way of enhancing the force's status. While the police's limited security role is partly the result of historical circumstance, the fundamental explanation is to be found at a deeper level. It lies in the legitimising role in relation to security of the external threat to

Israel's existence as a state. In most societies, the use of the military in an internal security role is a most unattractive option for government outside of a national emergency or of circumstances such as low level guerrilla warfare that the police are not equipped to handle. The reason is obvious enough. Deployment of the military constitutes a signal to the outside world of the existence of a serious threat to the state that is likely to detract from the state's legitimacy in an international context. In particular, any government seeking to convey an impression of normality to the outside world will deploy the police rather than the military, where it can.[16]

These considerations do not apply in the case of Israel. On the contrary, Israel's struggle for existence as a state in a hostile region enjoys much greater support internationally (and especially in the West) than would be forthcoming if Israel appeared threatened by internal conflict divorced from the threat of inter-state war. Consequently, treating the control of the Arab minority in Israel and the occupied territories as a function of the larger Arab–Israeli conflict by deploying the Israel Defence Forces in an internal security role, is a more attractive option for Israeli governments than attempting to present the control of the Arab population as a normal aspect of domestic policy. The treatment of the divide between Jews and Arabs in Israel and the occupied territories as a domestic question would invite damaging comparisons between Israel and other societies characterised by the political oppression of minorities, unless it was accompanied by far-reaching changes in the rights accorded to the Arab minority, including the right to give expression to their national aspirations. This in itself would pose a fundamental challenge to the Zionist ethos of the state. Paradoxically, in Israel's circumstances, enlarging the scope of civilian policing might give rise to greater international criticism of Israel's security policies than they seem likely to attract as long as they are viewed as part of the country's defence. If little change can be expected in the role of the Israel Police in this context, the main problems facing the force are likely to remain those of policing a majority community that accords greater legitimacy to the state – and, in the case of the religious, to the Halakha – than to the law.

Notes

1. M. Begin, *The Revolt* (London: Allen & Unwin, 1951).
2. M. Gurevitch, B. Danet, and G. Schwartz, 'The Image of the Police in Israel' (1971) 367–88.

3. *Israel Police Annual Report 1978* (Jerusalem: The Israel Police, 1979) p. 26.
4. S. Reiser, 'The Israeli Police: Politics and Priorities' (1983) 34.
5. Quoted in G.J. Bensinger, 'The Israel Police in Transition: An Organizational Study' (1981) 3.
6. *Israel Police Annual Report 1975* (Jerusalem: The Israel Police, 1976) p. 32.
7. Reiser, 'The Israel Police', 27.
8. Interview in *Law Enforcement News* (New York, 27 October, 1980) pp. 8–10.
9. See *The Karp Report: An Israeli Government Inquiry into Settler Violence Against Palestinians on the West Bank* (1984).
10. S. Lehman-Wilzig, 'Public Demonstrators and the Israeli Police: The Policy and Practice of Successful Protest Control' (1983) 44.
11. S. Reiser, 'Cultural and Political Influences on Police Discretion: The Case of Israel' (1983) 15.
12. A paramilitary unit within the Ministry of Agriculture.
13. A. Oz, *In the Land of Israel* (London: Fontana, 1983) p. 209.
14. A. Elon, *The Israelis* (Harmondsworth: Penguin, 1983) p. 301.
15. S. Smooha, *Israel: Pluralism and Conflict* (London, Routledge & Kegan Paul, 1978) p. 373.
16. See, for example, the chapter on Northern Ireland (Chapter 3) in this book.

7 South Africa

BACKGROUND

The South African state was founded in 1910. Since 1948 it has been under the control of the Afrikaans dominated National Party, which has pursued the policy of racial segregation and inequality we know as 'apartheid'. More recently, however, the South African state seems to be changing its form and practice. It is possible to compile an entensive catalogue of changes which have abolished some of the worst features of apartheid and extended new rights to Black South Africans.[1] It is moving away from a position Hanf once called 'uni-lateral conflict regulation' (where the interests of one group in society dominate over those of other groups), toward a position where the consent and co-operation of subordinate groups is more important in decision-making.[2] Speeches by government ministers are replete with references to the mistakes made in the past and how, in the new era of realism, the needs and interests of Black South Africans cannot be ignored. But most commentators are agreed that while the South African state is encouraging deracialisation in the economy and social life, it is resistant to full and genuine political deracialisation.[3] The state seems to be attempting to change apartheid without destroying White political supremacy. Hence the frequent reference by commentators to the gap between the appearance and reality of change in modern South Africa.

There is currently, therefore, a tension in South Africa between what can be called 'social liberty' and 'social control': there is a gradual opening up of South African society and an extension of basic rights to Blacks, but in practice Black South Africans remain subject to strict social control. Hence the paradox of the country: while things are changing, they also remain very much the same. This is so for two reasons. The extension of social liberties to Blacks is chimerical, for most of the rights are so bound with qualifications and controls that they do not greatly extend the range of actions which Blacks are free to do.[4] Secondly, many of the changes affect only a minority of Black South Africans, and actually involve a curtailment of the freedom of the majority by restricting the potentials for action which the majority are free to do. Thus one has in South Africa's case the contradiction of a state extending rights and protections to its

157

Black citizens, while still severely repressing activity which falls outside the narrow limits which the state defines as lawful and legitimate.

This affects policing. The orthodox portrayal of the South African Police (SAP) as the stormtroopers of apartheid, impervious to internal control, is simplistic. There is a change in SAP policy with regard to such things as the treatment of detainees, where it has adopted guidelines similar to those which the British government operates in Northern Ireland, the increasing use of open court in place of bannings, the easing of promotion prospects for Black policemen, and so on. But the need for the South African state to increase its legitimacy by consulting with Blacks and moderating its behaviour toward them is important to the state only to the extent that this does not conflict with the substantive goal of continued White political supremacy. Thus, many of the excesses of apartheid are being diluted only in such a way that does not prejudice this goal. This is evident, for example, in the reforms of the security legislation (where some of its provisions have been considerably strengthened), and in the treatment of detainees (where the code of conduct is so qualified as to permit monitoring only by government-appointed personnel). Above all this paradox is a feature of the policing of public order situations, where the state's policy changes still allow the SAP the autonomy to use considerable brutality to police the townships when protest becomes effective in threatening White political supremacy.

STRUCTURE, ORGANISATION AND FINANCE

The federal – and increasingly confederal – nature of South Africa's political system has produced a complicated juxtaposition of centralisation and local autonomy in the structure and organisation of the SAP. Table 7.1 shows that there are various police bodies functioning at national and provincial levels in South Africa. The largest and oldest is the SAP, which acts as a national force. For a time after union in 1910 each of the four provinces continued to maintain their own police force, but the SAP came into being in 1913. There also existed a separate military police known as the South African Mounted Riflemen, but their responsibilities were absorbed into the SAP in 1926. In the ensuing years, the SAP also took over the policing of the cities of Durban and Pietermaritzberg, who retained their own colonial police force for a long time after union, and in

Table 7.1 Police bodies in South Africa

National	Provincial/Local	African Areas Only
South African Police (now incorporating the former South African Railways and Harbour Police)	Municipal Traffic Police	Independent homeland police
Police Reserve (part-time)	Provincial Traffic Police	Non-independent homeland paramilitary forces
Reserve Police Force (part-time)	Area Defence Units (part-time)	Municipal Law Enforcement Officers in the townships
South African Police Wachtihuis (part-time)		Kitskonstabels

1939 the SAP assumed responsibility for the mandated territory of Namibia. The provinces have retained autonomy over traffic police. The Provincial Traffic Police is employed by each province (including Namibia) for traffic control in rural areas outside the jurisdiction of the Municipal Traffic Police, which is a force employed by the large municipal authorities for traffic control in the town's boundaries. At one time, there was another national force, the South African Railways and Harbour Police, which policed the transport services. In 1984, the manpower of the regular SAP totalled 44 696, while that of the Railways and Harbour Police was 7231, only slightly below its authorised complement of 7637. This was nonetheless large in relation to other transport police forces. The size of South Africa's transport police reflected the character of apartheid, for its officers policed the transportation of Blacks from the segregated townships, which are designed as mere dormitories for Black labour. It is also a measure of how politicised transport had become in the campaign of protest against apartheid. Partly for these reasons, the Railways and Harbour Police were absorbed into the SAP in 1986, which leaves the SAP as the only national force in South Africa.

This combination of national and provincial responsibility and central and local jurisdiction is further complicated by the separate political structures which exist for Africans. All the 'independent' homelands have developed their own police force under their control as part of their transition to so called nationhood, and some of the non-independent homelands have more *ad hoc* paramilitary forces under the direct responsibility of the Chief Minister. These forces have jurisdiction only within the borders of the homeland. The 1984 Annual Report of the Commissioner of the SAP revealed that 33 policemen from Transkei, 41 from Kwa Zulu and 38 from Ciskei had undergone training with the SAP in counter-insurgency and riot control. This is not only an attempt to prevent infiltration by guerrillas but also reflects how public disorder is also now occurring in the rural areas.

The development of African controlled city and town councils to administer African affairs in the urban townships has also given rise to a new police force operating at a local level. The power to have their own police force was granted to 32 African townships in December 1984; by February 1986, 750 Municipal Law Enforcement Officers had graduated from the Lenz Military Base, where they are trained separately from the SAP. Soweto Council (the largest African authority) had 270 officers by 1985 and spent R1.7 million on security, which only partly included policing. The powers granted by the central government insist that commissioned officers within these township forces be drawn from those policemen from the SAP who are attached to development boards, which are White-appointed bodies who once ran the townships and now act as advisors to the African councils. Indeed, the whole of Soweto's force in 1986 consisted of policemen formerly attached to the West Rand Administration Board. The role of Municipal Law Enforcement Officers is an auxiliary one to the SAP. They are charged with protecting the lives of African councillors and guarding municipal installations and government buildings, thus freeing the SAP to concentrate on policing the townships. The formal powers of Soweto's force, while consisting of conventional duties like supporting the SAP in maintaining law and order and preventing crime in the township, also include the overtly political role of ensuring 'the implementation of council decisions'. The force can also be required to assist the SAP in 'riotous conditions'. Thus, operationally, the township forces are in an ambiguous position for they are partly under the direction of the local African politicians (although their powers of control come from central government) and partly the SAP, whose responsibilities are avowedly not to the African councillors who administer the townships. In 1986, Black special constables were formed in the townships, known as 'Kitskonstabels', with similar functions to the municipal police. Unless otherwise stated, the focus of this chapter will be on the SAP.

The head office of the SAP is in Pretoria. For purposes of control South Africa is divided into 19 divisions, each commanded by a divisional commissioner. Each division is sub-divided into a number of police districts, each under the command of a district commandant. In 1985 there were 32 police districts. Each is sub-divided into a number of station areas, each under the command of a station commander. In 1985 there were 816 police stations and 39 border control posts in South Africa. The Commissioner of the SAP is responsible for the command, supervision and control of the force, under the direction of the Minister of Law and Order. The Commissioner is replaced every two years, which usually prevents him being able to stamp his personality and policy on the force. On completion of training all probationary policemen and women become members of the uniform branch, in which the majority of members serve. There are many specialist divisions in the force, including the criminal investigation branch, diamond and gold branch, commercial branch, narcotics bureau, stock theft unit and a special murder and robbery unit based in the large cities. In addition, there is a security branch. In 1984 a Special Guard was established to protect government buildings and government ministers. Major General Van Zyl, officer in command of the unit, likened it to the British Special Air Services. There is also a separate Special Task Force to counter hijacking and hostage-taking. The uniformed branch are assisted by a volunteer Reserve Police Force (established in 1961) and the Police Reserve, which consists of ex-members of the SAP who may be called to do duty for 30 days a year up to five years after leaving the regular force. In 1984, these two part-time forces had a manpower of 37 477.

The Security Branch is independent from the National Intelligence Service (NIS), whose forerunner was the infamous Bureau of State Security (BOSS). The Security Branch is part of the SAP and operates within its formal structure of authority, while the NIS reports directly to the State President via the State Security Council. In addition, there is also a Military Intelligence Branch dealing with 'military matters', which sometimes overlaps with the security branch and NIS. It is worth briefly dwelling on South Africa's secret services. In the 1984–85 financial year R84 million was spent on 'secret services', which did not include the SAP's Security Branch, representing a 25 per cent increase over the previous year. The NIS co-ordinates the various security services outside the SAP, although there is said to be rivalry between the security forces, with the NIS feeling that there is a need for only one security force independent of the SAP.[5] The State Security Council acts as a political overseer of security. This is the only Cabinet committee established in law and chaired by the head of government; it operates the network of Joint Management Centres which co-ordinate security at the local level. The committee decides upon the 'security matters' reported to it, but its composition suggests that it sees security in wide terms, with allegations being made that it involves itself in trade union affairs and in questions of land redistribution. It meets fortnightly, and in Parliament the State President, P.W. Botha, announced that its membership comprised, among others, 56 per cent from NIS, 16 per cent from the South African Defence Force (SADF), 11 per cent from the Department of Foreign Affairs, 1 per cent from the security branch of the SAP, 5 per cent from the Railways and Harbour Police and 1 per cent from the Prisons Service. A variety of government ministers have been co-opted, representing the ministries which are felt to touch security matters. These include the Ministers of Law and Order, Defence, Foreign Affairs, Justice, Constitutional Development and Planning, and Co-operation and Development, the latter two dealing with urban Black affairs. In as much as the committee has representation from the intelligence services, military and police, all of these have a *de facto* role in political decision-making.

The Police Act 1958 defines the functions of the SAP to be the promotion of internal stability in South Africa and its dependant territories, the maintenance of law and order and the prevention of crime. As in other societies where there are inhibitions on the development of a specialised administrative service, the SAP are also responsible for a variety of tasks tangentially related to these functions. These include administering the agricultural census in rural areas, guarding South Africa's territorial fisheries and manning customs posts along national boundaries. There is also a merger between policing and the administration of justice, for in all rural areas (where there are no public prosecutors) the police institute criminal prosecutions. In many smaller towns they act as assistant clerks and messengers of the courts, as well as excise officers, immigration officers, wardens and revenue officers. They also assist in the registration of births and deaths, serve as health inspectors, inspectors of vehicles and licences, postal agents and mortuary attendants. These duties evince that South Africa does not separate policing, the administration of justice and civil administration; this is a feature which is characteristic of other dimensions of policing in South Africa: it is symptomatic of the state's reliance on the police in areas which usually lie outside normal police work.

This reliance is effected, however, without there being an unusually large regular police force in South Africa. As Table 7.2 shows, in 1984 the regular force comprised only 44 696 officers. Despite the authoritarian nature of the South African state, this represented only 1.4 policemen and women per 1000 of the population, comparing favourably with liberal-democratic countries. The South African ratio has oscillated around this proportion since the inception of the SAP. In 1913, the ratio was 1.4 and reached its highest level in 1958 with 1.9.[6] In 1976, at the height of the Soweto disturbances, the ratio was 1.3, the same as 1931.[7]

Government ministers have applauded themselves on this low ratio and the zero rate of expansion of police manpower in real terms which it reveals. However, such is the nature of the South African state that a massive police manpower is not needed to police apartheid.

Table 7.2 Regular SAP manpower 1960–84

Year	Authorised manpower		Actual manpower		Civilian staff		Ratio per 1000 of
	White	Black	White	Black	White	Black	population
1960	13 365	14 642	11 938	13 786	514	–	1.61
1961	–	–	–	–	–	–	–
1962	13 545	14 780	12 778	13 853	543	–	1.59
1963	14 348	14 691	13 770	13 673	489	–	1.66
1964	15 592	15 177	14 528	13 812	600	–	1.56
1965	15 954	15 177	14 678	14 080	646	–	1.60
1966	16 606	15 689	15 437	14 056	820	–	1.61
1967	17 762	15 684	16 316	14 810	974	–	1.66
1968	17 926	15 701	16 587	15 166	1075	–	1.65
1969	18 422	16 026	16 376	15 532	1386	–	1.61
1970	18 587	16 199	16 346	15 531	1172	28	1.46
1971	18 629	15 924	16 776	15 333	1278	293	1.42
1972	18 638	15 876	17 063	15 218	1345	270	1.40
1973	18 877	16 603	16 366	15 222	1358	264	1.29
1974	18 870	16 320	16 862	15 713	1538	273	1.30
1975	19 016	16 507	17 179	15 903	1584	285	1.27
1976	18 883	16 752	17 799	16 638	1539	299	1.31
1977	–	–	18 817	16 202	–	–	1.29
1978	–	–	19 341	15 624	–	–	1.26
1979	21 118	17 447	18 464	15 612	1809	554	1.19
1980	–	–	18 307	15 907	–	–	1.19
1981	23 304	20 222	17 303	16 968	–	–	1.16
1982	23 540	20 464	22 152	20 375	–	–	1.41
1983	–	–	21 731	21 009	–	–	1.38
1984	22 997	22 564	23 206	21 490	2448	2770	1.41

Source: *Annual Reports* of the Commissioner of the South African Police, except for 1980 and 1983, which are taken from the annual survey of race relations published by the South African Institute of Race Relations. The ratio of manpower per 1000 of population is based on actual manpower, and excludes civilian staff. The population figures used to calculate this ratio were the United Nations' annual mid-year estimate, and can be found in *International Financial Statistics*, published monthly by the International Monetary Fund. The United Nations' estimates include the populations of the 'independent' homelands.

Ratios of this low order become understandable in the context of the amount of social control generated by the extensive range of political, economic and social institutions in the apartheid state. As Frankel has pointed out, the SAP have forged links with other agencies of control in both the public and private sectors, and the SAP's manpower is supplemented by the resources of other functionally compatible government agencies and by the embedding of police activity in a dense informal and quasi-informal social network.[8] The municipal and provincial traffic police, the part-time officers and the Black township police all complement the regular force. In a similar fashion, the legal obligation of White employers to report irregularities in the passes of Black employees means that a good proportion of the surveillance work required by influx control is provided by the private sector. White civilian volunteers are also integrated into police roles through the South African Police Wachtihuis, a force of amateur radio operators who act as a communications link, and through the Area Defence Units, which are a rural militia who monitor infiltration by guerrillas. In addition, the device of compulsory military service for young Whites has been used to channel servicemen into the SAP to offset manpower shortages. Around 1000 servicemen are directed into the SAP each year.[9]

However, the threat to public order posed by the township protests since 1976 has led to a rapid expansion of the regular police in order to rely on more formal policing agencies. From 1976 to 1984, regular manpower levels rose by 29.7 per cent. The projected manpower for 1987 of 87 000 would give South Africa an estimated ratio of 3.4 per 1000 of population, which would increase still further with the projections of police manpower up to 1995, when manpower is expected to have risen by another 100 per cent. There is one other reason for this expansion in the manpower of the regular force. Apartheid generates its own forms of control and surveillance, and now that the South African state is changing its form and practice it increasingly needs to rely on formal policing.

The apartheid state not only influences police manpower but also the command structure of the SAP, which is racially hierarchical. All of the volunteer part-time forces are exclusively White, while the commanding elite of the regular force is overwhelmingly so. Whereas in 1912 the ratio of Black to White policemen and women was 1:3, by 1984 there were many more Black policemen with a ratio of 1:1.07. As Table 7.3 shows, it has oscillated around this proportion since 1960. However, while there is increasing use of Blacks in the SAP, they are predominantly drawn in to fill the lower ranks. It was only in 1976 that Black officers were allowed to wear the same uniforms as White officers, and Black constables were given this dispensation in 1984. Blacks were allowed to join the SAP's Staff Association in 1979 and it was only in 1980 that a Black officer had authority over a lower

Table 7.3   Ratio of Black and White members of the SAP[1]

Year	Ratio
1960	1: 0.86
1961	–
1962	1: 0.92
1963	1: 1.00
1964	1: 1.05
1965	1: 1.04
1966	1: 1.09
1967	1: 1.10
1968	1: 1.09
1969	1: 1.05
1970	1: 1.05
1971	1: 1.09
1972	1: 1.12
1973	1: 1.07
1974	1: 1.07
1975	1: 1.08
1976	1: 1.06
1977	1: 1.16
1978	1: 1.23
1979	1: 1.18
1980	1: 1.15
1981	1: 1.01
1982	1: 1.08
1983	1: 1.03
1984	1: 1.07

Note:
1 Based on actual manpower and excludes civilian staff.

Source: Calculated from the figures in Table 7.2.

ranking White policeman. The first Black major was not appointed until 1978, the first lieutenant colonel in 1980, and the first Black station commander was not appointed until the same year. By June 1980 63 police stations were manned and controlled exclusively by Blacks (see Table 7.4). Discrimination in promotion, training and salaries was widespread, although it was abolished in pay, housing and pension rights in 1984. Recruits from the different race groups are still trained at different locations. Salary differentials were enormous. In 1980 the pay differentials for an Asian and Coloured constable were 12.2 per cent below a White constable at the bottom of the scale and 16.2 per cent below at the top. The equivalent figures for African constables were 39.4 per cent and 31.3 per cent. There is

Table 7.4 Command structure of the regular SAP by race 1983

Race	Rank				
	Major	Captain	Lieutenant	Warrant Officer	Sergeant
African	11	25	28	1138	2626
Coloured	1	8	13	246	505
Asian	2	4	14	247	330
White	470	741	1085	5337	4685

Source: South African Institute of Race Relations, *Annual Survey of Race Relations 1984* (Johannesburg: South African Institute of Race Relations, 1985) p. 786.

also a gender hierarchy. Women were not allowed into the SAP until 1972, and the number of Black policewomen is even smaller. The Cape Province had its first three Black women police constables in August 1985. At that time, there were only 10 Black women Municipal Law Enforcement Officers.

Apartheid also impinges on other features of the organisation of the SAP. The SAP tries to ensure that Blacks police their own areas, which is an attempt to ensure better compliance with (and enforcement of) the domestic laws of the country. This policy also reflects a recognition by the state of the shortage of White manpower and the unfavourable publicity attracted by White policemen brutalising Black citizens. In this regard, Black policemen play an important ideological role. On the one hand they allow some of the policing of apartheid to be carried out by Blacks themselves, while, conversely, this very fact counteracts some criticism of their methods. Police violence acts as a good example of this ideological role in operation. On the twenty-fifth anniversary of the deaths of 69 people in the 1960 Sharpeville massacre, a protest march by 2000 Blacks was fired upon by the police without warning, leaving 40 people dead. It was significant, President Reagan said, when discussing the deaths at a press conference, that Black policemen had been involved and had done the firing. In anticipation of views such as this, White policemen have been withdrawn from the Black townships as far as public disorder allows. This in turn parallels a wider process in state policy toward Blacks, whereby the worst effects of apartheid are being administered by Blacks themselves through various Black Parliamentary and local government structures.

Clearly the nature of the apartheid state allows strong policing to be achieved without an excessively large regular police force. However,

Table 7.5   SAP finance 1960–61 to 1985–86

Financial year	Finance (Rm)	Annual percentage increase	% of finance spent on 'Arms, Equipment and Ammunition'	Finance as % of government expenditure
1960–61	36.854	–	–	4.03
1961–62	38.396	4.18	1.12	3.91
1962–63	40.800	6.26	1.36	3.76
1963–64	45.870	12.42	2.31	3.76
1964–65	49.192	7.24	2.57	3.24
1965–66	56.358	14.56	2.44	3.42
1966–67	58.697	4.15	3.94	3.17
1967–68	66.950	14.06	5.05	3:22
1968–69	72.130	7.73	2.31	3.18
1969–70	85.590	18.66	2.98	3.16
1970–71	94.288	10.16	2.16	2.74
1971–72	104.422	10.74	2.42	2.78
1972–73	111.993	7.25	3.30	2.74
1973–74	118.980	6.23	2.73	2.87
1974–75	153.127	28.69	2.55	2.81
1975–76	168.027	9.73	2.94	2.36
1976–77	176.900	5.28	3.17	2.13
1977–78	204.000	15.31	4.11	2.33
1978–79	220.450	8.06	6.90	2.19
1979–80	245.247	11.24	7.58	2.07
1980–81	309.765	26.30	10.22	2.33
1981–82	–	–	–	–
1982–83	–	–	–	–
1983–84	564.282	–	–	2.47
1984–85	795.640	41.00	–	3.00
1985–86	954.700	19.99	–	2.98

Sources: Figures for SAP finance are taken from the *Annual Statement of Accounts* by the Auditor General, except for 1983 onwards which are taken from various issues of the *South African Digest*. Statistics on government expenditure for the calendar year can be found in *International Financial Statistics*, published monthly by the International Monetary Fund.

the police budget has risen excessively over the years, not least because policing apartheid is expensive in man-hours, technology and equipment. It was only in the 1974–75 financial year that expenditure on education overtook that on policing. In the 1960–61 financial year the police budget was R36.85 million, but by 1985–86 it had risen by an overall annual increase of 13.9 per cent to R954.7 million. However, as Table 7.5 indicates, the police budget, as a proportion of total government expenditure, is still below levels that existed in the early 1960s, following the Sharpeville massacre and the banning of the main Black opposition movements. Nonetheless, township protests since 1983 have caused the police budget to rise at a fast rate. Between the financial years of 1983–84 and 1985–86 the police budget rose by 69 per cent, compared with a 21.4 per cent increase in the defence budget. However, with the involvement of the SADF in internal public order incidents during 1985, the SADF got R245 million of the extra R288 million awarded in February 1986 as an emergency provision. The police got R42 million. This is indicative of how much of the policing of public order incidents in the townships in 1985 was borne by the SADF.

The police budget is voted annually by Parliament and the Commissioner of Police is the officer responsible for all expenditure to the Parliamentary Select Committee on Public Accounts. The police budget does not cover military intelligence, but it is not clear whether it includes all the expenditure of the SAP's Security Branch. The Secret Services Accounts Act 1978 allowed for money to be made available for intelligence without Parliament knowing how it was allocated; after the scandal involving the Department of Information's secret accounts, this provision was changed to allow secret accounts to be audited by the Auditor General. However, most of the SAP's expenditure is publicly accounted for. But at the beginning of the 1985 Parliamentary session a Bill was tabled giving the SAP their own secret account. The Indian Parliament in the tricameral constitutional system rejected the Bill, which was the first example of the three Parliaments failing to agree. The Bill was referred back to the State President, who has the power to refer it to the President's Council (an adjudicating committee) for final decision, where it was accepted because of the National Party's majority on the Council.

FORMAL STRUCTURE OF AUTHORITY

Currently the Minister with political responsibility for the SAP is the Minister of Law and Order, although formerly there have been Ministers of Police. Also in the past this responsibility has not been separated from the administration of justice, with the SAP coming under the jurisdiction of the Minister of Justice. The undesirability of this led to the creation of the Law and Order post, although there is no department of this name. The formal powers granted to the SAP are extensive. The Police Amendment Act (No. 70) 1965 empowered any policeman or woman at any place within a mile of the South African border to search without warrant any person, premises, vehicle, aircraft or 'receptacle of any nature' and to seize anything found. Under an amending act in 1979 this was extended to within 10 kilometres of a border. Eventually in 1983 this power was extended to the whole country, when the SAP were also given the power to search any vehicle at road blocks. The Amending Act (No. 64) 1979 empowered the State President, in the event of war or other emergency, to employ the police to assist in the defence of the Republic, whether inside or outside the country. The State President may also place the SAP under the orders and direction of any person the State President may appoint. The Criminal Procedures Act says that such force 'as may in the circumstances be reasonably necessary' can be used to overcome resistance or stop a person fleeing. It goes on to say that the killing of a person who cannot be arrested or stopped in flight by other means will be deemed to be justifiable homicide. This power has to be seen in the context of the arms policemen and women carry. Every recruit, Black and White, is issued with a side arm and a R1 rifle. The rifle is kept in the strongroom of the station and never taken home, although the side arm can be with permission. In 'riotous circumstances' and border control the SAP are issued with sub-machine guns and shotguns, as well as other riot control technology.

There are powerful legislative controls on the disclosure of police misconduct. The Police Act 1958 prevents the publication of 'untrue material' relating to police misconduct, with the onus of proof of the veracity of the material resting with the publisher. The Police Amendment Act (No. 82) 1980 lays down that no person is allowed to publish information relating to the constitution, conditions, methods of deployment or movement of any force concerned with the prevention of terrorism, including the SAP and Railways and Harbour Police; all such information has to be cleared with the Commissioner of Police first. There are also statutes which prevent the publication of photographs or sketches of people in police custody. There are powers which also limit civil prosecutions arising from police misconduct. The Indemnity Act (No. 90) 1977 gives indemnity to state officials in respect to any action or statement arising from the policing of 'internal unrest'. With this power, the number of deaths and woundings in the course of police duty is high since the current period of unrest began in 1976; and it is still rising as

Table 7.6   Number of deaths and woundings in the course of SAP duty
1976–84

Race	Killed		Wounded		Total by race
	Adult	Juvenile	Adult	Juvenile	
Black	1630	134	4065	579	6408
White	26	2	112	9	140
Total by injury	1792		4765		6557

Source: J.D. Brewer, *After Soweto: An Unfinished Journey* (Oxford:
Clarendon Press, 1986) p. 122.

the unrest escalates. Table 7.6 provides figures for the SAP only and
does not include other policing agencies. In the first six months of
1985 the Railways and Harbour Police shot and killed six people and
wounded 10. In addition R6.9 million has been paid by the state in
compensation for assault, wrongful arrest and injury arising from
SAP action between 1976 and 1984: roughly 1 Rand for every four
citizens. The human stories behind these statistics reveal horrific
torture, brutality and inhumanity on the part of the SAP, something
for which it has become rightly infamous.

The legislation which the SAP upholds has the same blank cheque
quality as their formal powers. Apartheid presents Black South
Africans with far greater potential for trouble, while at the same time
they are monitored more closely by the police, and subject to less
challengeable and more severe legal processing penalties. Turk has
shown that between 1970 and 1978 Parliament passed 62 acts dealing
with the control of Blacks, with the Police Act being amended eight
times. He estimated that nearly 16 per cent of the legislation passed
constituted efforts to make the internal control system more
effective.[10]

Unlike the situation in the USA where civil liberties are entrenched in amendments to the constitution, the South African
constitution contains few entrenchments. The only protections in
South Africa are insubstantial: respect for tradition, heritage, political checks and balances and the like. These have afforded little
protection to the invasion of civil liberties. The principal security laws
allow for people to be banned and detained without trial, for meetings to be prohibited and for organisations to be declared unlawful.

But in addition the SAP have at their disposal such acts as the Public Safety Act 1953, which allows for a state of emergency to be declared and which can be used to suspend most laws. The Post Office Act 1953 allows for mail to be intercepted if it is suspected of containing evidence of crime, authority for which rests with the Ministers responsible for the intelligence services. The Protection of Information Act 1982 gives the State President the power to declare any place or area a 'prohibited place', and anybody found there 'for any purpose prejudicial to the security or interest of the Republic' can be jailed for 20 years. The Intimidation Act 1982 makes it an offence to intimidate a person by threat or assault, and is frequently used in industrial disputes. The Demonstrations In Or Near Court Buildings Prohibition Act 1982 bans protests near court buildings in support of prisoners. But the main security laws are the most infamous.

Detentions were first used on a wide scale after the Sharpeville shootings in 1960 when 11 727 people were detained on the first day of the state of emergency. Since then many hundreds of thousands of people have been detained at some time or other, the number of suspicious deaths in detentions goes into hundreds, and the number of people, organisations and publications which have been banned runs into hundreds of thousands. Between 1980 and 1981 the Rabie Commission reviewed the security legislation which bestowed this degree of control. The Commission deliberated against a background of domestic and international pressure opposed to bannings, in the furore over a spate of suspicious deaths in detention, and in a climate when political dispensations were being formulated to grant Coloureds and Asians a role in central government. The Commission concluded that while the legislation was regrettable, it was necessary given the conditions in South Africa. It suggested consolidating the various Acts as well as instituting a new and more effective monitoring system. Another recommendation was to urge the use of open court against political opponents, rather than banning them by a decision of the executive. Following this, bannings on all but five people were cancelled. But this was accompanied with an increase in the severity of the charges laid against opponents. Recently the state has resorted to using the charge of treason, which carries the death penalty.

In 1982 the government implemented the Internal Security Act as its legislative response to the Rabie Commission. In the midst of some reform, security legislation was strengthened under the Act. The Act identifies various categories of detention, lays down procedures and conditions for detentions, redefines a number of offences and modifies powers relating to sentencing and the onus of proof. Under the old Terrorism Act a person had to prove innocence 'beyond reasonable doubt', but the onus of proof is no longer as severe: a presumption created in law may be rebutted with proof 'on the balance of probabilities'. The offence of terrorism, however, is more broadly and loosely defined. Briefly, it consists in the commission by a person of an act of violence with intent to overthrow or endanger the state's authority, or to achieve, bring about or promote any constitutional, political, industrial, social or economic aim or change in the Republic, to threaten or attempt such an act, or to perform any act which is aimed to achieve or threaten violence. The offence of subversion is equally broad, consisting of the commission of an act with the same intent as that of terrorism, which endangers or prejudices the state or community, or where a person conspires with, incites or encourages any person to commit such an act. Charges of terrorism or subversion can, therefore, be laid against workers in industrial disputes, schoolchildren boycotting classes and against participants in peaceful demonstrations.

The Act allows for preventive detention, the detention of witnesses and detentions for interrogation, but with a number of new controls. Preventive detention is now subject to review by a committee of three appointed by the State President on the recommendation of the Minister of Justice. Detainees may make representation in person to the committee. However, if the committee finds against the Minister, he is not obliged to free the detainee, for he can appeal to the Chief Justice, who is an appointee of the State President on the recommendation of the Minister of Justice. The wording of the Act does not allow for the committee to be composed of persons who are independent of the executive, nor is membership of the committee made public. The Attorney General has unrestricted power to hold state witnesses until court proceedings have ended, or for six months if no proceedings are instituted. There is no review with respect to 'political cases'. This gives the SAP free rein to intimidate defendants and witnesses. Under Section 29 of the Act people may be detained indefinitely if it is believed they are withholding information from police about a security offence. They need be released only when 'the said person has satisfactorily replied to all the questions in the interrogation'. No access by legal advice or family is permitted until an arrested person is brought before the court, and the individual may not be given bail if the Attorney General objects.

Like the old Terrorism Act, the Internal Security Act allows for persons suspected of involvement in terrorism and subversion to be held indefinitely for interrogation. People can be detained on the directions of a senior police officer of the rank of lieutenant colonel or above. This power should be set in the context of the Police Amendment Act (No. 45) 1982, which allows for the Minister of Law and Order temporarily to promote any officer of the SAP, thus giving police officers of all ranks the potential to detain at their discretion. The Minister of Law and Order must, however, give a written authorisation for any detention which lasts in excess of 30 days. After six months, the SAP must provide 'adequate' reasons why the detainee should not be released. A review committee looks at the detention after six months, but the Minister of Law and Order is not bound to accept their recommendations. There is no appeal against the Minister's decision. So in effect police discretion to detain is accountable to the Minister who takes responsibility for the police, but the Minister is responsible to no one: neither the courts nor Parliament have a right of review. Under the Criminal Procedures Act 1977 the police have the power of short-term detention, being able to arrest and detain 'in specific situations of unrest' without good cause having to be shown for a period not exceeding 48 hours, unless extended to 14 days by a magistrate, when good cause has to be shown. Most detentions, in fact, come within this category, which the SAP can employ at their own discretion. The review procedure does not apply to this Act, only to detentions under the Internal Security Act 1982.

While it is possible to monitor the operation of some of South Africa's security laws, the checks are very weak because they are not independent of the executive and political bureaucracy. This is also the fault with the guidelines established to govern the treatment of detainees. The SAP's uniform and security branches have a justified reputation for considerable brutality in their treatment of detainees, especially toward those detained for very short periods for whom no review procedure exists. A code was adopted in 1982 just after the death in detention of Neil Aggett, and it is laudable in its sentiments. It requires that a detainee be treated humanely at all times; that a detainee be not assaulted or ill-treated; nor subject to humiliating or inhuman treatment; and that a detainee be not deprived of exercise or sleep. Other directions include the immediate medical examination of detainees upon arrest and after complaints of illness, injury or assault. Members of the police violating the code are liable to disciplinary and criminal proceedings. Complaints are investigated by police officers not connected with the occurrence. Under the code, the District Commissioner of the uniformed branch is held to be responsible for seeing that the guidelines are followed, rather than members of the Security Branch. While the constraints in the code are an improvement on previous practice, the code is still only monitored internally by the SAP; moreover, in the past, the prosecutions brought against members of the police have been leniently treated by magistrates, and charges of murder are invariably reduced to culpable homicide. What is more, low ranking Black policemen are the officers most frequently brought before the courts, which does not reflect their greater duplicity but their marginality within the force, with Black policemen not being able to draw on the same organisational loyalty as White members of the SAP. One other caveat exists. The code's force can be temporarily suspended and officers given indemnity from prosecution when a state of emergency is promulgated.

The South African Government declared a state of emergency in 36 districts in 1985 and again throughout the Republic in June 1986. In the seven-and-a-half months in which the first emergency was in operation, nearly 11 000 people were detained for some period and the death rate due to the unrest averaged 100 per month. Some of the emergency powers were already available under other Acts but were consolidated into the emergency regulations. Offences against the regulations were punishable by a prison sentence up to 10 years.[11] Among the offences promulgated were: verbally threatening harm to another person; preparing, printing, publishing or possessing a threatening document; hindering an officer in the performance of his duties; destroying or defacing any notice of the regulations; disclosing the name or identity of anybody arrested under the regulations before their name has been officially confirmed; making statements calculated to subvert the government or legislature; inciting people to resist or oppose the government; causing fear, panic and alarm, or weakening public confidence; advising or inciting people to stay away from work or dislocate industry. Clearly the SAP had a wide range of offences with which to charge citizens, and such was the broad character of some of them that the SAP had considerable discretion effectively to detain and arrest whomsoever they wished.

The emergency regulations gave the SAP widespread powers of detention. While under the Internal Security Act 1982 detentions had to be ordered by a senior police officer, under the regulations 'any policeman, soldier, railway policeman or prison officer of any rank' could arrest 'without warrant any person to keep law and order'. Detentions were limited to 14 days unless extended by the Minister of Law and Order. While in detention people were forbidden to sing and whistle, make unnecessary noise, cause unnecessary trouble or be a nuisance. Anybody committing these 'offences' could be placed in solitary confinement, deprived of meals and, if the detainee was under 14 years of age, given six strokes. Detainees were not allowed to study or receive food parcels. The proclamation also allowed for gatherings to be banned, premises to be closed, traffic to be controlled, any area to be sealed off, people to be removed from particular places and curfews to be imposed. Magistrates and police officers could use or authorise force 'including force resulting in death' if people refused to heed instructions given in 'a loud voice'. The state and its officers were indemnified against civil or criminal lawsuits arising from actions taken under the emergency decree.

After the end of the state of emergency in February 1986, the extensive emergency powers were incorporated into a series of Bills which the White Parliament eagerly passed in order to control commemorations of the tenth anniversary of the Soweto uprising in June 1986, although the other Black Parliaments delayed their passage sufficiently to require a second state of emergency to be promulgated in order to deal with the anniversary. In the midst of the second emergency the Bills were eventually passed and entrenched the emergency powers, thus ensuring in future that draconian powers exist without the state having to signal to domestic and international opinion that the situation is serious enough to call a state of emergency.

This legislative context to policing in South Africa reveals that the South African state is caught in a cleft stick between the need of a reforming state to control the worst excesses of policing apartheid, which it does through various forms of monitoring, and the historical tradition of policing in South Africa, where the police rarely needed to be circumspect in their treatment of Black South Africans. This cleft stick produces a conflict within the state bureaucracy between some sections of its political arm, who are aware of the need to liberalise and of the domestic and international ramifications of police brutality, and some elements of the state's law enforcement agencies, who in practice are able to operate with an autonomy. The consequences of this can end in considerable embarrassment for reformist politicians. This is the dilemma of a state in the first throes of limited liberalisation, and is paralleled, perhaps, by Argentina after the transition to civilian government. The current changes in state policy result in a tension between police autonomy and accountability, which explains the curious oddity in South Africa of a state issuing daily press releases announcing the toll of brutal deaths for which its law enforcement agencies are responsible.

POLICE–MILITARY RELATIONS

The SAP has a strong paramilitary character. The roots of this lie in its origins as a colonial force and more generally in the cultural traditions of the Afrikaans community which fuse civil and military activities, which itself extends back to the Afrikaners' own colonial experience under the British. This paramilitary character is enhanced by the need of the South African state to control the many threats to public order which apartheid by its very nature generates. This is reflected in the training of the SAP. Basic police training covers all aspects of law and criminal investigation, but also hand-to-hand combat, self-defence, general emergency procedures and weapons knowledge and skills. Specialist police training includes instruction and familiarisation in use of mortars, machine guns, automatic weapons, the use of grenades, aspects of anti-vehicle and anti-personnel mine warfare, booby trapping, bush survival, tracking and ambushing.[12] These are skills the police have deployed fighting against guerillas in Namibia and Zimbabwe. Tours of duty in South Africa's own operational areas are the rule for all policemen under 50, so the SAP also have on-the-job training in all aspects of counter-insurgency; members of the SAP have also worked for periods in the Israeli police. In 1985 the force had this training extended to cover 'riot control in urban areas'. Up to that time this was restricted to specific units, but in February 1985 it was announced that all police officers were to undergo this training, and 22 400 police officers had passed through the training programme by November 1985. Riot control in South Africa is thus not a 'skill' restricted to specialist or elite squads but is a part of basic training.

Such was the threat to public order posed by internal unrest during 1985 that the SAP were withdrawn from border duty to enable them to focus on urban areas, with their duties on the border being assumed by the SADF, and the SADF had some of its forces redeployed to help the SAP counter the threat in the urban areas.

This is symptomatic of an overlapping division of labour between the police and defence forces, whereby the state regards them as complementary. Organisationally the links between them are strong. Young national servicemen can undertake their national service in the SAP, and joint staff courses at the SADF College have included officers of the SAP since 1977. As Grundy emphasised, Defence Department White Papers repeatedly make reference to collaborative links, and it is part of the formal duties of the SADF 'at all times' to 'assist the SAP in preserving internal order'.[13] According to the Official Yearbook of the Republic, the Army's training, strategic deployment, strike power and mobility are adjusted to this role, and the organisation of the Army is such that a localised situation of unrest can be countered by them without declaring a state of emergency or mobilising forces by proclamation.[14] Indeed, from the insurrection of the early 1960s the Army has continually been used as a subsidiary of the police in urban areas. Therefore the use of troops to quell civil disorder in 1984–85 was not, contrary to public perception, a new departure, although it was certainly dramatic.

PUBLIC ORDER SITUATIONS

In Great Britain it is possible to discern a process whereby political protest is being criminalised through public order legislation, which, it is argued, reflects the changing nature of the British state. This process has always existed under the South African state, where it operates alongside a second process, the politicisation of crime, whereby 'ordinary crime' is seen to have a political content. These two processes are reflected in the state's definition of 'public disorder', which seems to include all political activity outside the narrow limits which the state considers legitimate, where 'political' is itself defined widely to include economic, industrial and social activity. However, a distinction needs to be drawn between this definition as it is enshrined in legislation, such as the definitions of terrorism and subversion in the Internal Security Act 1982, and as it appears in practice as revealed in the policing of public order situations. In practice there seems to be an even wider definition, for in policing unrest the SAP have in the past seen disorder to include such things as industrial disputes, work stoppages, peaceful mass demonstrations, stay-aways, funerals, prayer meetings, motorcades and carol singing. This situation is not just a product of the authoritarian nature of the South African state, but also of the perpetual challenge to public order which the apartheid state generates from its Black citizens.

What is characteristic of Black politics in South Africa, where few formal channels of protest are available, is that many ordinary aspects of Black life are opportunities to express their protest against apartheid. This is true of education, religion, work, industrial relations and poetry and literature (among other things) which all, therefore, come to have ramifications for public order. This is clearly seen in the legal definitions of terrorism and subversion, which are general enough to include all these areas. What is also a feature of Black protest is that, after a long period of quiescence following Sharpeville, it has intensified, especially since 1976. Public order has thus become much more problematic for the South African state in recent years; hence police intrusion into such things as industrial relations, religious services, classroom boycotts, poetry readings and township demonstrations has likewise intensified. This is reflected in the passing of special legislation to pursue policing in these areas – such as, for example, the Intimidation Act, which prohibits pressure being applied on people to participate in industrial disputes, school boycotts and stay-aways. This pressure also comes within the definition of subversion in the Internal Security Act 1982. Thus the legislative context of public order in South Africa is fluid, with new laws frequently being introduced or old ones amended to cope with new exigencies and changed circumstances. This intensification of SAP involvement in public order situations is also reflected in the deployment of specialist sections within the SAP, such as the Task Force dealing with counter-insurgency, and in the inclusion of riot control in the basic training of all members of the SAP.

One further feature of Black protest since 1976 is the increasing violence with which it is pursued by Black South Africans. In part this is a response to increasing state violence, but it is also a barometer of how intense the political struggle against the apartheid state has become. One manifestation of this is the escalation in the incidence and ruthlessness of guerrilla insurgency in South Africa, with over 50 innocent civilians being killed in terror attacks on 'soft targets' since 1980. This escalation has affected the policing of other public order situations. The state often alleges that the unrest is organised and inspired from abroad, and specific allegations have been made about the involvement of the main guerrilla group (the African National Congress) in collective protests, mass demonstrations and industrial disputes. One particular effect of guerrilla insurgency on policing public order situations is that industrial disputes, mass demonstrations and so on are policed with as much vigour, ruthlessness, repression and brutality as is usually reserved for terrorists. In one year between September 1984 and October 1985, the SAP and police officers attached to the development boards killed 514 people in incidents of unrest, and imprisoned 4806. This puts the deaths resulting from guerrilla attacks in context. This effect is shown in the policing of formally legal strike activity, where many workers have been shot or deported to the homelands while participating in a legal strike. It is also evinced in the brutal suppression of peaceful mass demonstrations and funerals. One funeral in Uitenhage in March 1985 ended in 19 deaths as a result of police action.

The Kannemeyer Report into the Uitenhage incident placed no blame on the police for the deaths – as no official commission on similar incidents has ever done. But the report did criticise the actions of the SAP: they ignored political directions to use minimum force; they fabricated part of their evidence, wrongfully alleging that the marchers were carrying arms which they were about to use; accordingly they gave false information to the Minister of Law and Order, who then misled Parliament; conventional riot control weapons were discarded for live ammunition; and the police made provocative and inciting remarks to marchers. The report also revealed that a security policeman had misused the law to ban a funeral, which sparked the demonstration. This gives a glimpse of SAP conduct in public order situations, revealing that the problem is not an absence of administrative and organisational rules and instructions governing police conduct in public order situations, but an autonomy on the part of the local officers to discard them. This autonomy explains why some funeral processions, industrial disputes and the like end in the death of participants, while others remain peaceful with the police taking a background role. But even when formal rules are discarded by the SAP, the state has great difficulty in apportioning blame to the police. The criticisms the Kannemeyer Report made of the police were damning, but in contradictory fashion it absolved them of the blame. Likewise, despite widespread allegations of torture made by the churches, international organisations and foreign politicians, the State President and other Ministers made a number of speeches supporting the police, calling for loyalty to them from the public. The allegations were abused as 'half truths, lies and distortions'. But with a death rate in the 1985 state of emergency averaging over 100 per month, a political response by the state was necessary, especially given the changes in form and practice which the South African state was introducing. When it came, the political response was muted. P.W. Botha instituted a complaints procedure under the responsibility of the Attorney General, allowing members of the public to press complaints against the SAP and SADF for actions arising inside and outside the Republic's borders – the latter provision being aimed at police action in the 'independent' homelands. In the midst of the unrest Brigadier van der Westhuizen, officer commanding Eastern Province Command, urged the SAP to be disciplined, respectful of human dignity and courteous. The Minister of Law and Order attempted to lessen fatalities by a change in riot control technology. Along with live ammunition, tear gas, plastic batton rounds and sneeze machines, the police were instructed to use water cannon. But above all, politicians responded by prohibiting the reporting of the unrest in order to limit unfavourable publicity; and without this constraint the numbers of deaths more than doubled in the month after the ban compared to the month before.

Notwithstanding the frequent ministerial assurances that the SAP do not take advantage of the vast opportunities for arbitrary and intimidating action which they are afforded, the practical experience of police activity in public order situations suggests that the SAP often exploit their freedom to act in a relatively unrestrained capacity. This creates political dilemmas for a reforming state like South Africa, resulting, as we have seen, in various attempts to control the worst excesses of police activity. Thus, as an example, after it became known that during 1985 the SAP were giving magistrates lectures and videos on the unrest, the Department of Justice accepted a recommendation of the Judge President of Natal that no magistrate who attended should preside at political trials arising from the unrest. But the partial nature of the reforms which the South African state is implementing requires that these constraints be minimal when confronted with a sustained and effective challenge to White supremacy. This situation creates a dilemma for the SAP which is even greater than the political dilemma of the South African state. Gauging how much abuse a detainee can sustain, or how forceful to be when confronted with a Black crowd, is no easy task and the SAP usually make mistakes which reformist politicians find embarrassing. At the same time, the SAP are under equally strong pressure from the same politicians to get information and to contain the threat to public order. So the SAP are given effective *carte blanche* and then periodically made to answer for their use of it in open court, government commissions or the media. This creates enormous tactical problems for local commanding officers, resulting in decisions which can be disastrous in terms of loss of life and political embarrassment. When this occurs the SAP resort to lying on a massive scale, as the Kannemeyer Report revealed. Such deceit is an essential concomitant of the dilemma of policing under South Africa's partial reforms. Thus, on one hand, it is the case that there are few authoritarian states that have the prescience of the South African state to implement such rules as those governing the humane treatment of detainees, but, conversely, there are few authoritarian regimes that end up being so hypocritical because they escape the need to rationalise and excuse the breaking of these rules.

PUBLIC PERCEPTIONS OF THE POLICE

Most Black South Africans are alienated from the police. There are a variety of issues which give rise to this feeling, such as the SAP's excessive brutality, their lack of impartiality and the protective attitude of the state toward police misconduct. This alienation is not evidenced in survey material but in more indirect ways. Many Black townships have vigilante groups as community-based alternatives to the SAP. This alienation is also shown in newspaper copy, political statements and (above all) in the attacks upon the police by Black radicals. In 1985, 65 police officers died in the execution of their duty, most as a result of the unrest. In October 1985, the Minister of Law and Order announced that 700 police officers had been injured, the homes of 500 had been attacked and 400 of them were gutted. Radical Black politicians and newspapers give legitimacy to these attacks by arguing that there are no Black policemen: supporting the apartheid system in this way makes them White. This alienation increases the marginality of Black policemen within their own community. Most of the deaths, in fact, are of Black policemen; only four White officers have been killed in unrest. This is not only because Black policemen arouse greater anger, but (living as they do in the townships they police) they are easier targets. During 1985 many Black police officers were forced to leave the townships and move to emergency camps. Some were reduced to living in tents at the back of the police stations.

The marginality of Black policemen affects their morale, which in turn influences recruitment patterns and operational policy in the SAP. The Annual Reports of the Commissioner of the SAP do not provide an ethnic breakdown of Black policemen and women, but it is clear that so effective is the social ostracism of Black policemen that the SAP increasingly depends on rural Black recruits rather than on urban Blacks, who are the more politically conscious and active. Therefore Black police officers are predominantly insecure and politically conservative migrant workers, and Grundy has claimed that this enables the SAP to deploy its manpower to manipulate tribal as well as political divisions, ensuring the SAP dutiful hoplites who are more willing to use force against fellow Blacks.[15] This breakdown in relationship between the SAP and urban Blacks has another effect on operational policy, which only reinforces feelings of alienation. Even the most routine patrols take on the character of military-style operations conducted from behind the barrier of wire mesh, armoured vehicles and other technology, creating an inevitable distance between the public and the police.

This alienation is not shared by the majority of Whites, especially Afrikaners. Adam and Moodley quote a survey among Whites which showed that 74 per cent approved of the police and Army.[16] There is a stark contrast between the way White areas and the Black townships are policed, not least because of the different problems these areas present the police as a result of apartheid. Thus, the direct experience most Whites have of policing in South Africa encourages a more favourable view of the SAP. This positive view is enhanced by the common sense prejudice of Whites, who see Black South Africans as lawless, and by the restrictions placed on reporting police misconduct inside South Africa. This is symptomatic of the fact that most ordinary Whites are oblivious to what happens generally in the townships and fail to develop any familiarity with the problems of Blacks.

However, the changes in form and practice introduced by the South African state have made some White opinion leaders more aware of the needs and interests of Blacks. Reformist politicians are claiming they now champion the idea of equal (but still segregated) treatment for Blacks, a theme which has been taken up by some businessmen, academics and the press. This has affected the public portrayal of the police. Within the liberal English and Afrikaans speaking press, comment on police misconduct has been critical when police excesses have threatened the reformist policies of the state. This is one of the reasons why the editorship of Afrikaans newspapers has become so controversial, with some liberal editors being under pressure from owners, readers and shareholders because of their views. Criticism of the police is not shared by Right-wing Whites who reject the state's limited reforms. They tend to feel that police conduct is justifiable given the threat Blacks are supposed to pose; and it is significant that these Whites tend to come from the rural *platteland* and urban working class areas closest to the Black population and are that part of the local pigmentocracy most threatened (both economically and ideologically) by land reform and by the upwardly mobile Black community. In their view, police conduct is no more than a response to the problems the SAP have to confront, and certainly do not contribute to these problems. Thus the SAP is no different from any other police force in less divided societies. This is a view widely expressed in more conservative White newspapers. On the 17 July 1985 *The Citizen*, a conservative English speaking newspaper, carried an editorial which attacked the claim that the conduct of the SAP was contributing to the unrest.

> No community can be without the protection of the police. And no police force in the world would abandon its duty to maintain law and order . . . the continuing and widespread unrest is clearly aimed at making the townships ungovernable. In the circumstances, the use of the Army to assist the police is fully justified, though we urge the minimum of force . . . That [the police] have mostly acquitted themselves well, in trying and dangerous circumstances, should be gratefully acknowledged by all who believe in the maintenance of law and order.

The policy demand which follows from such views is for the SAP to be left free from political, administrative and organisational controls and instructions, which are said to impede the police in the maintenance of law and order. Conversely, those who support the liberalisation measures introduced by the state urge that the SAP come more under the political control of a reformist state. This is a policy demand supported by most liberal English speaking Whites and the majority of the English speaking press. Thus the Johannesburg *Sunday Times* wrote in an editorial on 7 July 1985:

> The police must drastically alter their methods. Turning such deep mistrust [of the police] around requires dramatic action not an edgy shuffling towards reform . . . Only by publicly cutting the rope which binds it to past policies will the government be able to shake off its nasty image and stop violence from hijacking reform.

There is an irony in such a view compared to the situation in Great Britain. There civil liberties are seen to be protected when the police come under local control independent from central government, for there is a notable shift to a more authoritarian political style in the British state which has affected police policy. In South Africa's case, the relation between popular perceptions of the police, civil liberties and the nature of the state is mediated by how the reforms in South Africa are seen. Many Whites in South Africa believe civil liberties for the majority of its citizens will be strengthened when the SAP come under the directions and control of the reformist elements within the government. In contrast, the government's Right wing, normally in favour of a more authoritarian apartheid state, demand that the SAP be given greater local autonomy in order to protect what these Whites consider to be their civil liberties against erosion from Black progress.

THE POLICE AS A POLITICAL INSTITUTION

There is a relationship between politics and policing in all political systems, but there are two dimensions to this relationship in South Africa's case: the police there act in an overtly political manner; and policing has been politicised as the political campaign against apartheid intensifies. All police officers are expected neutrally to uphold the constitutional order under which they function. The SAP face difficulties in this because South Africa's constitutional order is so closely identified with the policies of a particular political party. But even so, the SAP's conduct – such as their lack of impartiality, and their fervour and brutality – suggests that they act in an overtly political manner to uphold the policies of the National Party. They act in an overtly political manner when they manipulate tribal tensions in order to crush township protest, as they did in 1976 when they urged conservative migrant workers to attack radical students; or when they side with (and directly sponsor and support) vigilante and conservative elements in political disputes with more radical groups, as they have done for Inkatha or the Crossroad 'fathers'; or when they simply inconvenience rather than legally act against the government's opponents, whether White or Black; or when they physically attack government critics who are participating in formally legal protest activity. There are countless incidents of this sort which show political partisanship.

The frequency with which the SAP act to uphold the interests of a particular party has to be seen in the context of the recruitment patterns and operational role of the SAP. Apartheid generates opposition by the very nature of its injustices and inequalities, and in as much as opposition is defined by the state as a threat to law and order, the operational role of the SAP inevitably places it in conflict with the majority of Black South Africans from whom most of the opposition comes. The police, therefore, cannot but act in a political manner under apartheid. The occupational experience of the ordinary member of the SAP is one where Blacks are confronted as criminals and as threats to public order. This helps sustain a range of pejorative stereotypes of Blacks which pervade the occupational culture of the SAP, and these are stereotypes which imply Blacks are in direct conflict with the SAP. These images are reinforced by the recruitment patterns of the SAP. With the Afrikanerisation of the SAP that occurred with the National Party's electoral victory in 1948, White policemen and women are now almost entirely Afrikaans. The police have low status and reward, so much so that they attract mainly working class Afrikaners, many with an insular rural background.[17] Two consequences follow. The stereotypes they have of Blacks are drawn from their restricted Afrikaans upbringing and tend to be politically redundant or blatantly offensive.[18] White officers also tend to come from that section of the White community which is least economically privileged and therefore that part most threatened by the upwardly mobile urban Black community. So, by nature, most White members of the SAP tend to be loyal to Afrikaner hegemony, of which support for Afrikaans political parties is a component. Adam and Moodley have argued that Right wing sentiments are widespread among the SAP, especially the Security Branch.[19]

Traditionally, the mode of political representation for the SAP has been through the Afrikaans National Party, which has governed South Africa since 1948. In 1982 splits in the National Party arising from its limited reforms led to the formation of the more reactionary Conservative Party, which in turn has increased the competition between Afrikaans parties for the political representation of the police. Paradoxically, the Conservative Party is similar to radical Black politicians in seeing policing as a litmus test of the state's commitment to change. Radical Blacks infer from the way the SAP conduct themselves that the state is not seriously committed to change; the inference which the Afrikaans Right wing draw is that the state is giving too much too rapidly, and in the process is hindering the police in the maintenance of public order. Accordingly, the Conservative Party seeks to defend the SAP against what they consider to be direct attacks or implied criticism from reformist elements in the government. It is difficult to judge the extent to which the Conservative Party is mobilising support among the lower echelons of the SAP, although White policemen and women tend to come from that part of the Afrikaans social structure most threatened by the reforms implemented by the National Party and from which the Conservative Party draws its electoral support and power base. However, the Conservative Party is exploiting the contradictory position that the SAP have been placed in as a result of the changes in the form and practice of the South African state. The SAP are required vigorously to seek out crime, both political and civil, but they create political problems for the state if they go too far, resulting in the state acting against them in some form or another. This contradictory position is likely to increase the sense of alienation among ordinary members of the SAP, feeling that now they can no longer call on the same loyalty from the state as in the past. If this sense of alienation exists amongst members of the SAP it is possible that it will increase their support for more Right wing political parties who urge stronger loyalty to (and greater understanding of) the problems of the SAP. If such support exists, it will also increase support for – and, perhaps, participation in – Right wing paramilitary organisations who 'police' with the toughness and lack of restraint which the SAP feel they have lost. Indeed, there is some evidence that the paramilitary group Afrikaner Weerstandsbeweging (Afrikaner Resistance Movement) has support from sections of the SAP, who have been reluctant to move against the group when they threatened public order.

Whatever the case, the politicisation of policing in White politics will intensify in the future in a direction entirely opposite to the politicisation resulting from Black protest. The Right and Left of South Africa's political spectrum will place policing in the context of a wider debate about the state's commitment to reform, and the politicisation that occurs will be determined by their differing opinion of the changes the state is introducing.

Notes

1. 'Black' is the accepted and preferred term to describe the African, Asian and Coloured communities and will be used here to refer to all three communities.

2. See T. Hanf, H. Weiland and G. Vierdag, *South Africa: The Prospects of Peaceful Change* (London: Rex Collings, 1981) p. 17.
3. For example see from different perspectives: H. Adam and H. Giliomee, *Ethnic Power Mobilised: Can South Africa Change?* (New Haven: Yale University Press, 1979); S. Nolutshungu, *Changing South Africa* (Manchester: Manchester University Press, 1982); J. Saul and S. Gelb, *The Crisis in South Africa* (New York: Monthly Review Press, 1981).
4. For a discussion of social liberty see L. Crocker, *Positive Liberty* (The Hague: Martinus Nijhoff, 1980). As examples, see on trade union rights C. Hill, *Change in South Africa* (London: Rex Collings, 1983); and on the constitution see D. Welsh, 'Constitutional Change in South Africa', *African Affairs*, 83 (1984).
5. Noted by P. Frankel, 'South Africa: The Politics of Police Control' (1979–80) 486–7.
6. Figures taken from A. Sachs, 'The Instruments of Domination in South Africa', in L. Thompson and J. Butler (eds), *Change in Contemporary Southern Africa* (1975) p. 233.
7. Noted by Frankel, 'South Africa', 498.
8. Noted by Frankel, 'South Africa', 483.
9. Noted by K. Grundy, *Soldiers Without Politics: Blacks in the South African Armed Forces* (1983) p. 137.
10. See A. Turk, 'The Meaning of Criminality in South Africa', *International Journal of the Sociology of Law*, 9 (1981) 140.
11. The following details are taken from R. Omond, *The Apartheid Handbook* (Harmondsworth: Penguin, 1985) pp. 211–13.
12. Taken from M. Morris, *Armed Conflict in Southern Africa* (Cape Town: Spence, 1974) p. 289.
13. *Soldiers Without Politics*, pp. 136–7.
14. *South Africa 1985* (Pretoria: Department of Foreign Affairs, 1986) p. 319.
15. *Soldiers Without Politics*, p. 148.
16. H. Adam and K. Moodley, *South Africa Without Apartheid* (Berkeley: University of California Press, 1986) p. 109.
17. Noted by Frankel, 'South Africa', 486 and Grundy, *Soldiers Without Politics*, p. 143.
18. Noted by Frankel, 'South Africa', 492.
19. *South Africa Without Apartheid*, p. 67.

8 People's Republic of China

BACKGROUND

Although there is a national police force in the People's Republic of China, known as the Public Security Agency, the country has special features which make an analysis of policing more difficult than in earlier chapters. Some of these distinguishing features are China's sheer vastness, national diversity, economic under-development and the geographic remoteness and isolation of much of its population. China covers 6.6 per cent of the earth's total land mass, has borders with twelve countries running 20 000km in length and has 20 per cent of the world's population. Among its citizens there are 56 different nationalities and five main language groups. Although the Han Chinese are the largest group (representing 93.3 per cent of the total population in 1982) ethnic divisions are complicated by a rural–urban divide, with the remaining 55 nationalities dispersed over 60 per cent of the total area of the country.

The nature and size of the administrative structure of the Chinese state reflects this diversity and vastness. The country is divided into provincial administrative units, provinces, municipalities, counties and a whole range of smaller administrative units. In 1982 there were 30 provincial administrative units, 22 provinces, three municipalities and 2000 counties. But in order to cope with ethnic and national differences, there are also 'autonomous regions', such as Inner Mongolia and Tibet, which contain within them a number of smaller autonomous administrative units. In 1982, there were five autonomous regions representing 7.1 per cent of China's population. Many of these are peoples which previous Chinese states have colonised through military conquest. Thus, combined with the physical remoteness and isolation of its population, there are also ethnic and national differences which create a distance between the political centre and vast sections of the citizenry.

Features such as these have gone to ensure that the Chinese political bureaucracy does not collect – or, more importantly, disseminate to outsiders – statistical information about itself and its citizens to the same extent as other countries discussed in this volume. This includes statistical and other information on the police. One measure of this is the simple fact that there has been a national census on only three occasions since the formation of the People's Republic of China in 1949. Yet changes in state policy since 1978, including economic modernisation, birth control programmes and a less isolationist foreign policy, have made the bureaucracy more interested in statistically monitoring the population and more willing to disseminate information about Chinese society. This extends to information about the police, which is now beginning to emerge, although it does not match that of earlier chapters.

Nonetheless, policing in China is of singular interest. This is not only because so little is known about it but also because it has been affected by the changing nature of the state to a greater extent perhaps than other cases discussed here. The Chinese state has alternated between periods of social, political and ideological order and periods of marked change, disorder and reconstruction, which has affected policing. The ideology and practice of the Chinese Communist Party (CCP) has moved quite suddenly between acceptance of 'Leninist' models of order and 'Maoist' models, which stress the positive value of disorder and imbalance. Mao Zedong's 'mass line' sought to reduce the involvement of bureaucratic elites in decision-making, whether within the CCP or without, and to stress the integral involvement of direct action by the masses.[1] Whilst authorities differ over periodisation, there is a measure of agreement that 'Leninist' ideas of order (with their associated emphasis on efficient bureaucracy and codification) were a feature in the CCP and the state generally from 1949–54, particularly between 1959 and 1966, and from 1978 onwards. During the intervening periods 'mass line' and anti-bureaucratic emphases were the keynote. These were times of economic, political and social turbulence. These periodisations are by no means subtle but are useful in assessing the relationship between the police, the state and public order in the People's Republic of China, for at the outset they permit us to relate changes in public order policy to larger societal processes. For example, using this frame of reference, we more easily understand why mass demonstrations of economic and social dissent were in many places actually assisted by the police, army and paramilitary organisations in the early years of the Cultural Revolution (1966–76), yet these same organisations ruthlessly opposed seemingly similar demonstrations in later years.

However, while the dialectic of change within modern China is one which often produces alternate cycles of order and disorder, the underlying element of cultural and social continuity must not be underestimated. Further, in a vast country, where 80 per cent of the 1000 million people are peasants, and where there are 56 constitutionally recognised nationalities, the advancing and retreating 'waves' of differing kinds of development or change have an uneven effect; indeed, some isolated areas seem rarely to be affected by these tides. Yet to use these categories of 'order' and 'disorder' will allow us to look at key aspects of the relationship between the police, state and society. In the periods of 'order' there is an increasing emphasis on the codification of law, universal access to civil as well as criminal law, and a stress on standardised practice and application. There is less emphasis on the role of informal (mass) organisations and their policing powers and more on the mechanisms of 'formal' court-orientated 'routine' justice. The regular agencies of policing place reliance on constitutionally derived procedures and upon professionalism, as acquired through routine training. In periods of 'disorder' law itself diminishes in importance with *policy* emerging as the impetus in enforcement. In its turn, enforcement depends increasingly upon a range of 'mass' organisations, with the police often following new policy rather than enforcing existing laws. During these periods public demonstrations and conflicts within work-units aimed at fundamental change in local structures and personnel are – up to a point – regarded as 'normal', for qualitative change is needed to re-establish or renew the 'dictatorship of the proletariat'. Thus the processes of law construction and enforcement are themselves subject to criticism and significant review.

Whilst researchers may sometimes differ in their analyses of the relative merits and drawbacks of these periods, there is usually a strong reference to distinctions of this nature. Tom Bowden examines the public order problem from 1948 to 1968 using just such periodisations; James P. Brady uses concepts of 'bureaucratic justice' and 'popular justice' respectively in reference to the two kinds of period; while Leng and Chiu, looking at the emergence of what they describe as the 'jural' and 'societal' models of law in the Communist-controlled areas before 1949, contrast the initiation of a regular judicial system, and the development of mass agencies, extra-judicial organs and procedures.[2]

As defined above, China is currently experiencing a period of 'order'. Peng Zhen, Chairman of the Standing Committee of the National People's Congress, when looking back to the period before

1949, justifies building up a socialist legal system, with an emphasis on familiarity by all citizens with an increasingly all-encompassing corpus of law:

> Because there was no nationwide people's political organisation during the revolutionary war period, the Communist Party decided everything and party policies carried the weight of law . . . Generally we just followed party policies . . . some people [now] are not used to carrying out our policies in the form of laws, and think that party policy alone will do. They are wrong . . . All party members and cadres should set a good example by knowing and observing the law.[3]

Of course, such views are not characteristic of opinion throughout the history of the People's Republic since 1949. Leng and Chiu[4] report instructions by Mao Zedong during the Cultural Revolution to 'smash Gongjianfa' (police, procuracy, and courts). They further note a 1967 *People's Daily* editorial, 'In praise of lawlessness', which called for the complete destruction of existing law so that 'proletarian legal order could be established'; while in a 1968 document Mao is quoted as saying 'depend on the rule of man, not the rule of law'. It is through these distinctions that policing in China will be analysed.

STRUCTURE, ORGANISATION AND FINANCE

Before the establishment of the People's Republic in 1949, the CCP had been engaged in revolutionary struggle for more than 20 years. Under the previous Guomindang (Nationalist) government law enforcement had been arbitrary, and corruption and lawlessness became rife. Although it had gained limited judicial and policing experience in its own liberated base areas of the Civil War, the new CCP-led government felt obliged to abolish all Guomindang laws and judicial organisations, and totally to reconstruct the agencies of law enforcement. But the newly-created agencies faced severe problems. In the first four years of the People's Republic there was to be considerable resistance to the new government by the old secret societies; there were problems in the cities – the former Guomindang strongholds – with industrial sabotage, dissent and resistance. There were also riots and peasant disturbances in reaction to central efforts to impose a uniform taxation system. Further, the Korean War gave hope to old supporters of the Guomindang that Communist rule might not be permanent. In this context, it was hard to structure police policies on a systematic basis, for they were above all required to act, rather than to deliberate. During this time, the police were to be aided considerably by the militia, and at times by the People's Liberation Army (PLA).

The period from 1954 to 1957 was one of national consolidation. Relative stability was restored following the ending of the Korean War and the decline of internal dissent. During this time, China was to move into close economic association with the Soviet Union. For the legal system and the police, this led to an increasing emphasis on regular and constitutional methods of procedure. It also highlighted the need for 'specialists' in every area of economy and society. Thus training in police methods and in law began in earnest; an increasing familiarity with court procedure was required with the diminishment of the relative importance of mediation and quasi-legal procedures conducted by work units, youth, peasant, and women's associations and the like. However increasing professionalism laid the police open at times to attack from the left. For example, the 1957–58 Anti-Rightist movement, and the 1966–76 Cultural Revolution saw considerable criticism of officials 'isolated from the masses' and 'acting in bureaucratic manner'. The latter period saw seizures, by Mao Zedong-inspired Red Guards (young activists), of courtrooms and police stations, which were seen as 'bastions of bourgeois justice'; at this time many officials were relieved of their posts and 'sent down' to manual labour in the factories or countryside. Lo Ruiching, the national police chief was relieved of all authority and subjected to public criticism.

This period placed policy rather than law at the forefront; it thus gave power, as it was the author of policy, to the CCP. Whilst the police became of increasing importance as instruments of policy, they were far from being a relatively autonomous and professional organisation. They were subject to close party control. The police force, reformed in accordance with 'mass line' perspectives, worked in close association with the mass organisations and with the militia and PLA, not so much as an equal partner but as an instrument of new policies and interpretations.

Following the death of Mao Zedong and the removal of the 'Gang of Four' in 1976, China once again embarked upon new social, economic and political policies substantially different from those of the previous period. In a series of measures since 1978 it moved toward modernisation by an emphasis on stable hierarchies free of significant influence from mass organisations, and on the development of expertise in all fields. Both these aspects have been underlined by an increasing theoretical and practical separation of party from state. There has been an associated demotion of the role of ideology. The effect of the new policies in the economic sphere has been to increase activity domestically by encouragement of individual production in the agricultural sphere and by the loosening of regulatory controls on industrial and commercial enterprises. External trade has increased dramatically. The new policies have thereby generated increased pressure for legislation, civil as well as criminal.[5] An indication of this is contained in the intention of the sixth five year plan (1981–85) to 'maintain good public order . . . to ensure that the people can devote attention to the modernisation drive wholeheartedly . . . straighten out public order and resolutely strike against enemies against socialism and criminal offenders . . . resolutely clamp down on serious offences in the economic sphere'.[6] The police therefore have returned to the more distinct structure and organisation of the 'order' period.

However, even so, organisational questions relating to rank, territory and specialisation are not easily answerable owing to the paucity of primary data. Certainly in periods of 'disorder' distinctions of rank, whether expressed by organisation or visible sign such as uniform, are observed less. The effect of hierarchy within the police becomes muted by the involvement of the mass organisations, which at times may 'outrank' the regular service. It is noticeable throughout the whole period since 1949 that the most publicly-used distinction in rank is that between cadres (officers) and enlisted personnel. This is the case with the PLA, where (until very recently) the only major visible distinction between ranks was that officers' uniforms had four pockets and those of non-cadres had two. Whilst divisions of rank exist within the public security forces, they are rarely referred to either within or outside the force. However, within the public security organisations there is a strong awareness of who holds rank or seniority, largely because officers rarely work outside their own areas. (It appears that the relative lack of outward indication of rank does not lead to problems.) Several other branches with legal or quasi-legal powers of arrest and interrogation (such as the customs service) have recently introduced new Western-style uniforms with more prominent rank indications.

Specialised branches are similarly brought to prominence or diminished by current party or state requirements, in particular by economic and social policy imperatives. For example, during the 1980s the detection of crime has become a major priority, with a concomitant emphasis on development of specialised detection branches (whether in relation to economic crimes, crimes of violence, or other categories). However, this has still not resulted in a relatively well-defined separation along the lines of the uniformed and CID branches in Great Britain. As for territory, this has been a relatively constant factor throughout the period since 1949, with the provincial and county public security bureaux observing the basic local government divisions. China remains a predominantly non-mobile, rural-based society. Movement outside one's home county is quite rare, partly because of transportation problems, but also because of the relative self-sufficiency of localities. This aids the policing of public order and other criminal situations. Those involved in public protest or in other criminal activity will normally do so within the immediate vicinity of their own residence or workplace area. Without a developed road system, roving criminals or roving 'agitators' are rare; thus pursuit of them by local public security personnel rarely calls for interprovincial co-operation. In exceptional cases the PLA, with their ability to organise and sustain pursuit, may be called upon. Public security members are thus normally drawn from the area within which they work, and will live among the same community for most of their working lives.

Reorganisation in 1984 gave policing responsibilities for China as a whole to the Ministry of Public Security. Ruan Chongwu outlines this Ministry's relationship to the Ministry of State Security as follows: 'The Ministry of Public Security is in charge of law and order, traffic safety and fire control. The Ministry of State Security is in charge of anti-espionage work to protect national security. The two Ministries do not have much connection with each other in their work.'[7] Since 1984, the responsibilities of the police include protection of government and embassy buildings and other key locations. To assist in this function, 25 armed divisions were transferred from the PLA to the Ministry of Public Security. Apart from this particular Armed Police division, other categories in the force include traffic, criminal investigation, fire, foreign affairs, social security and census. Figures in 1986 indicate that China has 1.2 million security personnel, of whom 600,000 are armed policemen.[8] This gives a police/population ratio of 1.7 per 1000.

Two American academics working in the field of criminology, Richard Ward and Dorothy Bracey, provide one of the most recent surveys of the newly reorganised force. They remark that these classifications are in some ways comparable to those found in the West, but note that there is little mobility between the divisions, and considerable difference in training and recruitment procedures. In common with other authors, they note the tendencies toward a much more 'professional' role for the police. However, they perceive an underlying desire to maintain links with the 'mass line' perspectives:

> Professionalism is regarded more leniently under the present 'prag-matic' regime. Deng Xiaoping and his followers seem to believe that it is possible to cultivate at least some aspects of professional-ism without succumbing to 'bureaucratism' which is the stifling of the representation of the masses by the party or government . . . For the police, as for all other branches of government, conscien-tious following of the mass line should make it possible to benefit from the virtues of professionalism without suffering the vices of bureaucratism.[9]

The developments that they report, however – such as distinctive uniforms, imported computers, modern forensic equipment, all under-lain by a separate and distinct system of formal public security education – would seem to emphasise the development of a relatively autonomous and specialised role for the police in the latter part of the 1980s. A widespread system of training institutes is currently being developed, such as the new Public Security University and Police Officer University in Beijing. This is in line with wider plans for training of professionals in virtually all areas of public and commer-cial life. China's major cities and provinces are also reopening Public Security Colleges closed since the Cultural Revolution, and there are substantial plans to develop similar colleges at the county level. Since 1982 admission to the major courses of these institutes has been by competitive examination, adding once again to the ethos of 'profes-sionalism'. Indeed the Minister of Public Security, Ruan Chongwu, has stated: 'We want all police officers to have a university or college education, but we have not reached this level yet. At present about one-fifth of police officers have reached university or college level. We are working towards more specialised schools and vocational education to improve training.'

The formal structure of the current system is described by a leading official of the Ministry of Public Security as follows:

> The Ministry of Public Security is under the State Council, and the Social Security Bureau is a professional bureau under the ministry

and consists of a criminal investigation department, and an institute of forensic science and technology. The public security bureaus of the provinces, municipalities directly under central government and autonomous regions have social security and criminal investigation departments. The public security bureau at the prefecture level has a social security and criminal investigation section, and the public security bureau at the county level, a social security and criminal investigation team. In cities, the public security bureaus . . . have their social security and criminal investigation divisions or sections. At the grass roots, there are police stations.

One of the few accounts of local police station work is that of Elmer Johnson.[10] He, too, reports the current emphasis on blending ideas of professionalism and 'mass line' activity at the local level, for no matter how far the police in China have moved toward building a relatively autonomous and self-conscious organisation, its emphasis on 'professionalism' has been but recently regained. For some time this feature will be less apparent at the lower end of the hierarchy of authority.

FORMAL STRUCTURE OF AUTHORITY

At the grass roots, much of the authority is still diffused, although the police station remains a key focus. To provide the historical background to the powers local police have, from 1949 until the onset of the Cultural Revolution in 1966 there was a tripartite division of authority in the area of criminal justice – the police, courts, and procuracy (in some respects similar to the USA's District Attorney system). All these bodies were under the direction of the CCP committee at the appropriate level. Particularly in the earlier years of the People's Republic it was, in reality, the party committee which had the real powers of arrest, prosecution and sentencing.[11] The procurate was abolished during the Cultural Revolution, but reappeared, with enhanced functions, following the 1978 reforms.

Thus, even during periods of 'order', Party policy was a key factor in police work; it was even more so during periods of 'disorder', when 'popular' rather than 'bureaucratic' justice operated. However, with the increasing separation of the CCP from government, there have been considerable changes. Since 1979 the police have to obtain permission from the People's Procurate in order to detain and question, although this permission is often available under standing orders.[12] This relates only to serious crimes;[13] minor offences are often dealt with by a whole series of grassroots mass organisations. Although during the present period of 'order' their powers are somewhat less arbitrarily exercised, they are still extensive and important. There is seemingly no published code of conduct or procedure for the police beyond the constitution and related criminal law; rectification of a grievance against the police is more usually a matter of individual perseverance and ingenuity rather than that of using specified procedures. Thus arbitrariness is still a feature of enforcement at the local level. Further 'popular' elements of justice remains:

> [it] has been historically linked to *revolutionary line* ideals. Popular institutions do contribute to the protection of *social order*, but there is also an explicit commitment to *social justice* and egalitarian reform. The mass organisations at local workplaces and residential communities sponsor their own internal peace-keeping bodies which function as auxiliaries to the regular police and as lay representatives in the People's Courts. The mass organisations also have mobilised the populace for political struggle against erring individual officials, intellectuals and administrators, or whole social classes (such as landlords or capitalists) or general political problems within the government, Communist Party, or academy (emphases in original).[14]

The organisational basis of 'popular' justice was firmly established by the 1950s. In the urban areas there are residents' committees (with local offices, these supervise several thousand households and have a small permanent staff). The organisation in Canton, one of China's largest cities, is not atypical. In administrative terms the city is subdivided into six urban districts. Within each urban district are wards of some 2000 to 10 000 families. Each ward has its own police station. Thus the police structure in urban areas now parallels the administrative. These wards are further sub-divided for administrative purposes. Each ward has a residents' committee with a small permanent staff who liaise closely with the ward police station and its officers. As for the rural counties, here there are few police posts, and most villages seldom see a policeman but the mass organisations, similar to ward or street committees, work in a similar way.[15] Security defence committees operate within all major economic and social units – factories, educational establishments, street and village committees. These committees are co-ordinated by local public security authorities, and work in close association with police stations. Their duties today – in urban and rural areas – involve popularising the increasing number of new laws and supervising the implementation of key social policies, such as that of birth control, and assisting the police. Because the members of these committees know their neighbours and locale very well they are an indispensable source of information to local police stations. Knowledge of local people is increased by the role of these individuals in mediating civil disputes. And whilst the police are no longer empowered to search homes without a warrant, members of neighbourhood committees effectively do so under powers to inspect household registration certificates and checking for persons who are temporarily (or illegally) resident. The neighbourhood police station actually administers the registration of all local people; this is basic not only for residence but for employment, education and marriage. This system of supervision and control may appear stifling, almost totalitarian, but it must be remembered that this form of closely monitored society has its antecedents in Guomindang (Nationalist) and Imperial China. Chinese culture is one which emphasises the collective: indeed the word 'individualism' in Chinese has quite selfish connotations. Further, the normative acceptance of current CCP ideology is high; there is a strong emphasis in society on morality and correctness in behaviour. In rural areas, the degree of social control is even stronger. Traditional authority structures, emphasising the family and male control, are still influential. The relative lack of police presence in these areas is more a reflection of the strength of this social control than a shortage of resources. Thus, what Westerners may perceive as coercion, whether by police or mass organisations, may often be quite differently perceived in China.

However, for the maintenance of public order the police have, in the final analysis, considerable non-normative sanctions. Administrative sanctions without significant provision for judicial review remain. Under 1957 legislation, the police may impose small fines, issue warnings, or detain people for up to fifteen days. In 1979 the National People's Congress reaffirmed earlier legislation which permits police and civil administrative organs to send minor criminals for 're-education through labour' for a period of one to four years. It is clear that offenders against current political *mores* have been detained under this law without the necessity of court appearance. Note the distinction between 'reform through labour' and 'education through labour': they are two different concepts. The former involves punishment according to Criminal Law. On the other hand, 'education through labour' committees are set up by the government at all levels, and the Ministry of Public Security is represented on all of them. Administrative discipline may also be applied by the party to its members and by virtually any government or quasi-government body to its employees. They have the actual power (or sufficient normative influence) to summon, examine, and advise individuals within their jurisdiction. Many minor criminal 'offences' are also dealt with by these bodies, which have the ultimate sanction of reference to the police or the courts, who have a greater range of sanctions.

Thus, in the period of 'order' since 1978 there has been considerable emphasis on codification, regulation and supervision of the police and other units who have legal or quasi-legal powers with regard to public order. However, whilst this would appear to make law enforcement more closely aligned with ideas of constitutional rights, it is still a selective process, subject to the same kind of government and political imperatives that are seen at work in the liberal-democracies of the West. There are periodic 'crackdowns' on various types of activity ranging from 'anti-social behaviour' (which may cover political activities which thence become 'criminalised') through to more specific areas of crime, such as economic corruption. What distinguishes China from the West is that its social and cultural organisation is complemented by a series of interlocking agencies which enforce law, moral codes and policy. Importantly, the stress upon each of these three elements has differed considerably during the brief history of the People's Republic. The police have broadly followed these changes in political line, although they have not done this in a completely detached or uninvolved manner, as subsequent sections will indicate.

POLICE-MILITARY RELATIONS

The period from the founding of the CCP in 1921 to the inauguration of the People's Republic in 1949 was characterised by a series of bitter civil wars between the Communists and the Guomindang Nationalists. During these times the Communists established relatively large and stable base areas in the countryside areas outside Guomindang control. These base areas had their own distinctive forms of government, and their own laws and policing. Throughout, there was strong linkage and co-operation between the police and the PLA, the military arm of the CCP. Indeed police work was shared between these two bodies and local militia units – the PLA and militia tending the border regions, and the regular public security forces the more secure areas. Public security officers at this time were mainly recruited from the ranks of the PLA and militia, a practice which continues to this day, and may well increase as the PLA carries out its planned 25 per cent reduction in personnel between 1980 and 1985. In 1982, PLA strength was 4 238 210, equivalent to 4.17 per 1000 of the population.

These linkages continued to be firm between 1949 and 1953, a period during which there was considerable emphasis on mass line 'popular justice', although with growing consolidation of law-based 'bureaucratic justice'. During the majority of this period the CCP perceived considerable threats to the stability of the People's Republic: the Guomindang collapse in southern China had been rapid, leaving numbers of armed stragglers roaming the countryside; raids on the mainland organised from Taiwan were frequent, and industrial sabotage occurred, particularly in coastal cities. The Chinese entry into the Korean War gave increased opportunities for the Guomindang to initiate such attacks from their Taiwan bases. There was thus large involvement of the military in public order policing. There were also peasant disturbances related to economic policies. Because of the widespread nature of these problems, and because of the elementary organisation of the police in rural areas, the militia and PLA worked in close association with the mass organisations and People's Tribunals (the latter being specially oriented in this period to the land reform question).

In urban areas the PLA played a similarly decisive role. Because the cities were the last to fall to the rural-based Communists there was a substantial problem of organisation and order. With little experience of urban government, the new regime were forced to keep on many of the old administrators, including some key members of the police. As they could not be considered trustworthy, the PLA held considerable powers, some under martial law. However, urban militias and security defence committees were rapidly instituted; volunteers from these organisations were to constitute, along with the PLA, an essential adjunct to the newly-emerging police force in urban areas. As the regular police grew in strength, the need for PLA intervention decreased, and the kind of urban policing structure that exists today began to emerge.

By 1953 the economy and the defence of the country had been consolidated and land reform was proceeding; the growth of the mass movements had contributed considerably to the creation of this relative stability. The First Five Year Plan began that year and placed emphasis on economic and social stability. The emphasis was also on routinised and rationalised police work, and the PLA's role in public security and public order decreased considerably. Leng and Chiu describe the years between 1954 and 1957 as ones where there was a clear ascendancy of the jural model in what they called the era of 'China's constitutional experiment'.[16] Thus, in the area of law and order as a whole, a serious move was made to lead the country in the direction of stability and codification. It is too much to say that the PLA withdrew from law and order situations, but it is certain they were not to be of such crucial importance again until they were called upon in 1967 to restore order after the severe disorder of the first months of the Cultural Revolution.

Although initially starting as a reform movement aimed at creating a new socialist culture, the Cultural Revolution rapidly shifted its target from the academic to the political. Its key initiator was Mao Zedong, concerned at the degeneration of mass line ideals, the growth of bureaucracy and what he saw as bourgeois ideas within the state, society and the CCP itself. Whilst it involved a considerable power struggle within the highest ranks of the Party, it gave licence to aggrieved individuals and groups of all kinds to attack the representatives of the 'bourgeois headquarters', verbally and often physically. Thus authority of all kinds came under question and attack; order broke down completely in many parts of China. With party and state institutions (including the police) in disarray, the only body which could restore order was the PLA. During 1967 the central party authorities under Mao issued orders to the PLA to restore control. This move was far from the 'military coup' of the type seen in Third World countries. The PLA is bound by the constitution to accept party leadership in organisation and ideology, indeed its Commander has traditionally been the Chairman of the Communist Party. Whilst its members often play key roles in politics, the PLA itself has shown little sign of an enduring and consolidated desire to become permanently involved in politics and public order. On the whole the PLA seems content to be the 'Army of the Party', and accepts its control. The acceptance of the PLA's authority as legitimate in the realm of public order is heightened by its solid association with the achievement of liberation in 1949 – accomplished not only against the military might of Chiang Kaishek and invading Japanese forces, but also without any substantial aid from the Soviet Union. Basing its recruitment until very recently upon the agricultural areas, and involving itself in rural production, it has close associations with the peasantry. The PLA has a tradition of support for mass line policies and close involvement with farms and factories. It plays an extensive part in the creation of rural infrastructures and has a place in scientific and technical advance, as well as in cultural activities, with its ballet, music and literature units. Thus while they have the ability at times of weakness to reinforce the conventional public order forces, they have often done so as much on the basis of their ideological and social prestige as by force of arms.

However, the 1967 intervention incurred the wrath of some far-Left factions. Mao Zedong's exhortations at the outset of the Cultural Revolution had encouraged those wishing to see new forms of proletarian democracy. But his advocacy of mass line rather than 'bureaucratic' methods did not extend to sympathy with demands for 'proletarian power from below' as articulated during the short-lived Shanghai Commune, which used for its inspiration the Paris Commune of 1871. Proclaimed by the Revolutionary Rebels of Shanghai in January 1967, the example of the Shanghai Commune began to attract others. Mao was forced to issue his famous directive 'we must have chiefs' – thus elevating the Leninist principle of organisation and hierarchy over that of spontaneity and direct accountability. This directive was strongly resisted by anarchist-Leftists in many areas, whilst the Right continued to make armed stands against the intervention of the PLA on behalf of the 'non-anarchistic' Left of the CCP centre under Mao. The opposition in the huge city of Wuhan was particularly severe, with hundreds killed in battles between the warring factions; these events even shook many of the Leftist leaders of the Cultural Revolution, Mao Zedong included. The remainder of the 1960s was to see emphasis on the rebuilding of local government under a series of 'revolutionary committees' of workers, peasants and soldiers. This process involved use of the PLA's social prestige in a process of mediation much more than its force of arms in confrontation – although at times the latter did take place. As with Third World coups, the armed forces entered and directed politics at every level; unlike in other Third World countries the Army was to withdraw without too much protest, having consolidated power for the politicians rather than for the military. It should be noted that (whether military or political) these were actions initiated by the party rather than the military. Therefore, the PLA were the prime public order force in two ways. First, during the most destructive and anarchic phase of the Cultural Revolution (1966–69) they were called upon to restore order by force of arms in situations where either the Right or the ultra-Left were resisting the authority of Mao. Secondly, with the breakdown of existing administrative institutions, they played the key role in the newly-devised provisional organs of power at all levels of society. But the PLA were to return to military duties by the end of the Cultural Revolution.

Although nominally under the control of the PLA for most of the period since 1949, the militia has served various purposes during the history of the People's Republic. It has variously emphasised economic construction work, political activity, public security work at the local level, and assisted the PLA itself during times of major mobilisation.[17] Also the militia have been particularly active during times of ideological mobilisation in pursuit of collective economic or political goals. For example, during the movement to set up the Communes and the associated Great Leap Forward of the 1950s, militia membership climbed to over 220 million.[18] From time to time the militia has been used as a counter to other political forces, and even as a counter to elements in the PLA. During the Cultural Revolution there was a concerted move by Wang Hongwen, a prominent Shanghai-based member of the 'Gang of Four', to remove the militia from the control of the PLA, particularly in the urban areas. In his area, Wang transferred control of the newly-organised militia units to the trade union federation which he headed. These new units were well armed and focused on political intervention. Following the political realignments on the fall of the 'Gang of Four' in October 1976, the militia was once again unambiguously brought under the control of the PLA. By 1982 its active membership had fallen to some 5 million, yielding a ratio of 4.92 per 1000 of the population. The largely inactive reserve militia, numbering 75 million in 1982, has little autonomous political significance or public reputation. By contrast, despite a planned reduction of 1 million between 1985 and 1987, the PLA retains a prestige which neither the militia nor the police can rival, virtually guaranteeing its deployment, in instances of widespread public disorder, or in occasional serious disturbances in remoter areas.

PUBLIC ORDER SITUATIONS

The volatility of the Chinese political system since liberation in 1949 is not an unusual characteristic in socialist states, or indeed in any 'new' state, for in their early stages newly independent states often rely upon more tenuous charismatic leadership and authority. This creates problems, particularly for orderly succession and power transfer. In this respect, the situation in the USSR and Eastern Europe at the death of Stalin stands out as an example. The problem of public order in such situations is particularly acute. China's Cultural Revolution had as its background Mao Zedong's desire to ensure the continuation of mass line socialist policies beyond his death, and as such one would expect the challenge to public order to be strong. We have seen how the period of consolidation of CCP power following 1949 certainly did involve fighting real challenges to the state, yet during the often violent years between 1966 and 1976 the challenge to public order was very different. Public order was threatened by large-scale regime-sponsored attacks upon public figures, factions and institutions, who were no longer felt to be upholding the Maoist line. In Canton, the police lost control of the city to the Maoist Red Guards. Hundreds of deaths were reported. Industrial production was crippled in many areas and schools and universities closed.[19] However, while the police were not inactive during the period of the Cultural Revolution, they were secondary to the PLA as an enforcement agency. This is partly because the Cultural Revolution was an ideological disturbance of national significance rather than an outburst of criminal activity; it also involved a basic and political redefinition of 'criminal' along stark class lines. The police found themselves without the firm authority of undisputed law and often under public criticism as individuals. Many uniformed policemen chose simply to keep a low profile and to act only under direction from the new revolutionary mass organisations. However in some areas whole units of the plain clothes secret police were ordered by various leftist political factions to spread their members out into universities, factories, and other areas of unrest in order to act as a focus for demonstrations and other activities against rightist opponents of Mao.

The Red Guards moved against the courts and the police, thus weakening their ability to operate normally or to support Rightists in the ongoing power struggle. Following this the Bureau of Public Order was reorganised, its Minister dismissed and replaced by a PLA officer. These early stages of the Cultural Revolution were ones of demoralisation for the police; indeed after the most bitter of the fighting between rival Red Guard and rightist groupings in 1966–67 most of them tried to avoid official involvement in power struggles, leaving the PLA as the only national representatives of any semblance of 'law and order'. The police were to recover from this situation of demoralisation by being reconstructed in accordance with the mass line model. Senior police officers were sometimes sent for retraining at mass line cadre schools, and ordinary officers were exhorted to leave their desks and integrate their work with the mass organisations in factories, schools and communes. Indeed it was more the militia than the police who put down the April 1976 riot in Beijing's main Tian An Men Square – the first occasion on which organised and public mass opposition to the 'Gang of Four' was seen. The demonstrations occurred at the time of Qingming, the day when Chinese traditionally remember the dead, visit their ancestors' graves, and sweep them clean. In January 1976, China's highly respected Premier Zhou Enlai died. He had been subject to covert attacks from the Four, and both before and after his death there had been allusions that he was a 'capitalist roader'. The April 1976 Qingming remembrance in Beijing rapidly and spontaneously developed into a memorial demonstration for Zhou Enlai. Over a few days, 2 million people visited the square, and piled up wreaths in his memory. As the Four had actively discouraged this demonstration, it also contained an element of protest against the existing regime. Plainclothes police were despatched to the enormous square to shadow those who had made speeches and to photograph the handwritten allusive memorial poems. Overnight on the 4 April, the authorities removed all the wreaths, flowers and commemorative poems. Public reaction was swift. The following morning crowds thronged into the square, overturning and setting fire to government and militia vehicles. Official accounts of the protest, now seen by the post-Mao government and party as 'revolutionary', emphasise the brutality of the authorities: 'Late in the evening the lights in the square were suddenly turned on. Police and militia armed with clubs encircled the mourning throng and began a bloody and ruthless assault . . . many innocent victims were brutally battered . . . [and] subsequently . . . witch hunts were carried out in all places of work . . . several hundreds were interrogated and put under surveillance. The entire capital was paralysed with fear'.[20] It is notable that the emphasis in these reports is not so much on the role of the regular police, but more specially on the militia and the plainclothes force, whose relationship to the regular forces remains shadowy and ill-documented.

Following the fall of the Four in October 1976, there emerged a new emphasis on legal codes and practice, nominally aimed at combating arbitrary use and abuse of authority. Yet this change of regime itself was not achieved by entirely democratic means, for the arrest of the Four was in fact accomplished by the elite 8341 unit of the PLA in alliance with anti-Gang CCP members. Further, it was to be the end of 1980 before the Four were brought to public trial. The rise of a new Centre-Right coalition from that date has completely overturned the philosophy and practice of the Cultural Revolution. It is committed to economic advance through the use of monetary not ideological incentives, and reiterates concepts such as 'expertise' and 'professionalism' throughout the economy and society. Whilst the police have in general found this move an easier one to accommodate they now face a very different but equally complex public order situation. Whilst many accounts of the fall of the Four highlight the broad-based and eager acceptance of the new regime, there were in contrast pro-Leftist demonstrations and strikes of considerable intensity in Shanghai, Fujian and Hubei. Again, a variety of approaches were found in the short-term response of local police towards these changes.

The social and economic changes induced by the new 'liberal' economic policies have had effect on public order situations and their perception by the police. Whilst income levels for many peasants have risen, the salaries of cadres, and the wages of industrial workers have hardly improved. With considerable price inflation (particularly with regard to food), real income levels have fallen for many people. Unrest arising from this cannot be described as serious but during the latter part of 1985 the management of several factories in the Beijing area were forced to call in teams of cadres, including public security workers, in order to head off strikes. Public protests by young people at the rapidly increasing volume of Japanese imports and direct investment in China were first noted in 1985, and it was necessary to prevent student demonstrations against government economic policy breaking out in April 1986. First-hand reports from Universities in Beijing indicate that students (especially those of 'Beida' – Peking University itself) were intending to marshall demonstrations in Tiah An Men square at the time of Qingming remembrance. Orders were given by the authorities that all institutions of higher education in the

area should organise compulsory activities on their respective campuses for that day. Individual students were threatened with expulsion should they not attend these special meetings, which mainly
focused on the need for 'advance through discipline'. Several newspaper articles by prominent politicians were published around this
time emphasising that whilst discussion was 'a good thing', 'disorders'
– or demonstrations – were decidedly not.

While there is a rebuilding and reconsolidation of law and associated democratic reforms, it should be noted that, according to
Womack, the basic purpose of these reforms is not the limitation of
government by citizen rights but the strengthening of public rules to
limit the arbitrary behaviour of officials.[21] This leaves the state with
powers to define just who are the minority who oppose the people's
interest. For example, members of the short-lived 'democracy movement' in China which arose after the fall of the 'Gang of Four', were
an ill-defined aggregation of groups and individuals, who were rarely
hostile to Marxism; indeed many of them were ordinary workers
armed only with the desire to improve the socialist system. For a
short time their publications flourished, and were often on open sale.
However by March 1979 the authorities moved to halt their activities;
the Public Security Bureau was effectively given a new and authorita-
tive definition of 'those who oppose the People's interests'. From that
point onward the police – particularly the plainclothes branch – once
again became involved in the criminalisation of political dissent,
whether it was expressed by 'Rightists' or 'Leftists'.

PUBLIC PERCEPTIONS OF THE POLICE

There is little available data on public perception of the police. One
of the few sources – Whyte and Parish's survey of urban life in
contemporary China – concludes that the police are more likely to be
unpopular than the average neighbourhood leader. However, their
data is mainly from the late 1970s, a period when there was much
pressure on the urban police to ensure that youth sent to the countryside in the Cultural Revolution did not return. As a result, there were
frequent late night raids on households – a feature which certainly
soured police–public relations.[22] Further, it is very difficult in such a
diverse country as China to speak of the police as an aggregate, and
any available data can be misleading. However, despite new constitutional safeguards against arbitrary arrest, the police still possess a

relatively formidable set of powers over the ordinary citizen. They have the authority to impose terms of detention – on their own, or in association with other quasi-judicial units. They are also responsible for public health and census registration, which effectively gives them right of investigation of any person's home or background. For most of the period since 1949 police permission was required for all but local travel. Indeed, without endorsement of the previously essential ration card by the 'home' authorities, basic foods could not be obtained outside the locality. Thus the power to authorise or prevent family contact or work mobility was often in the hands of the police. The work unit has a similar power over mobility of Chinese workers. However such is the nature of policing that neighbourhood security committees and police know most individuals, and their powers are very much those of persuasion. For example, in the area of juvenile delinquency, Leng and Chiu[23] report that 'in minor cases of law infraction, teenage offenders are turned over to neighbourhood organisations, parents and teachers for help. Educational aid teams are organised by street committees, residential groups, schools, factories, enterprises, parents and the police to re-educate the problem youth'. Similarly, powers of persuasion in the area of social and political conduct are exercised by work units. As with the neighbourhood units, the work units will for example take a firm interest in the policing of family planning policies. First hints of an infringement of the one-child policy would bring friendly chats, followed if necessary by group discussions and, eventually, criticism. These kinds of pressures would also be brought to bear in the area of deviance from current political norms. Thus the twin *loci* of work and home are powerful socialising – and, in the final analysis, policing – agencies. Thus much of the public order in China is self-imposed by these agencies, which filter out many of the conflicts that might in other societies be left to the more formal areas of legal action such as the police and courts.

Further, even if during periods of 'order' the mass line perspective in police work decreases, it still remains as an ideological underlay. Ever since 1958 there have been regular 'Love the People' and 'Cherish the Police' campaigns. However strange these may sound to the Western ear, they are certainly taken seriously in China, for people are well acquainted with the philosophy of the mass line, which stresses friendly and open co-operation between officials and people. During these campaigns the police will undertake community projects, be particularly attentive to the needs of old people, children, the disabled and so on; in turn, the local people will be urged to go out of their way to do good deeds for their own police officers. Whilst Westerners might not recognise the terminology of these campaigns they would without doubt recognise the validity and utility of this application of 'community policing'.

The public security forces have not established themselves in a solid and unmistakable manner as a national force in the perception of the public. China's turbulent political history since 1949 has emphasised such differing conceptions of law and order that both national and local police organisation and practice has exhibited considerable inconsistency. It has also been seen to serve different political factions, rather than standing as a body with consistent practices that derive from constitutionally directed duties. Whilst the police are continually and consistently present in Chinese public and private life, they are not equally prominent. Formerly, they were regarded as but one part of the public order system involving security committees, military and paramilitary forces, and the myriad complex of other committees of youth, women's, and trade union organisations that exercised social and political control functions.

One reflection of this is that policemen have (until very recently) rarely featured in film or television drama or documentaries – unlike army or militia men, or indeed party secretaries. The economic reforms since 1978, designed to modernise and rationalise China's economy, have promoted a renewed emphasis on social order. The Ministry of Public Security wished the police to emerge from this policy change as upholders of the new legal codes, acting in a non-partisan and 'scientific' manner. Reflecting this, a number of films have now focused on the role of the police in the detection and rehabilitation of offenders. As yet, this emphasis is not widespread and has hardly extended to television. Curiously, though, there have been several opportunities for Chinese audiences to see Western-produced cinema films and television drama series about the police in other countries. In so far as the new economic, social and political policies continue, it is likely that the media will reflect the increasingly specialised role of the police. However, for many years to come the predominant public impression of the individual officer is likely to be that of someone associated with authority and the state rather than one who wears the badge of a separate and neutral body.

However, while it may be possible to 'cherish the police' at the local level, this may be more problematic at other levels. Both in the cities and countryside, mobile patrols operate in order to seek out trouble and to monitor potential public order situations. Similarly, a vast number of plain clothes or secret police take the guise of regular workers and are assigned to public places where disturbances may occur, such as bus and railway stations. Police 'roving spies' are also assigned to other areas designated as 'critical'.[24] Whilst this may be reassuring to the public insofar as it offers a deterrent to petty crime, it does mean that very little occurs without the knowledge of the police and their extensive information network. It is clear that Chinese people are beginning to share the fears of those in other countries of the operations of hidden and unaccountable agencies.

CONCLUSION

The central argument of this chapter is that the rapid social, economic and political change currently occurring in China has been the major factor in determining the relationship between police, state and society. Certainly, the police are an organisation which have contributed to this process of change in their own right, but this is secondary to the effect which larger social processes have had on shaping the police. For example, the period since 1978 has seen a marked increase in 'professionalism' in China's police services as a result of the policy of modernising the economy. Emphasis is placed upon legal procedures, upon structured hierarchies and chains of command. New distinctions in uniform emphasise differences between ranks and branches of the service, and thereby increase the clarity of boundary between responsibilities. Regularised and routine training increases police self-consciousness of itself as a relatively autonomous agency regulated by the demands of codified and specified law, rather than by seemingly arbitrary and changing 'policy' emanating from the CCP. The increasing routinisation of police work and China's membership of Interpol in 1984 again reinforce the image of relative autonomy for the police. However, part of the image of professionalism and autonomy owes to the increasing use of new technology itself related to the growth in complexity of work following the post-1978 emphasis on internal and external trade development; China's police now have to deal with credit card and computer fraud, drug trafficking (with some Chinese cities used as *entrepôts*), and (increasingly) motoring offences. However, it is quite apparent that the criteria of selection in enforcement still owes considerably to the influence of outside agencies; both CCP and government have urged periodic 'crackdowns' on robbery, corruption, and – under other names – on strikes and other forms of economic and political dissent. In August 1983, for instance, the government, fearful that its 'open door' strategy which accompanied the modernisation programmes was being threatened by bands of roving criminals, ordered a massive law and order campaign. It demanded the rounding-up of more than 100 000 suspected criminals by February 1984, at least 5000 of whom were reported to have been executed by January.[25] Those arrested were charged with offences ranging from murder and rape to armed robbery and the 'public humiliation' of women. The imposition of such draconian measures, involving the dispensation of summary (if not arbitrary) justice flies in the face of the apparent trend towards a more legalistic style of order-maintenance and suggests that the oriental despotic tail is still capable of wagging the modernising dog.

Notes

1. The translation of Chinese to English has long been problematic; many different systems have co-existed. In the main, this chapter uses the system currently in official use in China. Whilst this may create a few initial problems to those more familiar with older systems, most names and terms will be recognisable, for example, Mao Zedong/Mao Tsetung, Guomindang/Kuomintang, Beijing/Peking.
2. See: T. Bowden, *Beyond the Limits of the Law*, (1978); J.P. Brady, 'The Transformation of Justice Under Socialism: The Contrasting Experience of Cuba and China' (1981) 5–24; J.P. Brady, *Justice and Politics in People's China* (1982); S. Leng and H. Chiu, *Criminal Justice in Post-Mao China* (1985).
3. Peng Zhen, 'Importance of Improving China's Legislation' (1984) 16–17.
4. Leng and Chiu, *Criminal Justice*, pp. 17–18.
5. For example, Article 37 of the 1978 constitution states that no citizen may be arrested except with the approval or by decision of the People's Procurate, or by decision of a people's court. Arrests must be made by a 'public security organ'. Unlawful deprivation or restriction of citizens' freedoms by detention or by other means is prohibited. So is unlawful search of the person and of a citizen's home. The freedom and privacy of citizens' correspondence is protected by law, except in cases of public or state security or where a criminal offence is suspected. While these rights are newly established, in practice (as we shall see) the state is able to negate them with some ease.
6. Detailed in *People's Republic of China Year Book* (Beijing: Xinhua Publishing House, 1982).
7. For evidence of this see, for example, an interview with the then Minister for Public Security, Ruan Chongwu, 'Minister on Social Order in China' (1986) 12–16.

8. Ruan Chongwu (Beijing Review) cites these figures.
9. R. Ward and D.H. Bracey, 'Police Training and Professionalism in the People's Republic of China' (1985) 36–8.
10. E. Johnson, 'Neighbourhood Police in the People's Republic of China' (1984) 8–12.
11. Leng and Chiu, *Criminal Justice*, pp. 20–4.
12. This is reported in T. Saich, *China: Politics and Government* (1981) pp. 160–85 *passim*. See also *The Criminal Law of the People's Republic of China* (Beijing: Foreign Languages Press, 1984).
13. On the basis of 1985 figures, Ruan Chongwu (*Beijing Review*) claims China's crime rate to be the lowest in the world at 0.53 per 1000. Whatever the accuracy of the figures, or his claim, they suggest that most 'crime' is dealt with *outside* the courts.
14. See Brady, 'The Transformation of Justice' 16.
15. This structure is detailed in M.K. Whyte and W.L. Parish, *Urban Life in Contemporary China* (1984) pp. 18–23; 288.
16. Leng and Chiu, *Criminal Justice*, pp. 13–17.
17. See Saich, *China*, p. 147.
18. In 1958, 220 million represented over a third of the total population of the country. The implication is that most of the adult population were automatically enrolled as members of the voluntary, part-time militias during this period. The overwhelming majority would have been enrolled as reserve rather than active members of militias.
19. See Bowden, *Beyond the Limit's of the Law*, p. 196.
20. 'The Tiananmen Incident – Ten Years After', *Beijing Review*, 29, 14 (1986) 18–19.
21. B. Womack, 'Modernisation and Democratic Reform in China' (1983) 417–260.
22. Whyte and Parish, *Urban Life*.
23. Leng and Chiu, *Criminal Justice*, p. 78.
24. Bowden, *Beyond the Limits of the Law*, p. 201.
25. See the China supplements in the *Financial Times* of 19 October 1983 and 29 October 1984.

9 Conclusion

The preceding chapters illustrate both the differences and similarities that exist among a diverse range of states in the realm of public order policing. Conflict is, of course, an endemic feature of all societies, but the causes and expressions of conflict vary. However, what unites our chosen countries is their imperative need to maintain internal order. How this need is met, by whom it is satisfied, and the extent to which it is fulfilled provide telling indicators of the quality of the relationship between state and society. The focus on the issue of public order is particularly instructive since it affords insights into the values, rules and procedures that underpin the distinction between legal and illegal protest.

Whether one adopts a liberal or a radical perspective of the state, the police occupy a strategic role in the regulation of political conflict. In the former case, the state derives its legitimacy from its representation as the embodiment of broadly-agreed values and the neutral and equal application of the rules governing acceptable political conduct. From this standpoint, the state must not be a forbidding presence in society, but rather a lofty and dispassionate arbiter of conflict. This abstract and minimal conception of the state is transcended by delegating authority to institutions that mediate conflict, notably the police. They are invested with the features embodied in the idea of the state itself: that is, as disinterested custodians of public order. This contrasts with the radical view, whereby the state is portrayed as intrusive and expansive, functioning not as the benign guarantor of broadly-agreed values, but as a bastion whose primary purpose is to defend the interests of the powerful. This representation of the state as an instrument of domination controlled by a minority which is motivated to uphold their interests is realised in the actions of its agencies of social control. On this view, the police support and protect those groups whose interests are fostered by the state and they are therefore defined as partisan enforcers of minority needs as well as agents of political control. Whereas the liberal view emphasises policing by consent, the radical alternative recognises the police only as an instrument of coercion.

Though these somewhat stereotypical characterisations provide contrasting explanations of state–society relations and of the role of the police, in practice all states need to control internal order and the emphasis placed on consent and coercion is variable. While in liberal-democracies (like Great Britain, the USA and the Irish Republic) the conduct of the police is closely circumscribed by law, it is not unusual for them to breach formal constraints and to act outside the law, whether in the detection of ordinary crime or in the prevention and quelling of disorder. Conversely, even the most authoritarian of states (like China or South Africa) impose certain limits on police conduct affording their citizens some form of legal protection, although the idea of legality is invariably preached more than it is practised. Irrespective of their ideological base or political system, all states must maintain internal order. It is this defining activity that governs the equation between the police, public order and the state. The focus on public order policing thus throws into high relief the condition of the relationship between state and society. By examining concrete instances of the policing of public order, it is possible to construct a framework for the comparative analysis of order-maintenance and to provide cross-national insights.

A COMPARISON OF THE POLICING OF PUBLIC ORDER

This section will discuss the main lines of convergence and divergence between our case study countries, examining the extent to which there are commonly experienced problems of public order and the implementation of similar solutions. The subsequent sections will identify the implications that follow from these comparisons and develop a typology of state strategies toward the policing of public order.

Despite the contrasting nature of the states covered in this volume, our case studies reveal that there are commonly experienced problems of public order. Quite often instances of public disorder follow a similar pattern across societies, with groups asserting fairly minimal demands and sometimes precipitously finding themselves in full-scale confrontation with the state. But the nature of the problems which provoke disorder varies considerably. Such is the ubiquity of international terrorism that most of the states concerned are forced to confront the threat it presents, although in some instances (most notably the Irish Republic) it is motivated more by external circumstances than by internal strife. Since the 1970s terrorism has been perceived as a major challenge to public order in many countries. This has taken a variety of forms. Of the case studies here, the USA,

Northern Ireland, Israel and South Africa have been affected by significant instances of terrorism of domestic origin. Northern Ireland, for example, has a variety of Loyalist and Republican groups, while Israel has both Palestinian and anti-Arab groups and South Africa has the ANC. In all these cases (except that of the USA), the external links of those domestic organisations engaged in terrorism has loomed as an important issue: neighbouring states are seen as providing safe havens or the groups are said to be financed from external forces. A much wider category of states has been affected by the issue of international terrorism – that is to say, terrorism carried out by groups without a significant political base in the society affected. Clear examples of this phenomenon are Armenian bombings in Switzerland and attacks by Lebanese groups in France, and it is apparent in less clearcut form among the case studies in this volume. Examples are attacks on Americans abroad, Loyalist actions in the Irish Republic and IRA bombs on the British mainland. The issue of state involvement in this terrorism has become a major concern of international politics. In domestic terms, it has provided a spur to authoritarian measures, such as the passage of tough emergency legislation in the Irish Republic following Loyalist bombs in 1972, and the amendment of the British Prevention of Terrorism Act to incorporate international terrorism.

The preceding chapters demonstrate that some of the issues which motivate public disorder relate to long-standing cleavages within society, such as sectarian divisions in Northern Ireland, racial inequality in South Africa, and the issue of the rights of national minorities, which Israel exemplifies well. More remarkably, previous chapters indicate that the degree to which society is divided along ethnic, religious or national lines does not necessarily match the extent of the challenge to public order. There are many instances where less systematic and over-arching cleavages within society prompt public disorder of equal intensity. These sorts of cleavages can relate to the immediate local circumstances pertaining in a particular neighbourhood (as is often the case in the USA and in Britain's inner cities), or to the effects of particular state policies, as exemplified by reactions to policies covering such things as industrial relations and the control of large crowds. China represents an interesting variation on this, for fundamental shifts in the state's official ideology have clearly in this instance provoked disorder. Often in China's case this disorder has been deliberately encouraged for its supposedly cathartic effect. Normally, however, states are only indirectly responsible for disorder, usually having to confront disorder which is linked to the actions of those who politically oppose the state for some reason of policy or practice. However, in some instances, the legitimacy of the state itself can be at issue, as it was in the first years of the Irish Republic and still is in contemporary Northern Ireland and Israel. But this is less the case in South Africa, an equally divided society, where it is more a question of what policy goals the state pursues towards Blacks.

The fact that the challenge to public order does not necessarily correlate with the depth of cleavage in society should not be interpreted as arguing that ethnic divisions are an unimportant source of public disorder. Indeed, it is significant that even in those cases where ethnicity is not the primary source of political division in the society (such as in the USA and Great Britain) it is still a major basis of disorder. Ethnicity does not appear as a public order issue in two of our case studies, for both China and the Republic of Ireland are ethnically homogeneous societies. It is also significant that ethnic divisions loom large as a source of conflict in divided societies within both dominant and subordinate communities. How the state handles disorder in this area is a measure of the state's capacity to stand above contending factions in society and to act as the guarantor of the rights of ethnic minorities. It is notable from our case studies that states which govern divided societies (such as Israel, South Africa and Northern Ireland) increasingly face public order problems arising from divisions within the dominant group, which intensifies the difficulties of order-maintenance. There are divisions between Ashkenazim and Oriental Jews, and between ultra-orthodox and secular Jews, which have a similar effect in Israel as the political and ideological divisions which sustain militant Loyalism in Northern Ireland and the Afrikaans Right wing in South Africa.

These cases provide good instances of how changes in the nature of the state affect public order. The change in the relationship between religion and the state in Israel has provoked disorder, whereas the more obvious change in the character and practice of the state in Northern Ireland and South Africa – represented by, respectively the Anglo-Irish Agreement and the policy of deracialisation – has provoked a backlash in the dominant group which has produced new and perhaps more difficult challenges to stability and order, creating dilemmas for policing in the societies concerned. The move to co-option in Northern Ireland and South Africa, for example, has changed time-honoured traditions of policing which have brought problems for the regular police forces. In Northern Ireland, it has forced the RUC to move against those sections of the Protestant community which threaten public order, such as banning or re-routeing Orange Order parades through Catholic areas, which has alienated many Protestants and intensified the risk the RUC face. In South Africa, the SAP are subject to new controls which force them to be circumspect in their treatment of Blacks and has lost them some state protection. This has affected the morale of many policemen in these two forces and led a minority of them to question their loyalty to the respective state.

In most of the examples discussed in earlier chapters, it is cleavages within the society which provoke disorder. Besides the example of international terrorism, there are other instances where external issues spill over into internal disorder. In such cases, the state has greater difficulty in controlling the events which precipitate public disorder. Public disorder in the Irish Republic, for example, is now virtually entirely related to events which occur outside its national boundaries. In some cases, this can lead to an ambiguous demarcation of responsibility between the police and the military (who are more usually seen as protecting national borders), and in some extreme examples (where the challenge to public order is seen to lie in external threat), it can result in an under-evaluation and lack of status for the police. This is so in Israel, and to a lesser extent in the Irish Republic. It is also the case that there are states where internal divisions are exacerbated by external forces intensifying the threat to public order, such as the impact variously of Zimbabwean independence and international sanctions on South Africa, the aspirations of the Republic of Ireland in the North and the Vietnam War in the USA.

Public order, then, can be threatened by many issues which provide parallels as well as differences across the states discussed here. The particular nature of these issues is important for police policy and conduct. For example, particular sorts of cleavage can affect how the police are perceived by an ethnic, religious, racial or national minority group, making them special targets of protest. Again, recruitment patterns to the police can be altered to overcome this alienation, and particular forms of policing can be introduced for the same effect, such as the renewed emphasis on community policing in Britain's inner cities. In societies with certain sorts of fundamental cleavage, it matters a great deal who the police are, and the composition of the force is an important variable in their ability to contain and regulate conflict. Hence the effort to open up police membership to minority groups in Northern Ireland, Israel, South Africa, the USA and Great Britain. This fact further reinforces the importance of the effect of ethnicity on the policing of public order.

The solutions to these commonly experienced problems of public order also provide some parallels. It is notable that irrespective of the political and ideological character of the state and the cleavages to which disorder is related, all the states covered in this volume have legislated for public disorder in similar ways. They all have public order legislation of some form or other – even China – which provides the legal framework within which specific public order offences are defined, as well as outlining the powers available to those who police them and the punishments which specific challenges to public order entail. In some cases there is a separate legal system which deals with public order (such as the Diplock Courts in Northern Ireland), but mostly it is the target which differentiates public order legislation. Thus there is legislation common in all the states which govern demonstrations, public gatherings and other forms of protest. The legally defined punishments vary from detentions, bannings and imprisonment, found both in liberal-democratic and authoritarian states, to China's 're-education through labour'. The availability of more extensive emergency powers is a common provision of all the states discussed here, despite their different complexion. In the case of the Irish Republic, this reliance on emergency powers reflects a situation where challenges to public order are infrequent enough for there to be little public order legislation. But in most instances it reflects the inadequacy of normal statutes to deal with increasingly frequent and intense threats to public order.

What differs across the states discussed here is the extent to which the powers conferred by public order legislation and emergency regulations are monitored by the courts or by special complaints procedures, and whether 'due process' or the norm of legality[1] is followed in pursuing public disorder. It fits our picture of authoritarian states for China and South Africa to have no monitoring system and for the rights of citizens to be trammeled by the state, but in practice the situation is more complex. The changing nature of the South African state has led it to introduce a very weak form of monitoring, which sits uneasily alongside very repressive public order legislation. Indeed, even in China's case, the move within the state towards modernisation of the economy has influenced policing, increasing pressure for a framework of legislation, a stress on the use of the courts and the development of professionalism within the force. In liberal-democratic states there are more developed forms of monitoring, especially where there is a Bill of Rights or a written constitution (as with the USA and the Irish Republic), although most citizens consider the monitoring systems too weak. This reflects the difficult balance which liberal-democratic states have to strike between civil liberties and the maintenance of public order, although (as the public order incidents discussed in the Great Britain chapter (Chapter 2) show) there are instances when a liberal-democracy tips the scales against civil liberties. This is particularly the case where specific governments within liberal-democratic states operate, for whatever reason, with a wider definition of public disorder than is usual, thus drawing into the realm of public order such previously innocuous behaviour as hippy communes and peace camps. In Britain's case, it is tempting to advance the argument that public order issues highlight the increasingly authoritarian nature of the British state.

One other variation in the cases discussed here is the frequency with which the emergency regulations dealing with public order are invoked: it seems that some countries are in a state of permanent emergency. In the Irish Republic's case this is because emergency regulations are the basic means for dealing with public order, whereas in South Africa it is due to the severity of the challenge to it. So intense has this challenge become in South Africa that the draconian emergency regulations have been incorporated into established law. A final variation between the states covered in this volume is the extent to which extra- or non-legal powers are available to the state or the police. Liberal-democratic states operate under the constraint of 'due process' or the norm of legality which restricts their non-legal powers. But by enacting new legislation which widens the definition of public disorder and therefore extends the range of public order offences, the oppressive nature of such changes is cloaked in the mantle of legality, as is the case with Britain's Public Order Act. This is also accomplished in some instances by a process of criminalisation, so that formerly legal or peaceful acts are criminalised in order to justify the severity of the state's response to them. Thus carol singing in South Africa becomes defined as a threat to public order because it is supposed to be linked to the aspirations (if not the actions) of terrorists, and picketing miners in Britain become portrayed as the 'enemy within'. However two different categories of criminalisation need to be distinguished. The first is affixing the label 'political' to action that is lawful in terms of the ordinary criminal law so that it is presented as illegitimate because it is held to fall outside the realm of normal political behaviour. This is a tactic not uncommon in respect of industrial disputes, and the South African government justifies criminalising certain kinds of church services and funerals on the grounds of their political character. In this case, the attribution of political motive to the act is crucial to delegitimising it. The other form of criminalisation is the flat denial of a political dimension to unlawful acts. This option represents the attempt to delegitimise behaviour by preventing the perpetrators from claiming that political motivation makes otherwise illegal acts legitimate, such as the denial of political status to Republican prisoners in Northern Ireland. A more subtle form of this is the South African government's representation of intra-Black violence as a form of mindless anarchy rather than a struggle that is a function of the larger Black–White conflict.

Other states, of course, give the police (as the defenders of public order) an autonomy which allows them in practice to have a wider definition of public disorder than the law allows (which is exemplified by the police in South Africa) or gives them a discretion in how offences are construed and which laws to apply. The miners' strike in Britain shows how the police had discretion in construing offences, with some pickets being prosecuted for riot, although the courts subsequently dismissed all such cases. Even the South African state has had some of its emergency regulations defined as non-legal by the courts, with prosecutions under them being dismissed, although many of the regulations have been redrawn. But even China's police force have restrictions placed on their powers by the need to obtain permission from the People's Procurate in order to detain and question. What differentiates these cases from the restrictions imposed in liberal-democratic states is the lack of independence of the judiciary and the fact that the police can be assured of judicial compliance with their wishes. As the chapter on China (Chapter 8) emphasises, permission is often available under standing orders, and South Africa's judiciary, with the exception of the Natal Bench, are not noted for their independence. This is particularly the case with magistrates, who are state appointees and who try all public order offences save those of treason, terrorism and sabotage.

But providing a legal framework within which public order can be protected and specific offences defined is not the only solution to problems of public order. It is notable in all the countries covered here that the protection of public order has been militarised. This is meant in two senses. In their defence of public order the police have been provided with technological equipment and arms which amount to their militarisation. In some forces this is restricted to functionally specialised and equipped units, while in others it is part of the duties and equipment of a multi-purpose force. Militarising the police in this way occurs in some states because of the preference for arming the police rather than using the Army in situations of public disorder, which sits more easily with liberal views of the relationship between society and the state. However, in some states the police are militarised in a second sense, in that they are aided in their defence of public order by the military, with whom they can have strong links. Militarisation in either of these two senses is a common solution to challenges to public order.

A regular or volunteer Army assists the police in public order situations in a wide cross-section of states, including the USA, China, Israel, Northern Ireland, South Africa and the Irish Republic; indeed in the liberal-democratic Republic of Ireland, the army has powers of civil arrest, as they do in South Africa. Sometimes this connection with the Army is a historical legacy of past conflicts (as in the Irish Republic), but more often it reflects the inability of the regular police to deal with intense threats to public order, either through manpower shortages, under-funding or lack of sufficient technological equipment. Manpower shortages (see Table 9.1) particularly affect the police in South Africa, where even employers of Black labour have policing functions, while under-funding (see Table 9.2) is a severe problem of the Israeli police, although in this case it also reflects the public's greater faith in the efficiency and effectiveness of the military. In China's case, it occurs because there is a close ideological relationship between the state and the People's Liberation Army (PLA).

This link with the Army brings its own problems. In both the North and the Republic of Ireland there have been difficulties of police–military liaison over their respective jurisdictions. It creates particular ideological problems for liberal-democracies, where the police are usually portrayed as the neutral arbiters who hold together the framework by which society's struggles are resolved peacefully. In these instances, the role of the military in civil matters has to be specifically justified, either by presenting the threat as an external one (as occurs in Israel), explaining it as a peculiarity of the nation's past (such as in the Irish Republic), or as a desire to separate the regular police force from the pejorative consequences which follow

Table 9.1 Police manpower ratios per 1000 of population

Year	Great Britain[1]	Northern Ireland	Irish Republic	United States	Israel	South Africa	China[2]
1960	1.69	2.96	–	–	2.7	1.61	–
1961	1.73	2.89	2.34	–	2.6	–	–
1962	1.78	2.51	2.31	–	2.5	1.59	–
1963	1.81	1.34	2.24	–	2.4	1.66	–
1964	1.90	2.24	2.25	–	2.5	1.56	–
1965	2.01	2.30	2.28	–	2.5	1.60	–
1966	2.07	2.22	2.27	–	2.8	1.61	–
1967	2.09	2.13	2.25	–	3.2	1.66	–
1968	2.09	2.14	2.24	–	3.2	1.65	–
1969	2.08	2.01	2.23	–	3.2	1.61	–
1970	–	2.50	2.21	–	3.1	1.46	–
1971	–	2.66	2.21	–	3.0	1.42	–
1972	2.22	2.76	2.31	–	3.0	1.40	–
1973	2.24	2.84	2.53	–	3.0	1.29	–
1974	2.35	2.95	2.56	–	3.2	1.30	–
1975	2.43	3.19	2.64	–	3.5	1.27	–
1976	2.45	3.42	2.61	–	3.8	1.31	–
1977	2.45	3.70	2.59	2.5	3.8	1.29	–
1978	2.46	3.97	2.77	–	3.8	1.26	–
1979	2.48	4.29	2.78	–	4.3	1.19	–
1980	2.49	4.48	2.85	–	4.2	1.19	–
1981	2.50	4.69	2.82	–	4.2	1.16	–
1982	2.52	4.92	2.87	–	4.1	1.41	–
1983	2.53	5.09	3.09	–	4.6	1.38	–
1984	2.51	5.15	3.17	–	4.5	1.41	–
1985	–	–	3.20	–	–	–	–
1986	–	–	–	–	–	–	1.17

Notes:
1 Men only.
2 'Security personnel'.

Source: Calculated from previous tables.

from their involvement in often violent public order incidents. This is part of the justification for employing the National Guard in periods of unrest in the USA, for it absolves the regular police force from association with the actions of those who police public order. This applies to some extent also to the Israeli police. This is one of the reasons why the public image of the police has not deteriorated in the USA to the same extent as in Britain, and it is one of the arguments used to justify the creation of a similar force in Great Britain. One·

Table 9.2   Police budget as a percentage of total government expenditure

Financial Year	Great Britain[1]	Northern Ireland	Irish Republic	United States	Israel	South Africa	China
1960–61	–	–	–	–	2.24	4.03	–
1961–62	–	–	–	–	1.90	3.91	–
1962–63	–	–	–	–	1.94	3.76	–
1963–64	2.6	–	–	–	1.57	3.76	–
1964–65	–	–	–	–	1.83	3.24	–
1965–66	–	–	–	–	1.72	3.42	–
1966–67	–	–	–	–	1.83	3.17	–
1967–68	–	–	–	–	1.66	3.22	–
1968–69	–	–	–	–	1.59	3.18	–
1969–70	–	–	–	–	1.53	3.16	–
1970–71	–	–	–	–	1.30	2.74	–
1971–72	–	2.5	–	–	1.16	2.78	–
1972–73	–	2.6	–	–	1.00	2.74	–
1973–74	–	3.0	–	–	0.85	2.87	–
1974–75	–	3.0	–	–	0.92	2.81	–
1975–76	–	3.6	–	–	1.03	2.36	–
1976–77	–	3.8	–	–	0.92	2.13	–
1977–78	–	4.2	–	–	1.19	2.33	–
1978–79	–	4.3	–	–	1.29	2.19	–
1979–80	–	5.1	–	–	1.33	2.07	–
1980–81	–	5.5	1.4	–	1.29	2.33	–
1981–82	–	6.3	1.5	–	1.30	–	–
1982–83	–	6.3	1.5	–	1.32	–	–
1983–84	4.0	6.3	1.6	–	0.91	2.47	–
1984–85	–	6.4	1.6	–	0.88	3.0	–
1985–86	–	6.5	1.5	1.15	–	2.98	–

Note:
1 'Law and Order and Protective Services'.

Source: Calculated from previous tables.

other reason advanced for the creation of such a force in Britain is that it would prevent the regular force from being brutalised as a result of their involvement in the violent suppression of disorder, with particularly disastrous effects on the wider public image of the police.

Northern Ireland provides a lesson for the British state here, for the special police units of the RUC have become increasingly embroiled in controversial instances of covert action which have affected their public image. Indeed, the RUC are in a difficult position for they have to justify their actions to a parent state which operates with norms of 'due process' and legality which are more appropriate to the divisions of British society than to Northern Ireland. The attempt by the British state to civilianise policing in Northern Ireland in the early 1970s has to be seen in the context of the British state's unwillingness to deviate from the liberal-democratic view of the police as unmilitarised citizens in uniform, a view supported by the Police Federation of Northern Ireland. This idea of the police as citizens in uniform is an eloquent if sanguine statement of the liberal view of the relationship between society and the state. The failure of this policy in Northern Ireland as a result of an intensification of political violence, demonstrates the constraints which public disorder imposes on police policy.

Another point is noteworthy about Northern Ireland. This policy of civilianisation of the RUC illustrates how, on occasions, police policy can be deliberately used to try and affect the state–society relationship, for it represents an instance where police policy was changed in order to improve or affect the divisions within society. The changes in police policy toward Orange Order marches in Catholic areas is another example of this in Northern Ireland, while the South African situation shows how changes in police policy with respect to the treatment of detainees and the opening up of police membership to Blacks has been used to improve the state–society relationship. However, in the short term the use of policemen and women from distinctive ethnic groups has in some instances provoked rather than prevented disorder.

Such is the saliency of public order issues in the contemporary world that even in those forces which are largely unarmed (like Great Britain and the Irish Republic), or those (like Britain) that have little obvious contact with the military, specialist sections within the force have been formed to deal with public order situations, and they can rely on a battery of riot control equipment and arms. Only in the case of South Africa are the regular force expected to employ these skills and equipment, although all regular policemen in Britain get at least some training in riot control. Thus, China has its Armed Police Division, Israel its Special Duties Division, SWAT and similar forces exist in the USA, the Special Task Force operates in the Irish Republic and Great Britain has the specially trained and equipped Police Support Units, District Support and Territorial Support Groups, who are drawn from the ranks of the regular force and deployed in incidents of disorder. In authoritarian states and divided societies the existence of these specialist forces presents no problems of justification, but in most of the liberal-democratic states covered in this volume, these specialist units were developed only after regular forces had unsuccessfully tried to counter threats to public order by traditional methods. Strikes by miners and inner city riots in Britain and the riot outside the British Embassy in Dublin were instances which convinced the respective states that specialist units and equipment were necessary. No longer do British police tackle major public disorder with dustbin lids and standard truncheons; this slow shift toward a militarised and specialist public order police reflects a reluctance on the part of some liberal-democracies to change the public image of the police as uniformed but unarmed men and women 'in the middle'. In Britain's case this reluctance hangs incongruously with the argument that there is a shift by the British state toward the right. This is especially so because the lines of political responsibility for the British police are plural enough to allow local police authorities some influence over chief constables. At one time, they could restrict a chief constable's access to weaponry, although this is no longer the case. Plurality in political responsibility is being supplanted by centralisation, and it can be argued that Britain now has a *de facto* national force, with all the danger this entails from state manipulation of centralised structures of authority and organisation.

Any police force is more open to manipulation and pressure from governments when the lines of responsibility are singular, which is the case in South Africa, Israel and the Irish Republic. As Chapter 4 illustrates, in the liberal-democratic Republic of Ireland there are instances where ministers have attempted to exploit this single line of responsibility for partisan advantage, which is almost a daily occurrence in the authoritarian state of South Africa. The degree to which political manipulation of the police occurs is also affected by whether the forces are national and centralised or regional and decentralised. It is clear from previous chapters that the more decentralised the police force the less a common policy and practice can be implemented and the less effect political pressure or manipulation from the central government has. The federal system in the USA, for example, has a significant effect on policing. As was emphasised, this federal structure can lead to an overlapping jurisdiction, duplication of effort and a loss of efficiency, but it also produces a fierce local autonomy which resists political pressure from the centre. In the USA, this localism even extends to differences in uniform, pay and conditions of service. Regionalising the organisation and structure of the police has a similar effect in unitary states such as Great Britain, although with the public order incidents which have occurred in Britain during the 1980s, there has been a tendency to centralise the police through the mutual aid system co-ordinated if not controlled by the National Reporting Centre.

In short, this volume demonstrates that there are commonly experienced problems of public order in the states which are discussed, and commonly implemented solutions. But more important, despite these parallels, there is considerable variation depending on the nature or changing nature of the state, the cultural and political traditions in society, the specific cleavages to which disorder is related and the organisational structure of authority in the police forces concerned. Therefore, analysis of the policing of public order successfully crystallises the state–society relationship and shows the complex variables that enter a study of policing.

CATEGORISATIONS OF THE POLICE AND THE STATE

Categorising police forces and their styles of policing on a comparative basis is difficult because police forces are complex organisations and the socioeconomic, political and cultural circumstances in which they operate vary. Nonetheless in order to present variations of experience in an organised fashion, Bayley has grouped police forces into three categories or styles, which he termed 'authoritarian', 'oriental' and 'Anglo-Saxon'.[2] It is worth focusing on his arguments, for they represent one of the first attempts to formulate a comparative typology of policing. What is also unusual about Bayley's work is that it does not concentrate on a narrow range or homogeneous set of countries, which other comparative studies have done[3], but rather extends the comparisons to encompass a world-wide perspective. There is another reason for drawing attention to Bayley's framework, for while he makes one qualification·about the dangers of holding a simplistic view of policing and of the police as an organisation, the whole tenor of his comparative analysis vitiates this warning. We contend that comparative analyses should not be undertaken in spite of this qualification, but should specifically address themselves to it.

'Authoritarian policing' occurs within totalitarian systems where the state assumes authority to regulate society in whatever way is required to achieve desired ends. The police intrude as they wish and minutely regulate the whole of society. People come under scrutiny for behaviour which is seen as precursory to criminality, so that the police intervene pre-emptively in private lives in order to ensure that public order is not threatened. Moreover, they act without legal restraint: often the police are empowered to enact their own regulations. Consequent upon these extensive powers, the police have a wide ambit of authority, acting as an omnipotent agency performing whatever administrative tasks the state requires. All this means that the police do not exist to help the public but to service the state; they do not placate citizens, but control and direct them. The emphasis is placed upon control through deterrence not prevention through amelioration. A sign of this, according to Bayley, is the martial appearance of 'authoritarian police', with their arms prominently displayed.

Whereas 'authoritarian police' attempt to control and overawe through fear, 'oriental police' emphasise service through community policing. The police are similarly enmeshed in the routine daily life of the local community, but control is maintained through persuasion, counselling and community support. This form of policing (common to Japan, Malaysia, Korea and China) places an obligation on the police to create a known presence in the community which provides an opportunity for them to identify with the locale. No matter is too trivial, no service irrelevant for the 'oriental' style of policing. For instance, Bayley cites the urban Japanese experience, where police may boil milk for babies' bottles when women call at their local police station while out shopping. Through such methods the police deliberately try to embed themselves in social life, providing community services as much as law enforcement and functioning as moral censors on virtue, patriotism, duty and so forth.

According to Bayley 'Anglo-Saxon police' are more specialised. They tend to concentrate more narrowly on tasks associated with law enforcement, so that they are not all-purpose administrative agents of the state or community welfare workers. Furthermore, they have legal but no moral authority, with their role in the community being minimal and restricted largely to emergency responses. Individual officers may succeed occasionally in immersing themselves in the community's daily life, but this is not enshrined as an organisational objective. There is no routine, low visibility interaction with the public, no large clandestine presence watching for signs of imminent criminality: they are like firemen, staying in their stations until times of need. The response they provide in such circumstances is determined by an extensive legal framework which governs their conduct and guarantees the rights of citizens. This is symptomatic of the fact that the authority of the state, like that of the police, is jealously guarded and limited by a public which is conscious of its rights and fearful of police intrusion. Bayley argues that this style of policing typifies the liberal-democracies.

Leaving aside the question of whether these styles are adequate to cover all the world's police forces, as Bayley believes, there is another problem which is more pertinent to our concerns. His attempt to compare police forces and their style of policing is based on the erroneous assumption that national forces are homogeneous and monolithic and operate with a single style which is suited to the traditions and character of the state and society. A functional breakdown of the tasks of the police in a wide range of different states, such as that presented here, shows that all these styles can co-exist in a national force irrespective of the nature of the state and society. This is clearly apparent in an analysis of public order policing.

On the basis of the comparisons drawn in the previous section, it is clear that the 'Anglo-Saxon' liberal-democracies have police forces, or specialist units therein, which, occasionally, discharge 'authoritarian policing' functions. For example, like authoritarian states, liberal-democratic states also have the task of information gathering, neutralisation of offenders and social control, where the state assumes authority to regulate the private lives of people considered to present a threat to public order. Taking Britain as an example, it has been shown how the information gathering and storage technologies available to the police have become increasingly sophisticated, and that the state has intruded in the private lives of people to the extent of preventing, for example, some hippies and miners from driving on the highway because they were deemed to pose a threat to public order. Likewise, even police forces in authoritarian states perform 'oriental policing': that is they have obligations to provide guidance, protection and other community services. While the police in South Africa perform the many administrative tasks for the state which are characteristic of 'authoritarian police', specialist sections of the SAP, for example, have responsibility for liaison with schools, help with drug abuse and other community programmes. In the supposedly 'Anglo-Saxon' style of the British police, a community police programme, reminiscent of the 'oriental' style, has been readopted to improve police–public relations in the inner cities. Similarly, the police in China have functions which transcend the 'oriental' style they are claimed to operate with. Especially in the realm of public order policing, the police there have 'authoritarian' functions, but, as the chapter on China (Chapter 8) emphasised, there are also burgeoning elements of the legalistic 'Anglo-Saxon' style.

A comparative analysis of public order policing shows that all forces discharge a wide range of duties which encompass all these styles. Bayley's typology also underplays the influence the state has on styles of policing. Indeed, the state is a taken-for-granted and passive agent in his work. Although Bayley's typology implies that geographically and culturally contiguous states exhibit similar policing styles, this seductive idea is misleading and fails to address explicitly the relationship between policing and the state. Yet it is clear from previous chapters that the state plays an important role in conditioning the styles of policing adopted by a force in particular circumstances, at different historical periods and when confronted with specific issues and threats. Any comparative typology of public order policing therefore needs to incorporate two features: differences in the police–state relationship and the varying mix of styles which states typically deploy to accomplish order maintenance.

With these imperatives in view, it may be productive to identify a range of distinctive strategies employed by all states, which are united by their common and primary requirement to maintain internal order. The focus on state strategies in the face of public disorder enables us to avoid the regional dimension and monolithic approach characteristic of Bayley's arguments and to offer a typology that we contend more easily facilitates comparative analysis.

A TYPOLOGY OF STATE STRATEGIES IN PUBLIC ORDER POLICING

Most states expect to face public disorder of varying degrees of seriousness on an episodic basis and consequently evolve procedures for the police to follow in the handling of disorder. If the threat to public order is discontinuous the state will not usually define mechanisms for the detailed political supervision of the methods of order-maintenance. However, where disorder occurs on a sustained and generalised basis states must necessarily intervene through high-level strategic decision-making, so as to meet the challenge of actual or threatened instability. This is especially so where the disorder reflects a community's alienation from the institutions of the state itself. Just as the authority of the state depends upon its effectiveness and the scope and intensity of popular consent, the same is generally true of the police. When, for instance, disorder appears as an irregular series of episodes in a normally tranquil society there is a tendency for a premium to be placed upon policing by consent. In such circumstances, the quelling of disorder is a matter of applying first aid to an otherwise healthy political system. However, where disorder (or the threat of it) reaches epidemic proportions, the emphasis shifts to police effectiveness and may require surgical intervention into an ailing society. The balance between these remedies is fragile. To either maintain or regain social wellbeing, states have at their disposal a variety of strategies. While it is impossible to provide an exhaustive account of the strategies potentially open to states faced with disorder, the response of the state can generally be fitted into three broad categories: criminalisation, accommodation and suppression. Since these are not mutually exclusive, they can be combined in varying forms in particular societies.

On one level, criminalisation involves the police treating public disorder as instances of ordinary breaches of the law without regard to the political context in which the offences occur. It may also entail the denial of the existence of any political context at all. The justification for such an approach is that it requires the application of the rule of law by the police as a universal principle without exception. In the face of sustained public disorder, this strategy generally restricts the police to the limited policy of containment, given the difficulties of bringing successful prosecutions in circumstances where the legitimacy of political authority has broken down. Criminalisation can also be a much more ambitious strategy by extending the scope of the criminal law beyond direct manifestations of disorder to cover actions previously regarded as innocent of criminal intent. In this case, too, the police rely on the universal applicability of law to justify the action taken to quell disorder. In effect, the state discounts the political dimension to disorder.

The strategy of accommodation attempts in some form or other to meet the grievances of the groups from which disorder emanates. The varying types of accommodation have different implications for police conduct. Some of the most common forms of accommodation are measures to remove discrimination against a group, affirmative action programmes and steps to tackle deprivation. Assimilation by a minority group into the host community is the most preferred form of accommodation in some states, while others reject integration, choosing a policy of cultural pluralism designed to protect the special needs of particular groups. Accommodation can also be effected by policies of devolution or decentralisation in order to meet the multifarious demands of some region. In the case of international terrorism, accommodation can take the form of an adjustment in the country's foreign policy, thereby acknowledging the need to find a political solution to an external conflict which spills across state boundaries. The police can be passive actors in implementing or upholding these forms of accommodation, or they can themselves be a mechanism by which accommodation is facilitated, such as encouraging recruitment to the force from disadvantaged or disaffected groups or having different policing policies suited to various cultural or socioeconomic groups. An example of this would be low profile policing in areas of high tension to avoid further alienating a community. This conflict avoidance is a form of accommodation. The advantage claimed for the strategy of accommodation is that it responds to the causes of disorder, and does not merely address symptoms. Depending upon the form that it takes, the strategy is open to the objection that it constitutes appeasement of disaffected groups. This criticism is particularly common in the case of the accommodation of terrorism.

Suppression constitutes a third option open to the state. It can be realised through suppressive legislation or through harsh police tactics. To crush manifestations of dissent, the police can resort to such methods as the banning of political organisations, detention without trial, the imposition of collective punishments, the employment of emergency powers, the introduction or tightening of controls over movement and even joint action with the military. A hallmark of the strategy of suppression is the state's recognition of the political character of the disorder, but through the police, among others, the state confronts rather than accommodates the challenge to its authority. Most states justify suppression by emphasising the seriousness of the challenge that disorder presents to the very existence of the state. While this may have the advantage of rallying support for the police against criticism of their conduct, it also signals to the outside world that the conflict threatens the country's political stability. Consequently, to be successful the police need to achieve more than just the containment of violence. The strategy is usually deployed in the expectation that it will not only quell disorder but that its sheer forcefulness will act as a deterrent against further violence. Thus the strategy aims at securing a disaffected community's compliance with the state's authority rather than positive acceptance of it. Most forms of suppression are a clear violation of norms governing human rights, and the operation of such a strategy tends to be criticised as evidence of the state's authoritarianism, leading to the charge that it constitutes a police state.

The advantage of this typology is that it sets public order policing in the context of its relationship to the strategies adopted by the state. While outlining them is a useful heuristic exercise, the case studies in this volume demonstrate that in practice states pursue a combination of strategies depending on a range of factors, to be discussed shortly, although the composition of the mixture can vary both among states and within the same state over time. The police therefore operate in a variety of different ways to control disorder. For example, with the move to deracialisation, the use of all three strategies is apparent in South Africa. All three have been employed by the British state in Northern Ireland, with greater emphasis being placed on one or other of the strategies at different times since the onset of violence in 1969. While a strategy of suppression has been used in Israel to meet the threat posed by Palestinian nationalism, accommodation has been the norm in the handling of disorder originating within the dominant community. China relies on a combination of criminalisation and suppression. Even in liberal states where the legitimacy of political authority is buttressed by the existence of a wide degree of consensus, there has been the implementation of some measures of suppression, especially in combating the threat of international terrorism, which is less amenable to the strategies of criminalisation and accommodation.

On this evidence, the attempt to portray public order policing as somehow insulated from political decisions about the choice and mix of state strategies to deal with disorder is not only misleading, it also obscures the chain of relations connecting the state, police and society. By the same token, to treat the police as mere ciphers dutifully implementing whatever strategy has been arrived at by the state elite is equally prone to error and mystification. Though police forces may prefer to style themselves as professionals engaged in the disinterested enforcement of law and order, their pivotal role at the junction of state–society relations leaves them with immense strategic significance. While their conduct is rule-bound to a greater or lesser extent, their extensive powers (coupled with the occasional arbitrary exercise of discretion) provides them with some relative autonomy from the state. This is enhanced if the police have powers of prosecution. There are many examples from our case studies which show that the police act autonomously in the area of public order policing in both liberal-democratic and authoritarian states. Therefore the police are not technocrats occupying a value free position: the stance they have is not in the middle but to one side of what can become a threatening divide. Their actions can either help or hinder the wider pattern of the relationship between state and society.

A number of implications follow from our framework. First, it becomes impossible to characterise the relationship between policing and the state in a simplistic and unidimensional manner. It is apparent from previous chapters that any account of this relationship should make reference to a number of variables, including the nature or changing nature of the state, the cleavages that exist within society, the specific functional specialisms of the police force concerned and the organisational structure and lines of responsibility within the force. There are implications, secondly, for how we characterise 'liberal' and 'authoritarian' states. For example, it is problematic to describe some states as 'police states' as such, for the strategy of suppression is not exclusively employed by authoritarian regimes, nor is this the only strategy utilised in these states. In turn, it is clear that liberal states also deploy the strategy of suppression, which fits uneasily with the traditional image of the police–state relationship in liberal-democracies. It is likely that as public disorder intensifies in liberal states the strategy of suppression will be increasingly deployed. Thirdly, as Turk has argued[4], policing in all states is politically partisan. This is obviously so in those authoritarian states where the police function to bolster the regime, but it is also true of liberal states, where the police facilitate stability, continuity and order and inhibit disruption, transformation and change. Moreover, policing will become more politicised and partisan, even in liberal-democracies, as public order issues become prominent. Irrespective of how transitory are the specific grievances which motivate disorder, it is certain that public order issues will become more conspicuous in the light of the greater transmittability and diffusion of protest which has accompanied developments in communication in the modern world. For this reason, particular instances of disorder do not have to be as intense as in the past for them to have the same or even greater effect; the partisanship of the police will rise in tandem. Accordingly, future debate about the police should not concern itself with whether they are partisan or not, but how the police should behave in different political contexts, what degree of autonomy they should have in certain situations and the amount of control local authorities should retain from the political centre. This acknowledges that in certain situations the exercise of partisanship by police officers is not necessarily to be condemned. Rather, the issue becomes one of deciding to whom the police should be accountable so as to prevent them from becoming a law unto themselves.

One final consequence worth stressing is that while public order policing is becoming a functional skill restricted to specialist squads, how these units conduct themselves still affects the perception of the police as a whole. This is a particular problem for liberal-democracies, where the liberal idea of the police is a potent image fostered by the police themselves and the state generally. Our case studies reveal that this image requires qualification. The policing of public order in liberal states demonstrates the inadequacy of the portrayal of the police as neutral arbiters who dispassionately defend the middle ground. The greater the number of citizens who perceive the image to be Janus-like, the more the liberal idea of the police is undermined. Evidence presented in earlier chapters showed that the public image of the police has been dented in liberal-democracies, especially in Britain. It is only a small step from attacking the liberal idea of the police to undermining the liberal idea of the state itself. In fact an important thrust of our argument is to claim that liberal states are becoming more suppressive and authoritarian in their strategies for order-maintenance, which exposes the liberal idea of the state as esoteric and fragile.

This does not surrender the field to those who advance the radical alternative to the liberal idea of the state, for the corollary of our argument is that popular conceptions of policing in authoritarian regimes also need to be qualified, which in turn affects the portrayal of the authoritarian state. Case studies of South Africa, China, Israel and Northern Ireland prove that pure coercion does not work: order-maintenance in such societies requires the deployment of a mixture of strategies, so that suppression is combined with accommodation and criminalisation. This has been a slow realisation on the part of the political leadership in authoritarian states, and has often only come about as a result of vociferous domestic protest and increased international pressure arising from wider acceptance of the norms governing human rights, equality and justice. But order-maintenance in authoritarian states is moving in a more legalistic direction.

This suggests that in the area of public order policing there is an increasing approximation between authoritarian and liberal states, which is reflected in a convergence of their strategies for order-maintenance. The two sorts of state are proceeding in oppposite directions from their respective poles and particular states within each type are journeying at varying speeds and have travelled different distances. Of the liberal states discussed here, Great Britain has gone furthest in deploying both suppressive legislation and police tactics. The Irish Republic has suppressive legislation but the police on the whole do not use suppressive tactics, while the reverse is the case in the USA. In contrast, China and South Africa have both gone some way from relying exclusively on authoritarian-style suppression. Nor is the journey necessarily forward. A change in government, policy or personnel within a state can reverse the direction by changing the mix of order maintenance strategies. The reforms in China and South Africa occurred after a change in leadership and their current policies are still fragile and susceptible to revision from the ultra-Left and the unreconstructed Right. Conversely, an alteration in the combination of strategies deployed by the British state is feasible under pressure from the centre and left of the British political spectrum. This illustrates how the mixture of order-maintenance strategies within a state can fluctuate, which helps to explain why states travel at different speeds and distances along the path to convergence.

Various factors explain both why a particular combination of order-maintenance strategies is decided upon and the lack of uniformity in the movement toward convergence. These include: the historical legacy, cultural traditions and popular perceptions that surround the image of the state; the extent to which state power is restricted by legal and political constraints which protect the rights of citizens; the legitimacy of the state; the degree to which the society is homogeneous and consensual; whether social cleavages are episodic and transitory or sustained and over-arching; and the extent to which the state is subject to (and prepared to countenance) domestic and international pressure. Further research is needed in order to assess the role these variables play, but on the basis of this volume it is possible to point to some influences.

Popular perceptions of the state may determine the extent to which a government can deploy suppressive measures against a section of the population. If for historical reasons the state has customarily needed to defend itself against internal threats, the use of the military, martial law and riot police may not constitute a break with tradition. The state has already established itself as an intrusive, supervisory and coercive mechanism; and indeed this posture may have been legitimised by widely perceived threats to the state's integrity. Alternatively, however, the concept of the state may have been diffused, either by federal structures of government or by traditions of local autonomy, so that the idea of the state is familiar through comparatively benign connotations such as the 'welfare state'. In these circumstances, such a state would need to argue that 'abnormal' events justified the 'abnormal' police response to disorder. In some cases the legitimacy which a state possesses is a product of its history, especially the extent to which it was established with the consent of its citizens. But in most instances it reflects the state's ability to measure up to the expectations and demands of the governed. Clearly a state that fails to satisfy sections of its population – for example by ignoring culturally distinct identities or permitting obvious levels of relative deprivation to persist – loses legitimacy. Consequently it is less able to police disorder without recourse to suppressive tactics. However, accommodatory techniques may be used where there is some chance of pacifying or reducing frustration among identifiable minorities. It therefore follows that a state composed of a homogeneous population will be less likely to employ suppressive modes of policing since there will be a broad consensus underpinning the ethos of the state. Where fundamental cleavages of a racial, religious or ethnic kind exist and perhaps overlap, the state is more likely to deploy a mixture of strategies, varying according to the relations that exist between majorities and minorities, the relative cost of accommodation compared to suppression, and the extent to which the segments that oppose the state are themselves cohesive. External pressure will work in a number of ways. An authoritarian regime may moderate coercive styles of policing in order to propitiate international norms regarding human rights, which economic incentives may reinforce. A liberal-democracy may shift its strategies for order-maintenance in a more authoritarian direction in order to demonstrate that it is able to keep public order in a part of its own territory. It is possible to envisage other external pressures which predispose a sensitivity to external opinion. One state may have grounds which enable it to speak for a minority in another state, or be able to threaten intervention to redress grievances through sanctions or through the support of terrorists.

Considerations of this character need to be made when describing the relationship between the state, society and the police. A comparative analysis of public order policing shows just how complex this relationship is. Future analysis should address this complexity, not obscure it.

Notes

1. For a discussion of this see D.J. McBarnet, 'The Police and the State: Arrest, Legality and the Law', in G. Littlejohn, B. Smart, J. Wakeford and N. Yuval Davis (eds), *Power and the State* (London: Croom Helm, 1978).
2. See D.H. Bayley, 'A World Perspective on the Role of the Police in Social Control', in R. Donelan (ed.), *The Maintenance of Order in Society* (1982).
3. See for example: J. Roach and J. Thomaneck (eds), *Police and Public Order in Europe* (1985); F.E.C. Gregory, *The Police, Public Order and Western Society* (Brighton: Wheatsheaf, forthcoming).
4. A.T. Turk, 'Policing in Political Context', in R. Donelan (ed.), *The Maintenance of Order*. Also see D.H. Bayley, 'The Police and Political Change in Comparative Perspective', *Law and Society Review*, 6 (1971).

Select Bibliography

ALDERSON, J. *Law and Disorder* (London: Hamish Hamilton, 1984).

ANDRADE, J. *World Police and Paramilitary Forces* (London: Macmillan, 1985).

Annual Reports of the Commissioner of the South African Police (Pretoria).

Annual Survey of Race Relations (Johannesburg: South African Institute of Race Relations).

AUDIT COMMISSION *Local Authority Performance Indicators: Vol. 3, Police and Fire Services* (London: HMSO, 1995).

BALDWIN, R. and KINSEY, R. *Police Powers and Politics* (London: Quartet Books, 1982).

BAYLEY, D.H. (ed.) *Police and Society* (London: Sage, 1977).

BENSINGER, G.J. 'The Israel Police in Transition: An Organizational Study', *Police Studies*, 4 (1981).

BENSINGER, G.J. 'The Israel Police and Terrorism Management', *Journal of Crime and Justice*, 6 (1983).

BENYON, J. (ed.) *Scarman and After* (Oxford: Pergamon, 1984).

BENYON, J. 'Policing the European Union: The Changing Basis of Cooperation and Law Enforcement', *International Affairs*, 70 (1994a).

BENYON, J. *Law and Order Review 1993: An Audit of Crime. Policing and Criminal Justice Issues* (Centre for the Study of Public Order, University of Leicester, 1994b).

BOWDEN, T. *Beyond the Limits of the Law* (Harmondsworth: Penguin, 1978).

BRADY, J.P. 'The Transformation of Justice Under Socialism: The Contrasting Experience of Cuba and China', *The Insurgent Sociologist*, 10 (1981).

BRADY, J.P. *Justice and Politics in People's China* (London: Academic Press, 1982).

BREWER, J.D. *After Soweto: An Unfinished Journey* (Oxford: Clarendon Press, 1986).

BREWER J.D. 'The Police in South African Politics' in S. Johnson (ed.), *South Africa: No Turning Back* (London: Macmillan, 1988).

BREWER J.D. *Black and Blue: Policing in South Africa* (Oxford: Clarendon Press, 1994a).

239

BREWER J.D. 'Some Observations on Policing and Politics – A South African Case Study', *Policing and Society*, 4 (1994b).

BRIDGES, L. 'Policing the Urban Wasteland', *Race and Class*, 25 (1983).

BROGDEN, M. *On the Mersey Beat* (Oxford: Clarendon Press, 1991).

CASHMORE, E. and MCLAUGHLIN, E. *Out of Order: Policing Black People* (London: Routledge, 1991).

CHIKOTA, R.A. and MORAN, M.C. *Riot in the Cities* (Cranbury: Associated University Presses, 1968).

COWELL, D., JONES, T. and YOUNG, J. (eds) *Policing the Riots* (London: Junction Books, 1982).

CRITCHLEY, T.A. *A History of the Police in England and Wales*, 2nd edn. (London: Constable, 1978).

DE VILLIERS, D.P. 'Change in Respect of Security Legislation', in D.J. van Vuuren, N. Wiehahn, J. Lombard and N. Rhoodie (eds) *Change in South Africa* (Durban: Butterworths, 1983).

DONELAN, R. (ed.) *The Maintenance of Order in Society* (Ottawa: Canadian Police College, 1982).

FARRELL, M. *Arming the Protestants: The Formation of the Ulster Special Constabulary and the Royal Ulster Constabulary 1920–1927* (Dingle: Brandon, 1983).

FIELD, S. and SOUTHGATE, P. *Public Disorder* (London: Home Office Research Unit, 1982).

FIELDING, N. *The Police and Social Conflict* (London: Athlone Press, 1991).

FINE, B. and MILLAR, R. (eds) *Policing the Miners' Strike* (London: Lawrence & Wishart, and the Cobden Trust, 1985).

FRANKEL, P. 'South Africa: The Politics of Police Control', *Comparative Politics*, 12 (1979-80).

GEARY, R. *Policing Industrial Disputes 1893–1985* (London: Meuthen, 1985).

GRIMSHAW, R. and JEFFERSON T. *Interpreting Police Work* (London: Allen and Unwin, 1987).

GRUNDY, K. *Soldiers Without Politics: Blacks in the South African Armed Forces* (Berkeley: University of California Press, 1983).

GUREVITCH, M., DANET B. and SCHWARTZ, G. 'The Image of the Police in Israel', *Law and Society Review*, 5 (1971).

HAIN, P. (ed.) *Policing the Police* (London: Calder, 1979 (vol 1), and 1980 (vol 2)).

HALL, S. *Drifting into a Law and Order Society* (London: The Cobden Trust, 1979).

HALL, S., CRITCHER, C., JEFFERSON, T., CLARKE, J. and ROBERTS, B. *Policing the Crisis* (London: Macmillan, 1978).
HILLYARD, P. 'Law and Order', in J. Darby (ed.) *Northern Ireland: The Background to the Conflict* (Belfast: Appletree Press, 1983).
HILLYARD, P. and PERCY-SMITH, J. *The Coercive State* (London: Collins, 1988).
HMSO *Inquiry into Police Responsibilities and Rewards: Report* (London: Cm 2280, 1993a).
HMSO *Police Reform: A Police Service for the Twenty-First Century* (London: Cm 2281, 1993b).
HOLDAWAY, S. (ed.) *The British Police* (London: Edward Arnold, 1979).
HOVAV, M. and AMIR, M. 'Israel Police: History and Analysis', *Police Studies*, 2 (1979).
The Irish Council for Civil Liberties, *The Emergency Powers Act 1976: A Critique* (Dublin: ICCL, 1977).
JEFFERSON, T. *The Case Against Paramilitary Policing* (Milton Keynes: Open University Press, 1990).
JOHNSON, E. 'Neighbourhood Police in the People's Republic of China', *Police Studies*, 8 (1984).
JOYCE, J. and MURTAGH, P. *The Boss* (Swords: Poolbeg Press, 1983).
The Karp Report: An Israeli Government Inquiry into Settler Violence Against Palestinians on the West Bank (Washington, DC: Institute of Palestine Studies, 1984).
KERNER, O. *Report of the National Advisory Commission on Civil Disorders* (New York: Bantam, 1968).
KINSEY, R., LEA, J. and YOUNG, J. *Losing the Fight Against Crime* (Oxford: Blackwell, 1986).
KRATCOSKI, P. and WALKER, D.B. *Criminal Justice in America* (Glenview: Scott Foresman & Co., 1978).
LEHMAN-WILZIG, S. 'Public Demonstrators and the Israeli Police: The Policy and Practice of Successful Protest Control', *Police Studies*, 6 (1983).
LENG, S. and CHIU, H. *Criminal Justice in Post-Mao China* (Albany: State University of New York Press, 1985).
LOVEDAY, B. 'Government Strategies for Community Crime Prevention Programmes for England and Wales: A Study in Failure?', *International Journal of the Sociology of Law*, 22 (1994).
LUNDMAN, R.J. *Police and Policing* (New York: Holt, Rinehart & Winston, 1980).

MARSHALL, G. and LOVEDAY, B. 'The Police: Independence and Accountability', in J. Jowell and D. Oliver (eds.), *The Changing Constitution* (Oxford: Clarendon Press, 1994).

MAYHEW, P., AYE MAUNG, N. and MIRRLEES-BLACK, C. *The 1992 British Crime Survey* (London: HMSO, Home Office Research Study 132, 1993).

National Economic and Social Council, *The Criminal Justice System: Policy and Performance* (Dublin: NESC, 1980).

NIEDERHOFFER, A. and BLUMBERG, A.S. (eds) *The Ambivalent Force* (Massachussetts: Xeros College Publishing, 1976).

PENG, Z. 'Importance of Improving China's Legislation', *Beijing Review*, 27, 35 (1984).

PLATT, A. and COOPER, L. *Policing America* (Englewood Cliffs, NJ: Prentice Hall, 1974).

POCKRASS, R.M. 'The Police Response to Terrorism: The Royal Ulster Constabulary', *The Police Journal*, 59 (1986).

Policy Studies Institute, *Police and People in London* (London: Policy Studies Institute, 1983) 4 vols.

POPE, D. and WEINER, N. (eds) *Modern Policing* (London: Croom Helm, 1981).

PUNCH, M., (ed.) *Control in the Police Organisation* (Cambridge, Mass.: MIT Press, 1983).

REIMAN, J.H. *The Rich Get Richer and the Poor Get Prison* (New York: Wiley, 1979).

REINER, R. *The Politics of the Police* (Brighton: Wheatsheaf Books, 1985).

REINER, R. 'The Politics of Police Research', in M. Weatheritt (ed.), *Police Research: Some Future Prospects* (Aldershot: Avebury, 1989).

REISER, S. 'Cultural and Political Influences on Police Discretion: The Case of Religion in Israel', *Police Studies*, 6 (1983).

REISER, S. 'The Israeli Police: Politics and Priorities', *Police Studies*, 6 (1983).

Report of the Advisory Committee on Police in Northern Ireland, (Hunt Report) (Cmd 535) (Belfast: HMSO, 1969).

Report of the Committee to Recommend Certain Safeguards for Persons in Custody and for Members of An Garda Siochana (Dublin: The Stationery Office, 1977).

ROACH, J., and THOMANECK, J. (eds) *Police and Public Order in Europe* (London: Croom Helm, 1985).

RUAN, C. 'Minister on Social Order in China', *Beijing Review*, 29, 34 (1986).

RUCHELMAN, L. *Police Politics: A Comparative Study of Three Cities* (Cambridge: Ballinger, 1974).

SACHS, A. 'The Instruments of Domination in South Africa', in L. Thompson and J. Butler (eds) *Change in Contemporary Southern Africa* (Berkeley: University of California Press, 1975).

SAICH, T. *China: Politics and Government* (London: Macmillan, 1981).

SCARMAN, Lord *The Scarman Report: The Brixton Disorders 10–12 April 1981* (Harmondsworth: Penguin, 1982).

SCHEINGOLD, S. *The Politics of Law and Order* (New York: Longman, 1984).

SCRATON, P. *The State of the Police* (London: Pluto Press, 1985).

SHANE, P.G. *Police and People: A Comparison of Five Countries* (St Louis: C.V. Mosby, 1980.

SILVER, A. 'The Demand for Order in Civil Society', in D. Bordua (ed.) *The Police: Six Sociological Essays* (New York: Wiley 1967).

SKOGAN, W. *Contacts Between the Police and Public: Findings From the 1992 British Crime Survey* (London: HMSO, Home Office Research Study 134, 1994).

STEAD, P. *The Police of Britain* (London: Macmillan, 1985).

STEYTLER, N. 'Policing Political Opponents: Death Squads and Cop Culture', in D. Hansson and D. van zyl Smit (eds.), *Towards Justice?: Crime and State Control in South Africa* (Cape Town: Oxford University Press, 1990).

SUMMERS, M.R. and BARTH, T.E. *Law and Order in a Democratic Society* (Columbus: Charles E. Merrill, 1970).

THACKRAH, J.R. (ed.) *Contemporary Policing* (London: Sphere Reference, 1985).

TURK, A. 'Policing in Political Context', in R. Donelan (ed.), *The Maintenance of Order in Society* (Ottawa: Canadian Police College, 1982).

US GOVERNMENT, *Task Force Report: The Police* (Washington, DC: US Government Printing Office, 1967).

WADDINGTON, D. *Contemporary Issues in Public Disorder* (London: Routledge, 1992).

WADDINGTON, P. 'Towards Paramilitarism?: Dilemmas in Policing Public Order', *British Journal of Criminology*, 27 (1987).

WADDINGTON, P. 'The Case Against Paramilitary Policing', *British Journal of Criminology*, 33 (1993).

WARD, R. and BRACEY, D.H. 'Police Training and Professionalism in the People's Republic of China', *Police Chief*, 52 (1985).

WEITZER, R. 'Policing a Divided Society: Obstacles to Normalization in Northern Ireland', *Social Problems*, 33 (1985).

WEITZER, R. 'Accountability and Complaints Against the Police in Northern Ireland', *Police Studies*, 9 (1986).

WHYTE, M.K. and PARISH, W.L. *Urban Life in Contemporary China* (Chicago and London: University of Chicago Press, 1984).

WOMACK, B. 'Modernisation and Democratic Reform in China', *Journal of Asian Studies*, 43, 3 (1983).

UGLOW, S. *Policing Liberal Society* (Oxford: Clarendon Press, 1988).

Index